T0322665

THE
LONG
SILENCE

THE LONG SILENCE

The True Story of James Hanratty
and the A6 Murder
by VALERIE STORIE,
the Woman who Lived to Tell the Tale

PAUL STICKLER

The
History
Press

First published 2021

The History Press
97 St George's Place, Cheltenham,
Gloucestershire, GL50 3QB
www.thehistorypress.co.uk

British Library Cataloguing in Publication Data.
A catalogue record for this book is available from the British Library.

ISBN 978 0 7509 9676 1

Typesetting and origination by The History Press
Printed and bound in Great Britain by TJ Books Limited, Padstow, Cornwall.

Trees for LYfe

'Dedicated to the memory of my beloved parents and all the many friends who held faith with me'

Valerie Jean Storie
1938–2016

'You dream, and very rarely, you are not in a wheelchair.'

Valerie Jean Storie

Contents

Foreword by Professor Adrian Hobbs CBE

Valerie Storie witnessed the murder of her boyfriend, Michael Gregsten; was shot and critically injured; saw the culprit convicted; and then expected to disappear from the public eye. It was not to be. For most of the rest of her life, she was pestered by the media and vilified for causing the conviction and hanging of James Hanratty. A pressure group was set up, books were written, television programmes produced and debates in parliament were held to support this false claim.

When, eventually, enhanced DNA techniques showed that Hanratty was indeed guilty, Valerie decided to write a book telling the true story. Although she started to write notes, the book was never completed. However, she had retained a comprehensive collection of material. This included transcripts of the police interviews and the trial, all of the published books, official reports, a comprehensive set of newspaper cuttings, scripts and recordings of television programmes and correspondence related to the case. It seemed important to ensure that her 'papers' were retained for future research into the case.

When he learnt of the papers, Paul Stickler expressed an interest in writing what could have been Valerie's book. Having processed all of the available material, both Paul and I were determined to ensure that the book was as factually correct as possible. It is almost an unbelievable story and a fascinating read. Fact can truly be stranger than fiction.

Acknowledgements

I owe a great deal of gratitude to Professor Adrian Hobbs CBE, friend and work colleague of Valerie Storie, without whom this story could not have been written. As executor to her will, he generously allowed me access to Valerie's papers in order that an account of her ordeal could be written. As a result, we are now very much more enlightened about the shocking events which occurred between 1961 and 2016.

I also wish to express my grateful thanks to David Sanders, Emeritus Professor of Psychology at the University of Sunderland who not only provided invaluable support to me in reading the script and making many suggestions to help improve the narrative but also in providing expert advice and guidance in my attempt to interpret the personality traits of James Hanratty. I am very grateful for his time. I would also like to thank Chief Constable Garry Forsyth of Bedfordshire Police who kindly allowed me access to the archived case papers in order that I could corroborate newspaper reports, earlier narratives and details recorded by Valerie.

Finally, a personal thank you to Mark Beynon, National Commissioning Editor at The History Press, for agreeing to publish the manuscript and to my literary agent, Robert Smith, for all his constructive advice throughout the research and writing process.

The Protagonists

Acott, Basil (Bob) Montague	Detective Superintendent in charge of murder investigation
Alphon, Peter Louis	'Suspect' in murder investigation
Blackhall, Edward	Key witness to driving of Morris Minor
Dinwoodie, Olive	Liverpool sweet shop assistant
Durrant, Frederick	Alias of Peter Alphon
Evans, Terry	Fairground worker in Rhyl
Ewer, William	Janet Gregsten's brother-in-law
Foot, Paul	Journalist
France, Carol	Daughter of Charles France
France, Charles (Dixie)	Friend of James Hanratty
Gillbanks, Joseph	Defence enquiry agent for James Hanratty
Glickberg, Florence	Alias of Florence Snell. Employee at Vienna hotel
Glickberg, Jack	Alias of William Nudds. Employee at Vienna hotel
Gregsten, Janet	Wife of Michael Gregsten
Gregsten, Michael	Murder victim
Hanratty, James	Convicted of the murder of Michael Gregsten
Hawser, Lewis	QC in charge of 1975 review
Hirons, Harry	Petrol pump attendant
Jones, Grace	Landlady of Ingledene guest house, Rhyl
Justice, Jean	First author of book on Hanratty and friend of Peter Alphon

Kerr, John	First witness to speak to Valerie Storie after she had been shot
Kleinman, Emmanuel	Solicitor for James Hanratty
Nimmo, Douglas	Detective Chief Superintendent in charge of review of Rhyl alibi
Nudds, William	Employee in Vienna hotel
Oxford, Ken	Detective Sergeant, assistant to Bob Acott
Rennie, Ian	Physician in charge of Storie's care
Sherrard, Michael	Hanratty's defence counsel
Skillett, John	Key witness to driving of Morris Minor
Snell, Florence	Employee in Vienna hotel
Storie, John (Jack)	Father of Valerie
Storie, Marjorie	Mother of Valerie
Storie, Valerie	Victim of the A6 attack
Swanwick, Graham	Prosecuting counsel
Trower, James	Key witness to driving of Morris Minor
Woffinden, Bob	Journalist and film producer

Introduction

Many people will recognise the name James Hanratty. He was hanged in April 1962, at the age of 25, having been convicted for what became known as the A6 murder. On a summer evening in August the previous year, he held a couple at gunpoint in a cornfield in Buckinghamshire after he had surprised them while they were sitting in their Morris Minor car. After keeping them captive for almost two hours he ordered them to drive under his directions through Middlesex on the outskirts of London and then north along the A6 towards Bedford. After a journey of around 60 miles, and having kept his two captives imprisoned for five hours, he shot the man in the head, raped the woman and finally emptied a number of rounds from his revolver into her body. Miraculously, despite one bullet penetrating her neck, she survived. The 22-year-old would be paralysed from the chest down for the rest of her life.

Hanratty would be convicted after a trial lasting almost four weeks but his execution marked the beginning of a forty-year journey of cries of a miscarriage of justice, media frenzies, legal arguments, criticism of the police, a referral to the Criminal Cases Review Commission and finally a Court of Appeal ruling in 2002 when DNA evidence would finally put an end to the furore; he was indeed guilty.

For many, that was the final curtain and nothing more needed to be said. Yet, among all the controversy, the newspaper articles, the television programmes and the books published that had begged for an overturning of the conviction, one person remained silent. She kept her counsel. She had been pilloried by the media for decades for sending an innocent man to the hangman's noose. Journalists had banged on her door for thirty-five years hoping to get the woman to break her silence, but she remained steadfast.

That person was the woman who witnessed her partner being shot at point-blank range while sitting in the front seat of his car. That person was the woman who was then raped alongside his dead body, who was then made to drag him along the road and was finally on the receiving end of a volley of bullets. That person was Valerie Storie. She gave evidence at Hanratty's trial but then withdrew from the limelight. From the confines of her wheelchair she read every written word, watched every television programme, making note after note.

When Hanratty's guilt was confirmed through DNA, she decided the time had come to write her own story. The personal story of how she came to be on the wrong end of a revolver, on the receiving end of a rapist's attentions, shot and left for dead. How the newspapers continued to hound her, to criticise her and to finally give up on her when the truth finally emerged. How she tried to live a normal life, her courage and the incredible fight against how her life had been turned upside down in August 1961.

Yet, she never wrote it; a few outline sketches of her memories she wanted people to know and hundreds of handwritten notes containing her thoughts gathered dust in her home, but it was not the full story. She died in 2016, her innermost feelings littered among the piles of paper upon which she had scribbled.

But now the story is told from her perspective; an account that places her at the heart of a murder hunt, the trial of a killer and its aftermath. The *Storie Papers* that have now come to light contain detail that never reached the courtroom or the journalists' pens; information that, though known at the time, was never brought out at the trial as it had no bearing on the identity of the killer. The words you will read are those that passed Valerie's lips and with no creative re-enactment. What the *Storie Papers* reveal are her personal experiences and her hopes and dreams as a young woman, all of which were, literally, shot away from her.

Left for dead in an isolated layby on the side of the A6, her body now paralysed, she remained sufficiently lucid and attentive to be able to relay the story from the initial kidnap through to the five-hour journey, the killing, the rape and the final attempt to silence her. Her story could have ended there, but it was only the beginning. She would be resolute in her recollections and underwent strong cross-examination at her attacker's trial about how she was wrong in her identification of the killer. Afterwards, many claimed, it was she who had sent an innocent man to the gallows.

After Hanratty was executed, her public abuse would continue for another forty years as repeated attacks were levelled at her and the police for malpractice. A self-appointed 'A6 Committee,' headed by a leading journalist and supported by an overzealous barrister, would, year after year, subject her to more and more pressure. Unsolicited journalists would visit her front door, questions would be raised in the Houses of Parliament and separate investigations into discrete aspects of the case would occupy the front pages for years to come.

In the meantime, Valerie tried to rebuild her life. She returned to work and she would refer to the events of 22 August 1961 as her 'accident'. Her parents, who cared for her, died. Yet still the headlines kept coming. Hanratty was innocent. Storie was mistaken. The police were corrupt. And because her partner was still in the process of separating from his wife at the time of his murder, she would receive letters at home saying she was a whore, a tramp and an adulteress. But in the face of adversity, she kept smiling and despite more newspaper articles claiming the police had got it wrong and the case referred to the Court of Appeal, she never doubted herself.

For forty years, she would remain in touch with the police officers who investigated the events of that August evening; police officers who were maligned and accused of being inept and incompetent and who had managed to let the real killer slip through their fingers. Many areas of the investigation were repeatedly cited as clear evidence of a police cover-up and the British psyche would become conditioned around a myth that grew into reality; those officers too, maintained a dignified silence.

Much of the fine detail has not been included in this account. To do so would detract from Valerie's experience of four decades of torment but critical aspects, which kept the story alive for forty years, are explained. It addresses criticisms aimed at Valerie, the police, the judiciary and the government and offers a different view.

When the courts finally confirmed Hanratty's guilt in 2002, Valerie's feelings were of sorrow for his family. His parents, she said, had gone to their graves not knowing the truth. She wanted the world to know the other side of the story and she picked up a pen and started to sketch out her thoughts.

She had remained silent for thirty-five years. Her book, she decided, would be called *The Long Silence*. But her jottings would lie in a cardboard box – until now. After her death in 2016, her friend and former work colleague, Professor Adrian Hobbs, was kind enough to release the papers in order that Valerie may realise her ambition and offer her own account.

It is time for her story to be told.

PART 1 — THE CRIME

Chapter One

Valerie and Michael

'Goodbye. I shan't be late.'[1]

These were the words called out by 22-year-old Valerie Storie to her parents on 22 August 1961 as she stepped out from her house in Anthony Way, Cippenham, on the western outskirts of Slough. She closed the door and followed Michael Gregsten to the grey Morris Minor parked on the small driveway of the semi-detached house in which she had been born. It had been a relaxing evening so far. Michael, dressed smartly in a jacket, shirt and tie, had taken time off from work that week but had collected Valerie from where they were both employed at the nearby Road Research Laboratory in Langley. They stopped briefly for him to have a haircut and then drove on to her parents' house for tea.

Marjorie and Jack Storie doted on their only child. She was bright, engaging and enjoyed life; to them, the perfect daughter. She had always been a bit of a bookish child although, to the horror of her teachers, she left Slough Grammar School at the age of 16, unwilling to go to university, but she was strong in character and liked to make her own decisions.

The job at the laboratory was her first and she loved being involved in the roadside experiments they carried out to identify causes of road accidents and, perhaps unsurprisingly, had developed a passion for motor cars. Better still, her role even required her to drive from time to time. With her steady wage of £34 a week,[2] she enjoyed the occasional holiday and ventured off to places such as Sweden, Austria and, more recently, Majorca.

The man she had brought home for tea was a physicist and both Marjorie and Jack knew that the two of them shared a passion for motor rallying and that they had agreed to arrange some sort of work event for the coming weekend. As far as they were concerned, their daughter and Michael were now heading off back to the laboratory to put the final piece of the plan together.

The reality was somewhat different.

Michael and Valerie had known each other for some time, having met at work at the rather mundane canteen committee where social functions were discussed. Over time, the pair had become attracted to one another, but beyond that, it was true that their shared passion was motor rallying and they had agreed to take on the responsibility for organising navigational rallies for club members. It was their plan that evening to drive to a nearby public house and, over a drink, make some final alterations to the event in Chesham that coming weekend.

The relationship, though, was complicated. Michael was fourteen years older than her and married with two children, though he was now in the process of separating from his wife, the probable reason why she chose not to discuss it with her parents. Valerie had been brought up in a very respectable, conservative household and for her to have a relationship with a man who was still married would have been difficult for them to understand. But Valerie found Michael 'dashing and handsome'[3] and would later say that, 'I suppose I was flattered that he took a shine to me.' In the four years that they had known each other they had grown closer and were now 'very fond of one another'. They had been sexually intimate for two years and, seemingly, marriage had been mentioned.[4] In reality, this was Valerie's first serious relationship; tragically, it would also be her last.

The Morris was Michael's aunt's car but she had recently given it to him due to her advancing blindness and the two of them had adapted it to their own tastes. It was quirky. The radio button was permanently stuck in the 'on' position and a home-made wireless aerial was fixed to one of the rear windows. They had attached reflective Scotch tape on the rear bumper to make it more visible in the dark. Valerie had stuck a white flower-holder to the inside of the windscreen in which she had placed small, pink, artificial flowers and miniature roses. The exhaust pipe leaked, a small point that would soon become a prominent feature in the few hours that lay ahead, but it was *their* car. They knew its intricacies. They had rallied together in it, Michael as the driver, Valerie the navigator. They had made love in it. It was special to them and captured their personal love of driving. It was their world and one that had made the friendship grow into something 'a little deeper'.[5]

The Station Inn at Taplow was a short drive away. They arrived around half past seven and people who recognised them said that they kept themselves to themselves, Michael drinking a single pint of Double Diamond beer, Valerie, a gin and Pepsi Cola. They discussed the rally, studied maps – this was Valerie's forte – and agreed the route and the clues they would give to the competitors. In practice, the rallies amounted to little more than treasure hunts carried out by car fans following various clues set down by the organisers, but it was fun. At work she visited various accident sites and over the years she had not only become a competent driver but she was somewhat of an authority on road names and numbers, and her sense of direction had become very acute.

Just over an hour later, around 8.45 p.m., they finished their drinks, returned to their car and set off. Michael drove; Valerie sat in the passenger seat.

They were not yet ready for home though. They had matters they needed to talk about, not least Michael's imminent move from his accommodation in Windsor to new rooms in Maidenhead sometime later that week. Both he and Valerie had already been to see the house and Michael had paid a week's rent in advance; the landlord recalled being introduced to Valerie as Michael's fiancée. Only the evening before, he had finalised the arrangements and been given the front door key. Everything seemed to be set up for the two of them spending their immediate futures together.[6]

Michael, though, was a bit of a worrier. He was concerned about money, his wife, his two children who he idolised and more generally about his own mental well-being. His marriage had been a bit difficult and the world had seemed to be turning in on him but now he was about to embark upon a new chapter in a new home. He needed to talk and having driven away from the pub forecourt they set off for the secluded spot they used sometimes when they wanted privacy; a cornfield in nearby Dorney Reach. It was less than 2 miles away.

There were houses in the area but this was mostly quiet countryside, even though only a few hundred yards from the newly built M4 motorway. No one could have known they were there or had planned to travel there as it had been a last-minute arrangement. Valerie would later say: 'If we hadn't been doing a rally for the laboratory, trying to plan a rally-cum-treasure hunt, we would not have been there at that time.'[7]

Michael drove the Morris no more than 6ft into the field, the car still clearly visible from the road. He extinguished the lights and switched off the engine. They were alone, nervously excited about the future, and started to talk.

Chapter Two

The Cornfield

Valerie's shopping basket rested on the back seat. It was full of her personal effects including her handbag, a wallet and a purse, a few pound notes and coins pushed inside them. Michael's duffel bag containing freshly laundered clothing rested next to it. A brown, check car rug was spread out; another small, personalised feature of the rallying Morris.

They had been here on a few occasions before, to make love or simply to spend time alone together. But tonight, they were talking. They had finished the planning for the weekend's rally, Valerie's maps folded away in her shopping basket. What was going to happen to them? Were they to marry? Was Michael actually going to leave his wife and two boys? Where was the money going to come from? He was a scientist at the laboratory and being a talented mathematician occasionally taught evening classes at St Albans Technical College, so extra money was coming in, but it nevertheless worried him. With some justification it seemed, since Michael had a tendency to spend willingly rather than save.

They were, though, generally relaxed talking in their cornfield. They had never been disturbed before and it was easier to talk here rather than anywhere else. They kissed only once. How much time had passed since they had pulled into the field is not absolutely clear since neither was paying particular attention but, Valerie would later estimate, after about thirty minutes their private conversation was disturbed. The two were facing each other, their arms resting on the backs of the seats as they spoke quietly when there was a tap on the driver's window.

Valerie's immediate instinct was that it was the farmer coming to find out what they were doing and to tell them to get off his land. It was not yet dark, but twilight had set in and visibility was not perfect. Michael wound down his window, only halfway, when a gun was thrust through the gap, its muzzle pointing directly at them.

'I'm a desperate man. This is a hold-up,' a man's voice said.

What Valerie then saw surprised her. The man was immaculately dressed. Through the window of the car and despite the fading light, she could clearly see that he was wearing a suit and tie with a white shirt. She was able to see only the body of the man between his waist and shoulders, but his smart appearance seemed at odds with his threatening behaviour. The sudden intrusion did not seem real. None of it made sense.

With the gun still pointing at them, the man said, 'I have been on the run for four months. If you do as I tell you, you will be alright.'

He demanded the driver hand over the ignition key.

Michael turned to remove it from the ignition but, in what proved to be a recurring feature of the hours that lay ahead, Valerie's force of character, perhaps even a hint of stubbornness, took over. Whether it was because she was in shock or perhaps still not believing this was really happening – she would never be sure – she was determined that this man, whoever he was, was not going to take advantage of them. She mumbled to Michael not to hand over the key and grabbed his hand to stop him. Michael reacted: 'Don't be silly. He's got a gun.'

The muzzle of the gun inches away from their heads reinforced the point and Valerie held back. Michael passed the key through the open window.

Fear now set in. The man was real. The gun looked real. Opening the rear door on the driver's side, the gunman climbed into the back, Valerie instinctively gathering her basket to make sure it was safe from the man's clutches. Now settled inside, he ordered Valerie to lock all the doors from the inside, telling them both not to look round but face the front. She recalled later how she remembered her reaction: 'I didn't scream. I sometimes wonder why I didn't. This is daft. I must be asleep.'[1] Before getting into the car, she remembered the man locking the driver's door from the outside and he now instructed Michael to lock the rear one he had just clambered through. He clearly did not wish to be surprised by anyone walking past.

With the man now sitting inches behind them, the weapon pointing in their direction, Valerie feared the worst and instinctively grabbed the hand of the man with whom she had started to plan her future. They looked at each other.

'What are we going to do?' she whispered.

Michael's response was terse.

'I don't know.'

Seemingly content he had everything under control, the gunman started talking. A young, cockney accent, Valerie thought. 'I'm a desperate man,' he repeated. Every policeman in Britain was looking for him, he claimed. He hadn't eaten for two days and he'd been on the run for four months. As he spoke, Valerie and Michael listened, their heads slowly turning towards the man wielding the gun, only to be stopped in their tracks with a sharp, 'Don't turn round. Face the front.'

They waited and then the cockney voice continued.

'If you do everything I say and don't make a noise you will be alright.'

This did not bode well. '*If you do everything I say*' had a worrying undertone. Michael, sensing that the man needed to be reasoned with, said, 'I'm sorry you haven't eaten anything. We've nothing to offer you but we're willing to drive you into town to get a meal or something,'[2] an attempt on his part to at least move to a busier, safer area. The response was blunt.

'Don't be silly, I have gone without before. Just keep quiet and you'll be alright.' A short silence.

'This gun is real,' he continued.

His uneducated voice, as Valerie would later describe it, now seemed to gather momentum. It was as if he had not really got a plan and was filling in time with pointless chatter.

'It's like a cowboy gun. I feel rather like a cowboy.'

He said it was a 'thirty-eight', though Valerie had no idea what that meant. It was loaded, he boasted, and tapped his pockets, which let out a rattling noise. 'These are the bullets.' He said that he had never shot anyone before and was waving the gun about as if to show it off, so much so that Valerie caught a glimpse of it against the silhouette of the failing light. 'It was black or dark and had a barrel about six to eight inches long,' she would later recall.

Each time the couple in the front tried to turn around to catch a better glimpse of their captor, a raised voice would order them to 'face the front'. Continuing to talk aimlessly, he repeated that he had not eaten and had been sleeping rough for a couple of nights. Valerie reflected on his tidy appearance and thought it odd that a man who had been without food and shelter for a couple of days would be so 'nattily dressed'. He was not making sense and frankly, she did not believe him.

Repeated requests by Valerie and Michael about what the man wanted were met with poorly thought-through answers. 'There's no hurry,' he responded on several occasions and often he used the phrase, 'Be quiet, will you. I'm finking.' His inability to pronounce 'th' was a prominent feature in his voice.

Their fears escalated when he suddenly exclaimed that if anyone walked past, he would shoot them. Almost as if boasting, Valerie thought, the man outlined how he had been to prison and ever since he was 8 years old he had been in remand homes, borstal, CT – an abbreviation that was meaningless to Valerie – and his next one coming up was PD, an equally meaningless abbreviation. He had also been to prison for five years for housebreaking, he said.[3]

The conversation continued with the gunman repeating phrases, yet often contradicting himself, Valerie and Michael both making desperate attempts at trying to establish what it was that he wanted. The longer it went on, the more they tried to reason with him. But now their terror heightened. They had been held captive for probably no more than five minutes, when the man wielding the gun handed the ignition key back to Michael and told him to drive further into the field. No lights, he instructed, just drive further in. This was it. He had clearly decided what he wanted to do.

Michael started the car and drove towards some haystacks, following the instructions of the man in the back seat, carried out a three-point-turn, and with the Morris now facing the entrance to the field, switched off the ignition and returned the key. The man's motive now became clear. He demanded Michael's wallet. Valerie, seemingly still able to think rationally under the extreme circumstances, urged the gunman not to take it as it was of sentimental value. The request was tempered with a promise that he would return it and Michael passed it back. It contained around £3. The next was for their watches, which they slipped from their wrists and passed backwards, looking forward all the time. Next came the demand for Valerie's purse, in her shopping basket, which she knew only held a few coins and she told him that in the hope it might make him change his mind. Moreover, she was concerned that she had a wallet in her basket that contained several pound notes and she was determined that he was not going to get his hands on it; she and Michael needed it for their future.

Her ploy worked but he now wanted her handbag. She had an idea. She asked whether she could keep her cosmetic bag, to which the man giving the instructions made a jocular response about women always needing their make-up. He agreed and Valerie removed her cosmetics, but also managed to retrieve her fountain pen, and she slipped them both into the glove compartment. The light had now practically disappeared, and in the darkness Valerie picked out her wallet from her basket, opened it and removed the pound notes. She grabbed her handbag out of the basket and passed it to the back, and slowly, without any sudden movement, secreted the notes inside her bra. There was no challenge from the back and she was relieved that her quick thinking had gone unnoticed. At least her money was safe and perhaps now that the man had got what he had come for, the ordeal would soon finish. He would just walk off or perhaps more annoyingly, make them get out of the car, and steal it. That would hurt, stealing their Morris.

But the pointless conversation continued.

He knew Maidenhead, he said, a town a few miles along the M4, said he had been to Oxford and repeated that he was a wanted man. But now he remembered he was hungry. Had they got anything in the car he could eat? They had not, but it gave Michael and Valerie an opportunity to suggest an escape. They told the gunman to take the car so that he could go and get some food. The suggestion was refused. They offered to drive him somewhere where they could buy some chocolate and then return to the field. This was also declined and it was now met with the idea that he would wait until the morning, tie them up and then go. There was no hurry.

Between them they urged the man to leave there and then, while it was dark. That way he would not be seen. He did not like that idea either. What did this man want? He had got their money – well, some of it at least – so why did he not just simply take up their offers of escape? The frustration continued. He now asked them whether they were married and they explained that they were not. He asked their names and they told him and in quick retort, Valerie asked for his. Unsurprisingly, he refused. They offered once more for the man to take the car but the same answer came from the back: 'There's no hurry.'

It was now about half past ten, almost an hour since the tap on the window and the weapon poked through. They had been held at gunpoint, robbed and had offered the man the opportunity to disappear into the night, but he seemed to be dithering. Suddenly, a light emerged from one of the nearby houses. A man came out and it looked as though he was putting away a bicycle in a shed. The gunman reacted: 'If that man comes over here, don't say anyfing. I will shoot him and then I'll shoot you.'

Valerie assured him that the man would not be able to see the car in the dark and there was nothing for him to worry about. The threat though was repeated. If he came anywhere near the car, people would die.

The man who emerged from the house had not seen the Morris. He simply put his bicycle away and went back inside, unaware of the drama unfolding a hundred yards away. The danger had passed but the tension inside the Morris was palpable. The man had now threatened to use the gun. Another hour of aimless conversation followed. It was in Valerie's words, 'a game of cat and mouse with the gunman'. It was as if he had got himself into a situation he had never envisaged and now couldn't work out how to get himself out of it.

It was another forty-five minutes before things changed. 'I can't stand it any longer,' the man in the back said. He was hungry and wanted to find something to eat. Pointing the gun directly at Michael, he told him to get out. He unlocked his door and stepped into the field, the gunman climbing out at the same time. Michael was told that he was going to be put in the boot of the car and he was instructed to open it.

What followed was another act of defiance from Valerie. She had already tried to prevent her boyfriend from handing over the ignition key, had secreted money in her bra and now she instantly took action realising what was just about to happen. Knowing that Michael would be trapped inside the boot, she prepared his escape. With the gunman preoccupied with Michael, she reached over and grabbed hold of the tags on the back seat. She tugged hard and pulled the seat away from the boot frame. Michael would now be free to clamber out if the opportunity arose. She had acted just in time. The gunman, who she could now see had a grey or white handkerchief across the bottom half of his face, gangster style as she described it,[4] leaned in, and grabbed the rug from the back seat saying he was going to put it in the boot. It was clear what was happening and both Michael and Valerie now made a false claim. The car had a leaking exhaust, they said, and if the car was driven with Michael in the boot, he would suffocate from the fumes. Incredibly, this had an effect on the man giving the instructions. He thought about it and changed his mind. The boot was closed and Michael was instructed to get back into the driver's seat.

The stress was starting to get to Michael. He had almost been bundled into the boot and had escaped merely by the exaggeration about the exhaust pipe. Had the threat been carried out, what would have happened to Valerie? Although trying to cut down, he was a heavy smoker and now needed something to settle his nerves.

'Do you mind if I have a cigarette?'

'No,' came the reply, and he pulled a packet of cigarettes from his pocket. There was only one left.

'Do you smoke? I'm sorry, I only have one left.'

'No, I don't like smoking.'

Michael lit the cigarette and drew heavily on it. He smoked quickly, and when he was halfway through, Valerie's level-headedness again came to the surface.

'Why not put it out and save the other half for later? You'll probably need it.'

Michael stubbed it out.

Valerie was analysing all the information she had taken in. The gunman, she thought, was probably local to the area owing to their relatively isolated location, and it would have been impossible for him to have known that they were going to be parked there that evening; it had been a last-minute decision. He was clearly ill-prepared, not knowing what he wanted to do and kept contradicting himself time and time again about locations he had visited and detail about his background. He was obviously a thief, but why this? Brandishing a gun made no sense. He was, she surmised, just a poorly educated, young cockney criminal who was enjoying being a cowboy for the evening. Despite this, she was petrified and her anxiety levels were just about to increase.

He told them that they were going to drive but he was going to do the driving. On the face of it, this did not make any sense. If the gunman was driving, he would presumably have made at least one of them get into the back seat, which would have made him vulnerable to being grappled with from behind. Despite this being an opportunity for them both, the couple talked him out of it, particularly, as Michael said, he knew how to drive the car. This comment would play an important part when later analysing the events that were about to begin.

The gunman seemed to agree with their sentiment and the ignition key was passed from behind. The self-styled cowboy was hungry and they were going to get some food, he told them. This was frightening. No longer would an escape from the cornfield be possible. They had been held captive for two hours and the Morris Minor, now with its lights on, edged slowly towards the entrance of the field and turned left onto Marsh Lane.

Chapter Three

On to the A6

The front-seat occupants of the Morris were now experiencing a cocktail of emotions; concerned for their lives but maintaining a small hope that the ordeal would somehow soon be over. What the gunman had done so far was serious enough and if he was ever caught, he would undoubtedly go to prison. It was a little ironic that only a few weeks earlier the government had announced a three-month amnesty on firearms in the hope that many would surrender unwanted weapons, many of which had hung around in people's drawers and cupboards since the end of the Second World War. The police had expressed deep concern about just how easy it was to get a gun and in the hands of criminals it would make the country a dangerous place. In fact, in the first week of the amnesty, more than 1,300 weapons had been handed in at police stations, which rather proved their point. [1]

Such a criminal and such a gun now appeared to be in the back of the car and the position was dire. Perhaps, though, the gunman had had his fun already and he would just simply slip away without any hint of who he was. Perhaps even, he would merely want dropping closer to his home. He would tell them to keep facing the front, clamber out and they would drive off. They would not be able to identify him. And if he made off with the ignition key to give him time to escape, Valerie had deftly slipped a spare one from the glove compartment into her make-up bag. She was thinking ahead.

Immediately after leaving the cornfield, the car crossed over the recently opened M4 motorway, prompting the gunman to demonstrate that he had not yet grasped the concept of how this new type of road worked. Asked whether they could get on the motorway there and then, the couple in the front explained to him that in order to join you needed to get to a particular junction for that to happen. Instead, they crossed over the bridge and met with the A4. A discussion took place between the three of them about which way to turn, the gunman giving out confusing messages about where he wanted to go. To the left were Maidenhead and Bath; he had had enough of Maidenhead, he said. To the right was London; he didn't want to go there either. Michael and Valerie asked again. There was no hurry, he retorted. He was 'finking'. Finally, he decided on Northolt, to the right, and they headed off.

Given that the man had said he was hungry, Valerie again suggested they look for a chocolate or milk vending machine so that he could get something to eat or drink and, passing through Slough, they pulled over at Nevill and Griffins dairy. They stopped next to a milk machine, which needed sixpences. No one had any, which gave Valerie the idea about another possible escape.

'Shall we try and stop someone to ask?' she suggested.

'No, don't do that.'

He knew a café in Northolt where he could get food. They were ordered to drive on.

Occasionally, when speaking to Valerie, the gunman referred to Michael as her husband and more than once she told him that they were not married. He did not seem to be able to grasp the fact. He asked where they both lived, and they told him. The conversation reinforced Valerie's view that this was a man in his twenties and had no idea what he wanted. He changed his mind several times over whether they were to return to the cornfield in Dorney once he had eaten but the mention of Northolt seemed to confirm that they were on a journey that would take them well away from the spot where they had been caught by surprise.

As they drove through Slough, the time on the post office clock showed 11.45 p.m. They had been in the car under threat of death now for over two hours and it would have struck Valerie that as they passed through the town, she was within a couple of hundred yards of her home where her parents would probably by now have been worried about their daughter's late arrival home. 'Shan't be long,' she had shouted back as she had left and now, four hours later, she was going in the wrong direction heading for Northolt and an opportunity at the milk machine to escape had been and gone. Being close to home, Valerie made a desperate pitch, suggesting to the gunman that he should just abandon them and take the car. It was not to be. The order to continue driving remained.

There were times when silence filled the car. Little was said as they drove in the general direction of London. Valerie and Michael exchanged glances, well aware that a gun was pointing directly at them.

The silence was broken.

'How much petrol has the car got?' the voice from behind said.

One gallon, he was told, and it would only go for another 20 miles, a desperate attempt by the two of them to encourage the gunman to make a decision quickly about what he wanted to do. In fact, it had 2 gallons in its tank. His response was not encouraging.

'We'd better get some petrol.'

Obviously planning on travelling a long distance, he wanted the car filled with 4 gallons of fuel. Afraid that a full tank would increase the prospect of them being held captive in the car for a long time, Michael lied and said that the car's fuel tank was not big enough to hold that amount. The man thought for a second and then said:

> I want you to go in and get 2 gallons of petrol. You'll stay in the car, wind down the window and ask the man for 2 gallons only. I have the gun pointing at you and if you try and say anyfing else or give the man a note or make any indication that anyfing is wrong, I'll shoot.

The Morris pulled over into a Regent petrol station just beyond the Colnbook bypass close to London airport and the gunman handed Michael one of the pound notes he had earlier stolen from his wallet.[2] If there could ever be a lighter moment in this terrifying situation, Valerie would later say that Michael was really fussy about which type of petrol he put in his car and would have hated having to put Regent fuel into his beloved machine.

In reality, Valerie was now absolutely petrified. This was a time well before automated fuel pumps dominated garage forecourts. Motorists requiring fuel needed to pull alongside a petrol pump and wait until the garage attendant approached them. The driver would then tell the attendant how much fuel to put into the tank and once completed, pay the garage employee, waiting, if necessary, for any change that was due.

Much later, Valerie reflected on how a man, masked with a handkerchief across his face and brandishing a gun, could get away with pulling on to a garage forecourt and being seen in the rear seat dressed so inappropriately. She could never be sure, since she was being permanently reminded to face the front, but she sensed that he must have been removing the handkerchief at certain times to ensure he did not attract unnecessary attention. It would have been easy for him to simply lower the gun away from any prying eyes outside yet keep it aimed at its potential victims.

All Michael had to do, though, was put one foot wrong, a minor deviation from the plan that unnerved the cowboy, and she would be shot dead. But, with the gun pointing directly at her head, Michael did exactly as he was instructed, told the garage attendant he wanted 2 gallons, handed him the £1 note and received 10*s* 3*d* in change,[3] which the man in the back immediately demanded. In another act of misplaced humour, the gunman handed the threepenny piece to Valerie and said, 'You can have that as a wedding present.'

The instruction was given to drive off. Once again, an opportunity to escape had passed them by. Had one of them tried to alert the garage attendant or even simply tried to run from the vehicle, it could have ended in disaster. But with the car now containing around 4 gallons of fuel, the Morris drove from the garage forecourt capable of driving over 150 miles.

The instructions now came thick and fast. 'Turn left here. Now turn right.' Hesitation, and then more instructions. It was apparent that there was no clear plan but, given his directions, it seemed clear that he did not want to go in the general direction of central London. Trying to take advantage of the situation, both Valerie and Michael gave their kidnapper numerous opportunities to just take the car and abandon them, but each time their offer was refused. There was no hurry. He was 'finking'.

There was more conversation about food and the need to get to Northolt as they made their way through the Middlesex suburbs of Hayes and Stanmore, just outside north-west London. Michael was stressed and told the man that he needed some cigarettes and for a moment, the voice in the back became distracted. As they passed a cigarette vending machine he gave Michael the opportunity to buy some.

'You can stop and get some there. You can get out but don't do anyfing silly because I am pointing the gun at the girl.'

They pulled over, and before he stepped out, Michael kissed Valerie on the cheek and told her not do anything silly while he was away.[4] He went to the machine, bought a packet and returned to the vehicle. Again, neither took the opportunity to attempt an escape. The risks were too high. Michael climbed back into the driver's seat and offered a cigarette to the man.

'Do you want one?'

'Yes,' came the reply, despite him earlier saying that he did not smoke. 'But go on driving.'

Valerie took the packet from Michael, removed two cigarettes and placed them in her mouth. She lit both and handed one to Michael, the other to the gunman. As he took it from her, she saw for the first time that he was wearing a pair of black gloves. She couldn't tell whether he actually smoked the cigarette as he continued to call out his indiscriminate directions.

He told Michael to be careful, somewhere near Stanmore, Valerie thought, as he said there were some roadworks around the corner. He was right, there were; he clearly knew the area. Probably realising he had given away a piece of information about himself, he quickly tried to claw the situation back.

'I suppose you think I know this area but I don't,' he said.

More nervous commands followed. 'Mind that crossing,' he once said. 'Be careful of those traffic lights' and 'mind this corner'.

Desperate to make sure no harm came to them, Valerie tried to develop some form of human connection with the man wielding the gun by engaging him in conversation. His apparent nervousness provided an opportunity.

'Can you drive?' Valerie asked.

'Oh yes. All sorts of cars.'

The conversation continued about vehicles and at one point he asked Michael to explain the position of the gears on the gear lever, perhaps an indication that he planned on later stealing the car but also that maybe he was unfamiliar with this type of vehicle. A striking feature about the man's knowledge of cars arose when Michael needed to change down to third gear, at which point the gunman asked why he hadn't selected first. 'He certainly didn't know much about cars, certainly very little about Morris Minors,'[5] Valerie would later say.

They never did stop for food or drink. Instead, they drove aimlessly through Middlesex, never actually getting to Northolt due to them taking a wrong turn, and eventually driving into southern Hertfordshire. Valerie specifically recalled just missing Watford, going through Aldenham and then Park Street, a terminal entrance for the M1 motorway.[6] Approaching a roundabout, Michael asked for directions.

'Which way do you want to go?'

'St Albans.'

From this point on, the road turned into the A5, reinforcing the point that they were on a long journey, now nearly 40 miles away from home.

With the car travelling along at speeds between 30 and 50mph, the engine noise provided the opportunity for Valerie and Michael to communicate with each other through eye movements and by whispering in undertones. Valerie would later say that, 'He didn't seem to bother what we were saying, just as long as we faced the front and didn't turn our heads. He didn't seem to worry.'[7] The man was preoccupied, she felt, most likely considering his next move.

They too were scheming and their whispered plan of an attempt to escape or at least to frustrate the gunman was remarkable.

'We had a plan,' Valerie later told a jury. 'If we saw a policeman, Michael would pretend to have a steering problem with the car and pull up on the pavement next to him. I was going to hit him [the gunman] with a screwdriver I had armed myself with. However, when you want a policeman there is never one available and we didn't see *one* on our journey.'

She would later allegedly tell a journalist that she had also armed herself with a box of matches and she was considering lighting some of them and throwing them into the gunman's face, but this never featured in the accounts she would later tell the police. Quite how the 'policeman' plan was discussed without the gunman being alerted is remarkable. But, with no policeman in sight they continued their journey north.

They persisted with more ideas. Valerie suggested to Michael that when driving in built-up areas, they should slow down in an attempt to draw attention to themselves but when in the de-restricted areas, they should speed up. This was going well until the order came from the back to not go over 50mph.

Desperation had kicked in and they put the next part of their whispered conversation into place. The Morris was fitted with a reversing light, which was operated by a single switch underneath the dashboard to the left of the driver and which could be switched on and off without anyone in the back seat realising. As they idled along, Michael started to repeatedly switch it on and off in an attempt to alert someone – anyone. He flashed his headlamps at motor cars as they came towards him, switching between main and dipped beam. It had no effect, though quite what he hoped to achieve is not clear.

The Morris Minor rumbled along, Michael still making attempts to speed up in the quieter areas, before they eventually approached St Albans.

'Go to St Albans,' came the direction.

'This is St Albans.'

'No it isn't. This is Watford.'

Watford was about 8 miles south of where they were but the gunman would not accept the point. It was clear that he did not know where he was, what he wanted or where he was going. The couple chose not to argue and they drove on. Approaching yet another roundabout, they asked for further directions.

'Straight on.'

They were now on the A6, north of Luton, 50 miles from the Dorney cornfield and Michael continued to flash his reversing light.

Half a mile behind them, driving to work, Rex Mead and his passenger were distracted by the vehicle in front of them, a rear white light flashing on and off. Mead estimated that the time was around 12.20 a.m. He travelled behind it for a while, for about 500 yards, he thought, and decided that 'it was doing nothing silly,' and 'only doing about 25–30 miles per hour,' so he opted to overtake. As he passed slowly by, he looked to his left and saw three people inside. Two were in the front and the other was in the rear, offside seat. Mead's passenger gestured to them in an effort to establish if everything was alright but none of them seemed to notice him. With everything apparently in order, Mead accelerated past them.

His observation of the threesome in the Morris tends to support Valerie's later thoughts that the man in the back would occasionally remove his mask to avoid people staring at him. It would have been a simple enough task.

Mead did not know that inside the car he had spotted with the flashing reversing light, tensions were high. This had been the opportunity both Valerie and Michael had been waiting for, yet they did not react. They did not start to drive in an erratic manner to grab Mead's attention. They did not sound the car's horn. They did not wave frantically to make it obvious that there was a gun pointing at the back of their heads. They simply carried on driving, hoping that somehow the overtaking driver, in his 1956 Hillman or 1954 Ford Anglia, Valerie thought, would instantly recognise the dangerous situation they were in and do something about it. But, of course, he did not. He could not have known. They had devised a plan, put it into action, and then did nothing.

The man in the back, though, was nervous.

'What did they want?' he demanded. 'They must know something is wrong.'

In an effort to defuse the tension and scared that he would overreact and shoot them, they made a suggestion.

'One of the stop lights might have gone out. One of the bulbs is loose, isn't it Mike?' Valerie quickly, misleadingly, suggested.

They were instructed to stop. Michael switched off the reversing light, was ordered to surrender the ignition key and the man stepped out and edged towards the back keeping his hand on the rear door.[8]

He got back in and said, 'They are OK [the lights]. You must have done something.'

The ignition key was handed back and Michael was ordered to carry on with the journey, but it was clear that the gunman had become unnerved.

This had probably been their only real opportunity for them to have driven off and left the gunman on an unlit stretch of the A6. But it was over in an instant. He was out of the car for only a few seconds and did not give the couple in the front the time to grab the spare key, put it into the ignition and drive off. The kidnapper would have easily had the time to jump back in and take whatever revenge he thought necessary. Limited though it was, this window of opportunity had now gone and once again they were heading north, now almost 60 miles from home.

The subject of food had long since disappeared from the conversation. Perhaps the shock of the overtaking car had had some effect on the gunman. He had held Michael and Valerie captive for over three hours and been giving constant directions, albeit without any measure of confidence. At one point he handed back the watches he had stolen from them, perhaps the first hint that the man's motive for this treacherous journey was not to steal. Valerie slid both of them onto her left wrist and told Michael that she 'will put yours on my wrist, darling'.[9] She could detect that the man in the back kept on looking at his own watch, before saying that it would soon be daybreak, told them again that there was no hurry and that he was 'finking'. It had become monotonous. But suddenly the instructions changed. He needed to sleep, or to use his exact phrase, he wanted 'a kip'.

With her skills in map reading and navigation, Valerie distinctly remembered driving through the villages of Barton-le-Clay and Silsoe, Michael still earnestly flashing his reversing light, as the gunman looked for somewhere that they could stop. Ronald Chiodo, an American airman who had just finished work, remembered driving south on the A6, between 1.30 and 1.45 he recalled, when he saw in his reversing mirror the flashing light on the back of a car travelling in the opposite direction. He thought it strange but carried on.

Suddenly, the gunman shouted out.

'Turn down there,' he commanded, pointing to a road on the left.

Michael did as he was told and turned slowly into a narrow lane. As the car edged forward, Valerie saw a sign that read, 'Private. No parking.'

In a remarkable step, which seemed to defy all attempts to try to escape, Valerie blurted out, 'We can't stop here. This is a private road and we'll draw attention to ourselves.'

It will never be known exactly why Valerie said what she did. She would never elaborate on the point. Perhaps she felt that anyone disturbing them would spook the gunman into acting irrationally at a time when the journey was hopefully coming to an end. Yet, she and Michael had spent the last three hours trying to find an opportunity to attract attention to themselves; it had been their secret plan as they journeyed along from London. More likely though, she was simply scared, finding themselves in an isolated spot, perhaps too isolated for her own comfort, the ideal location for the gunman to put a bullet in each of them. Whatever her reason, the gunman agreed with her and ordered Michael to turn the car around and head off north along the A6 towards Bedford.

Minutes later, another small turning on the left presented itself. The gunman was alert.

'Go down there.'

Once again, the car turned into the lane and after about 50 to 100 yards a row of houses appeared. Michael stopped the car, but there was more reaction from Valerie.

'We can't stop here. Someone will see us.'

For the second time, the gunman agreed and ordered Michael to carry on and start looking again.

They now hunted along the A6 searching for somewhere to pull over, somewhere where they would not be disturbed and the gunman could have his 'kip'. This was a double-edged sword. A quiet location could prevent the gunman from overreacting to a passing motorist; there was little chance of a pedestrian passing at that time of the night since it was approaching two o'clock in the morning. Such a spot, though, would also present the perfect opportunity for the man to shoot them. No one would see or hear anything and they would be dead. But the gunman's demeanour did not suggest he would kill them on the side of a road. He had had an opportunity to do that four hours ago when he first approached them in the cornfield. Surely, his confused behaviour indicated that there was no plan and that all he wanted was to sleep.

The car crept through the silent streets of Clophill village and edged slowly north, the occupants' eyes searching for an obvious spot. The A6 north of the village meanders to the left before swinging back to the right, stretches out and then bears back round to the left. The road then climbs gradually, known locally as Deadman's Hill, an RAC box a few feet in on the left-hand side. At this point, the road was flanked with wide verges and telegraph poles. Fifty yards further along, a small opening appeared in the verge and the gunman shouted, 'Go in there.'

By the time he shouted out his instruction, Michael had already passed the entrance and was told to turn the car around and go back. He carried out a three-point turn in the road, his second that night, and headed back in the opposite direction, purposely driving past the entrance. Unsurprisingly, the order came to turn around again. Michael complied but it had been his attempt to frustrate the man who had been tormenting him for hours. This time, when reaching the entrance he turned in and then immediately turned right again along a concrete strip. 'I thought it was a disused runway,'[10] Valerie would later say. It led almost immediately to a cul-de-sac with a pile of gravel blocking the way ahead. The instruction came to turn the car around again, stop and 'turn all the lights out'.[11] This was it. The journey seemed to have come to an end. The fear began to surface again and in a vain attempt to still try to attract attention, Michael kept the reversing light switched on, but it was noticed and he was told to turn it off. The ignition key was passed back.

The view of the car's position from the A6 was partially blocked by the low verge, well over 20ft wide and with a single tree and a few wild flowers 3 or 4ft tall. With its lights out, any passing motorist would have been excused for not seeing the silent Morris. The abducted couple had now been held prisoner for four and a half hours and were over 60 miles from home. It was two o'clock in the morning. It was dark. No cars were passing. The handkerchiefed cowboy, gun in hand, pointed it at his victims.

Chapter Four

Clophill

The gunman, now in total control of the situation, picked up Michael's green-and-white-striped laundry bag and ordered him to put it somewhere in the front. He placed it on the floor by the gear lever.

'I want to kip,' he said, 'but first I must tie you up.'

The gunman demanded to know whether there was any rope in the car, perhaps a tow rope in the boot, but when he was told that there was not, he suggested cutting up the rug on the back seat.[1] But there was nothing that could be used and Michael was forced out of the car.

'Let me look in the boot to see if you have any rope.'

He clearly did not believe them. Back in the cornfield when he had thought about putting Michael into the boot he had seen just how crammed it was with clothing, tools and other car paraphernalia and probably suspected there would be something there that he could use. At gunpoint, Michael was ordered to open the boot. A small piece of rope was found in a toolbox, which was grabbed by the gunman, and Michael, with the gun waving directly at him, was told to get back in the car.

Now back in the rear seat, he continued his orders. 'Give me your tie,' he said. The scientist removed it and passed it backwards and Valerie at this point was ordered to turn slightly. She turned to her right and was facing Michael. She was petrified, but she was very aware of what he was trying to do. He told her that he wanted to tie her hands and ordered her to hold them out in front of her. She complied, and he first wrapped the tie tightly around her wrists and then ordered her to extend her fingers so that he could force her thumbs together. But in an effort to engineer another escape opportunity and as a measure of self-protection, as the man tied her wrists, she pulled them apart so that they would not be bound tight. He thought they were, she told a court later. Thinking, though, that he had his prey under control, he went one stage further and used the rope he had found in the toolbox to tie her bound wrists to the rear passenger door handle. Now, he must have thought, she was safely pinioned.

He was mumbling, Valerie remembered. Something about needing to find something to do the same to Michael. She took advantage of his mind apparently being elsewhere, pretended to drop something on the floor and leaned down. With her hands out of sight, she wriggled one of them free, immediately slipped it back into the now-loosened rope and straightened herself up. If an opportunity arose, she could now escape.

Throughout the ordeal of fetching the rope from the boot, the removal of Michael's tie and the binding of Valerie's wrists, the couple pleaded repeatedly for him not to shoot, to spare them their lives, to take anything he wanted but each time got the answer, 'Na, I'm finking.' He repeated that if he was going to shoot them, he would have done it by now. At one time he suggested that he would release them at daybreak but that seemed just another idea made up on the spot.

Hearing him getting restless about how to secure Michael, Valerie said, 'Why don't you tie us up together, just leave us outside and tie us up and then you can go?' She even suggested that he tie their feet together. The idea was dismissed. He was insistent on dealing with the driver. He reconsidered cutting the rug but abandoned the idea again when it finally dawned on him that there was nothing in the car that could do the job.

'Why not use *your* tie?' Valerie persisted.

'Oh, no,' he said, 'I need that.'

For the gunman to have made a point that he needed to keep his own tie is an important aspect and its significance would become apparent much later.

He made his next move.

'Give me that bag up,' he demanded, indicating the laundry bag he had passed forward only a few moments earlier.

He had obviously decided to search it and Michael bent forward to carry out the instruction. He picked it up and passed it backwards, over the front seats. As his body turned slightly, there were two, quick, successive loud bangs. Valerie described it as 'a terrific noise' and instantly, 'there was the smell of gunpowder'. Michael's body lurched forward and it fell onto the steering wheel. 'I could hear blood pouring from his head,' Valerie later said. He had been shot twice in the back of the head with no warning and for no apparent reason. His body was twitching, and for the first time Valerie lost her composure.

She screamed, 'Mike, darling,' before turning her attention on the gunman.

'You shot him, you bastard. Why did you do that?'

'He frightened me. He moved suddenly. I got scared,'[2] came the reply.

'Well, you told him to move the washing back.'

'Well, I know but I got scared.'

A later post-mortem[3] would confirm that Michael was shot at close range, two bullets entering the head, close to the left ear, no more than an inch or two apart. They had passed straight through and exited through his right cheek and though probably he was unconscious, the cause of death was asphyxiation due to inhalation of blood. The stark reality was that Michael now lay dead, murdered, in the front seat of his car, inches away from Valerie, who had witnessed the whole drama.

Valerie was now hysterical. She looked at the twitching body in the driver's seat and watched as it jolted backwards, its head slumping over the back of the seat. The horror of what had just happened started to dawn on her.

'Oh, for God's sake, don't kill me. Just let me get him to a doctor quick and I'll drop you anywhere.'

Her pleas were met with more illogical and contradictory replies, the gunman first denying Michael was dead but then acknowledging the obvious reality. She begged time and time again to allow her to get him to a doctor. While her hands were now free, she kept them held together to make it look like she was still under his control. She continued to cry out for the man to get assistance but her plea was greeted by the now all too familiar, 'Be quiet will you. I'm finking.'

Quite why Valerie said what she said next would never be explained but she asked, 'Well, what is your name? What shall I call you?'

It was as if she knew she needed to calm the man down and appearing to be friendly with him might have the right effect. The response was astonishing. After a momentary pause, possibly caused by the shock of being asked the question in the first place, he said,

'Call me Jim.'

She would tell the police that she presumed that this was not his real name.[4]

The question seemed to have an effect, though, and he again asked Valerie for her name. Again, she told him. Perhaps this would work and he would soften his attitude towards her. Her mind was rushing. She was being met with indecisiveness, denial, even indifference. She tried something else.

'If I see a car coming I'll stop them and ask them to give you a lift. I won't say anything that's happened as long as we can get help.'

The obvious implausibility of her last plea, though unknown to her at her moment of terror, would have been apparent to the gunman. He had no intention of getting a lift with someone and quite how this woman would not say anything when she had a dead man in her arms was beyond comprehension.

This surreal drama was acted out for twenty to twenty-five minutes, Valerie later estimated, and throughout, Michael's bleeding body occupied the tiny, cramped area inside the Morris Minor. During this time the gunman, now turned murderer, repeatedly asked Valerie her name as he couldn't seem to remember it. It would not have been obvious to her at the time but the gunman had not dealt with the situation he had created by killing her immediately afterwards, ridding himself of any human being who could testify against him. The reason for that was about to become apparent.

The duffel bag had fallen onto the back seat of the car and the killer, who was immediately behind the bloodied body, delved in and pulled out a pair of pyjamas.

'I'll cover him up. He's dead.'[5]

Seemingly unmoved by the atrocity of his murderous act, he placed the pyjamas over Michael's face, slid across the seat and sat behind Valerie. He was ready for his next move.

'I know your hands are free. You can throw the ropes away,' he bragged.

Instinctively, Valerie tried to grab the gun, which was being waved inches away from her face, but he pushed her back. He looked at her.

'Kiss me,' he said.

Only a small gap separated them.

'No,' she nervously replied.

She would describe this moment as her 'greatest anguish' since she was not sure that Michael was dead and, for all she knew, he was being mentally tortured by having to listen to the gunman's latest demand.[6]

He made it several times again, and then said, 'If you don't, I will count five and then I will shoot you.'

He started to count and Valerie turned to allow him to kiss her. It was brief. But now she was literally face to face with the killer and as she stared at him, by luck a car drove past, travelling north, and its headlights lit up the attacker's face. He seemed oblivious to his sudden exposure, or perhaps he simply did not care.

'He had very large, pale blue, staring, icy eyes,' she told a jury five months later. 'He had a pale face as I should imagine anyone would have having just shot someone.'

The passing headlight lasted only a few seconds, but it was enough.

Perhaps emboldened by having now seen him, she tried once more to grab the gun, but she was again pushed away. He was too strong.

'That was a silly thing to do. I thought you were sensible. I can't trust you now,' he said.

This comment was perhaps indicative of the killer's intentions and what was about to happen. He openly declared his mistrust of her not only because of her attempting to seize the weapon but influenced probably by his annoyance with the couple's behaviour – the use of the reversing light and the untying of the rope.

He continued with his advances towards her.

'Come and sit in the back of the car with me. I will count five and if you haven't got in I'll shoot.'

To reinforce his message, he got out of the car, opened Valerie's passenger door and pointed the gun directly at her.

'Come on, get in.'

'No.'

The gun's muzzle almost touching her, he repeated, 'Get in.'

It was no use resisting any further. If she refused to do as she was told, there was no doubt he would shoot; Michael's body was proof of that.

She moved slowly in the hope that a car would pass but there was only silence. She clambered in and slid across, Michael's pyjama-covered face hanging immediately next to her in the dark. The duffel bag rested between her and the rear door. The man got in, slammed the door behind him and sat facing her, his gun rested on his lap. She saw that he was still wearing his black gloves, which she thought were silk and tight-fitting. He tried to kiss her and started to grope her breasts. She then remembered the money she had removed from her wallet and had secreted in her bra. She was determined, even as she was being sexually mauled, that he was not going to get his hands on it. As he continued to fondle, he ordered her to undo her bra and as she obeyed the instruction, she grabbed the pound notes and deftly slipped them into her Mackintosh pocket. He seemed not to notice.

'Take your knickers off,' came the next order.

'No.'

'Come on.'

She again refused but this was swiftly followed by another threat to shoot. Reluctantly, fearfully, she complied.

Now naked underneath her skirt and petticoats, the attacker manoeuvred himself and casually placed his gun on the rear parcel shelf to enable him to remove his gloves. But he struggled and with Valerie awkwardly laid back against the upright of the seat and the duffel bag, he ordered her to remove them. She pulled one off, which he put in his pocket.

Up to this point, Valerie had been wearing her glasses; she needed them for everyday use. He told her to remove them and she put them into her coat pocket. Then he pushed her further into the duffel bag and unzipped his flies.

'Put me in,' he ordered. Valerie did as she was told and with her now half-lying, half-sitting, he raped her.

It was over quickly, 'a very, very short time, a minute or so,' she would later tell the police. 'He didn't seem particularly excited. He seemed sort of anxious to get it over with. He didn't seem sexually excited.'

She pushed him away, forcing him to withdraw, and as if the indignity so far had not been enough, he said to her, 'You haven't had much sex, have you?'

Valerie's response was clinical. 'Can I put my knickers on?'

She was allowed and the murderer, now also rapist, zipped up his flies, put his glove back on and retrieved his gun from the parcel shelf.

Valerie was first to talk.

'For goodness sake, go. Take the car, it's almost daybreak.'

It is impossible to be sure about the exact time that Valerie spent sitting in the car with her rapist and dead boyfriend. Their journey of terror had been unwittingly witnessed by Ronald Chiodo when he saw the reversing light on the car sometime between 1.30 a.m. and 1.45 a.m. when he was fifteen minutes south of the layby at Deadman's Hill. The time the Morris arrived at its final resting place, therefore, is likely to have been between 1.50 a.m. and 2.05 a.m. In broadest terms, Michael had been shot around two o'clock and Valerie had been raped by half past. Suggesting that it would soon be daybreak was a genuine mistake on Valerie's behalf. In fact, it would be another four hours before the sun would rise.

'Be quiet, will you. I'm finking,' uttered the man, whose unimaginable acts of violence seemed to have reached their conclusion. He paused for a moment, staring at the body in the front seat of the car.

Seconds later, he said, 'We'll have to get him out. I'll leave you here and take the car.'

He seemed to have at last recognised and accepted Valerie's offer of escape. Michael was dead but at least she would survive the ordeal.

Both got out. The instructions continued.

'You'll have to get him out. I mustn't get blood on me,' the gunman said.

Not only had she been raped but now she was being told to remove her boyfriend's blood-soaked body from the vehicle. She opened the driver's door and saw that Michael's hands were still gripping the steering wheel, as if he had somehow instinctively grabbed it when the bullets had pierced his skull. She gingerly touched them and felt that they were cold. Blood had poured from his nose, and his jacket, shirt and trousers were soaked. Knowing that this could be her last opportunity to be rid of the killer, she grabbed Michael's shoulders and tried to pull him from the seat. But he was too heavy, plus, she thought, his legs had caught around the pedals. She pulled again but through either sheer fright or simple lack of strength, she could not tug him free.

'You'll have to help me,' she told the gunman, who was standing some distance away, probably to ensure no blood got on his own clothes.

He reluctantly edged forward, grabbed Michael's legs and pulled them free from the pedals. Together, they dragged him out of the front seat and his body slumped onto the gravelled road. Realising the man wanted to get into the front seat, Valerie dragged the body away from the driver's door, around the rear of the car and laid it on the edge of the grass verge running alongside the layby. She looked at her watch. It was just after 3 a.m.[7]

Valerie desperately hoped that the end was in sight. She could soon be free from this nightmare, but she had a request.

'Let me have my things out of the car.'

She wanted her basket, which contained items she needed for work. She had just witnessed the murder of her boyfriend, had been raped, had dragged the body along the road but now wanted her basket and seemed to be focusing on the time she would be going back to the laboratory.

'It has some rally things for work. I must have it,' she reiterated.

The gunman had no desire for her belongings and allowed her to recover them. She grabbed hold of her basket from the front footwell, Michael's duffel bag and a few items out of the glove compartment. This was their car, their belongings, their life. This man shall not have them. But she was not finished. One of her most cherished items was still in the car. The white artificial flower-holder was stuck to the windscreen with its three artificial pink flowers and miniature roses. She pulled the holder from the screen and put it in her basket. If she had thought quickly enough, she would have recovered the Valentine's card in her basket,[8] but things were moving too fast. At least some of her personal items were salvaged.

Her last-gasp pleas now fell out of her mouth. She told him to go and again said that she would not tell anyone. She would do nothing, just sit there and not go for help.

His response was strange. He needed her to show him how the Morris gears worked and where the light switch was. She had much earlier come to the conclusion that the man was not familiar with the car and was, she thought, a nervous passenger. Even though she was surprised by the request, she was only too eager to do anything to get rid of him, showed him the light switch, explained the gear movements, including selecting reverse and even started the engine for him. She stepped back but as she did so, the engine stalled. She re-started it and the man climbed inside. Everything was ready for the moment when the ordeal would end. The killer had got into the car having already folded the car rug over the front seat, presumably an act to stop him getting any trace of blood on his clothes. He was clearly very conscious about getting contaminated by any of Michael's blood and she watched as he wiped the steering wheel clean. With the car engine running she returned to Michael's body lying at the side of the road, the pyjamas still draped over his face.

She knelt down on both knees, legs tucked up underneath her, looking at Michael. But the gunman had followed and now stood over her.

'I fink I had better hit you on the head or somefing to knock you out or else you will go for help,' he said.

'No, I won't. I won't move. Just go. Hurry.'

Her cunning and resourcefulness remained. She pulled from her pocket one of the pound notes that she had managed to switch from her purse, to her bra and finally to her raincoat pocket and offered it to him: 'There you are. You can have that if you'll go quickly.'

Appearing shocked, he said, 'Where did you get that from?'

'Oh, it was just in my pocket.'

This person had just murdered a man and raped a woman. Hours earlier he had started the ordeal by stealing their valuables and now, five hours later, he casually took the pound note and walked away.

He walked, Valerie estimated, about 6 to 10ft, but suddenly turned and pointed the gun directly at her. He started to shoot. She saw the flame. She immediately felt something hit her, at the top of her left arm, and she screamed out. A second bullet struck, around the neck, and she immediately lost all sensation in her legs and collapsed to the ground. Now lying on the uncomfortable gravel, unable to move, more shots were fired, two or three she thought. Something hit her. She then heard the frightening noise of clicking and the obvious sound of reloading. The killer was not going away. He was going to finish her off. More shots rang out, though she was unsure whether any hit her; she sensed that they went over her head. Then she heard the clicking again; the gun had been emptied once more.

She was still alive, for some reason not feeling any pain, but quite unable to move. She heard footsteps approaching and she lay perfectly still and purposely held her breath, hoping to convince her attacker that she was dead. He walked up to her, touched her either with his hand or foot, and seemingly satisfied that she was dead, turned and walked back towards the car. She let out a hushed breath and she listened to his footsteps fading away against the throb of the Morris engine. Seconds later, the car door slammed shut and she saw the headlights suddenly burst into life. The car started to move forward and slowly its engine faded into the distance and its lights disappeared from her view.

It was over.

She was confused. She tried to turn over onto her back but was unable. She thought to herself, 'What am I to do now?' She tried again to move, hoping that perhaps she could somehow roll along the layby and on to the road. That way, someone would surely find her and help would arrive. But no matter how hard she tried, nothing seemed to work. She simply could not move.

Her emotions were mixed. She would later tell the police that at one point she thought she was going to die. Indeed, she prayed that she would, but then changed her attitude. 'If I die,' she thought, 'no one will know who to look for.' More importantly, she could not afford to die as her grandmother was ill in a nursing home and news of her own death would probably kill her. She had to think more clearly.

Luckily, her arms could move and she decided that she would somehow try to write the description of her attacker using stones from the road. She knew she had to sketch out the words 'blue eyes' and 'brown hair,' but her fumbling around in the dark found nothing to help her.

Time passed and after thirty minutes or so, she heard a car approaching. She started to scream to attract attention but the sound of the engine just passed her by. No wonder. She was mostly hidden by the verge, a good distance from the main road, and it was dark. Another one passed and she desperately grabbed hold of her petticoat and tried waving it. It was not seen. William Clark drove by, he estimated, at around 5.30 a.m. and saw what he presumed was a sleeping hitch-hiker in the layby. There was no need to disturb him, so he carried on with his journey.[9] Eventually, Valerie either fell asleep or, more likely, wandered in and out of consciousness.

She had no concept of time but the next thing she recalled was a pair of legs standing next to her. It was now daylight. The man was putting a jacket over her.

She remembered telling the man her name and address, Michael's name and even managed to accurately give the registration number of the car, 847 BHN. Their attacker had large eyes and brown hair, was in his twenties and he had driven off towards London. At one point she remembered saying, 'Stop that car.'

The next thing she knew was seeing ambulancemen and a police inspector as they lifted her into an ambulance. Her next stop was Bedford hospital, but for now, the layby at the side of the A6 was about to be put under the microscope. A woman had been raped and shot, a man lay dead and the ground was littered with spent cartridge cases. The killer had stolen £4.

PART 2 – THE INVESTIGATION

Chapter Five

The First Two Weeks

About 6.40 that morning 67-year-old labourer Sidney Burton was walking past the layby on Deadman's Hill. His home was just under a mile away in West End, Haynes and he was heading in the direction of Luton. To his right he heard a mumbling noise. He looked across and saw a man and a woman lying side by side, and as he moved closer he noticed the woman was moving. He could not understand what she was trying to say, saw that both she and the man had blood on their clothes and assumed they had been involved in an accident. In the distance he saw a man standing next to an RAC box, approached him and described what he had just seen.[1] The man's name was John Kerr. He was an 18-year-old Oxford undergraduate who, as a summer job, was part of a team carrying out a census of vehicles on the A6. He had been there for the past two days filling in forms provided by Bedford County Council.

When Burton first approached him, he told him that there was a man and a woman lying in the road and the woman seemed to want something; he thought she was a foreigner, he said. And with that, Burton simply walked off. What Kerr did next would be subjected to extreme scrutiny for the next forty years and would result in one of the principal criticisms to be levelled at the police. He walked to where the people were reported to be and as he made his way along what he called the service road, he found the young woman lying on her back alongside a man. He saw that her skirt was pushed above her waist but her underclothing showed no sign of interference. Her clothes and face were spattered in blood and immediately realising something was seriously wrong, he asked her what had happened.

'I've been shot,' came the response.

Shocked, he looked at the man and saw that his face was covered in what he described as 'a piece of blue towelling like a face flannel'.[2] The woman asked him to stop a passing car, which he did and asked the motorist to inform the police. He returned and again asked her what had happened. In his statement that he made to the police later that day, Kerr said that the woman told him: 'We picked up a man at Slough at 9.30 p.m. He held us up at gunpoint. He said he had a .38.'

He asked her what the man was like and she replied, 'He had big staring eyes, fairish brown hair, slightly taller than I am, and I am 5ft 3½in. When he left us he took our car which is number 847 BHN.'[3]

When Kerr made this written witness statement at Bedfordshire Police headquarters later that day, neither he nor the officer who took the statement could have realised how important it would become. Kerr's statement was short and his only additions were that he had placed his jacket over the woman to keep her warm and that he tried to feel the pulse of the man but could not find one. He had also seen two empty cartridge cases on the roadway close to the woman's body.

The call to the police was logged at 6.55 and one of the first officers on the scene was Inspector Edward Milborrow. Within four minutes he had spoken to the woman, established that her name was Valerie Storie and had circulated the registration number of the stolen Morris. He also recovered six spent cartridge cases that he found close to the two victims.[4] As more police officers arrived, they were concerned with preserving the scene and keeping at a distance a number of members of the public who were beginning to gather.

Meanwhile, an ambulance had arrived to attend to Valerie and as she was being placed on a trolley, Sergeant Peter Wortley recalled Valerie saying, 'He shot me three times in the head, I pretended I was dead.' He asked her if she knew who her assailant was and she replied, 'No, I reckon he was mad. He said he had been on the run for four months. He promised not to touch us.'[5] Constable William Robertson noticed that on her left wrist she was wearing two watches, one a gent's the other a lady's.[6] She was placed in the rear of the ambulance and within an hour of her being found by Sidney Burton, she was being treated in Bedford hospital.

Sergeant Wortley was one of the officers who was required to move the increasing number of members of the public away from the area. While doing this he spoke to John Kerr, who identified himself as the man who had first spoken to Valerie. He observed that Kerr appeared to be very distressed, and he asked whether he could return to the RAC box to carry on with the census. Wortley obtained his details and allowed him to leave.

More senior officers were now arriving, including Chief Inspector Oliver, Superintendent Morgan and Detective Superintendent Charles Barron, who would be in charge of the investigation. Certain formalities were being carried out such as placing canvas screens around the scene and a doctor examining Michael's body to certify his death.[7] Chief Inspector Oliver found a number of spent bullets on the ground, including one in a nearby ditch and one in the green and white duffel bag close to the victim's head. He took possession of these as they would be needed for a later forensic examination.

Superintendent Barron would have been briefed about the nature of Valerie's injuries, the initial story that the attack had started in Slough almost 60 miles away possibly after picking up a hitch-hiker, and that there was an outstanding stolen vehicle, the registration number of which had already been circulated. He would also have been aware that Valerie had said that she had been attacked by someone who she thought must have been a madman who had said he had been on the run for four months. One matter that needed urgent attention was a circulation of the description of the killer. Officers had been sent to the hospital in the hope that they would be able to speak to Valerie, but given the nature of her injuries, there was a strong likelihood that doctors would not allow them access to her, and even that she might die.

Instructions were given for a national police broadcast to be made (one not designed for public consumption) and it was circulated by telex at 10.50 that morning. It stated that the description of the man was aged 25, smooth face, big eyes, smartly dressed in dark grey or black suit and it said 'alleged that suspect gave his name as Brown'. The registration number of the missing car, 847 BHN, was also included.

When compared to the description given by Kerr in his statement, which said, 'He had big staring eyes, fairish brown hair … When he left us he took our car which is number 847 BHN,' it can be seen where errors and confusion start to occur. The size of the eyes and the registration number are common between the two, but brown hair had now become Brown, a surname. The most likely source of this confusion was a statement made by a motorist who was passing the scene, saw the commotion, and stopped to see if he could help. He spoke to Valerie and asked her name. She told him, although, only hours later when he made his statement, he could not remember it. But he said, he then asked her: 'Who done it?'

She replied, 'Brown. He's taken my car.'[8]

In any event, the scene was being searched, a description of the killer had been circulated and Valerie was receiving medical attention.

A couple of hours earlier, Detective Sergeant Douglas Rees and Detective Constable Gwendolyn Rutland had arrived at the hospital. When Rutland first arrived, she saw Valerie in a private ward, where she described her as conscious but obviously very distressed and being treated by doctors. Before this, upon arrival at the Casualty Department, Valerie's upper clothes had been cut to remove them – her cardigan, blouse and bra – and had now been thrown away. However, the shoes and raincoat she had been wearing had been preserved. Consultant orthopaedic surgeon Andrew Pollen was now overseeing her examination and treatment and over the next few hours he would treat her wounds, give Valerie a blood transfusion and carry out a number of X-rays. He saw, he thought, seven wounds around the neck, face and left upper arm area and realised that her lower limbs were completely paralysed. The right side of her jaw and left upper arm were fractured and X-rays revealed two bullets lodged inside her chest. Despite this being a serious, life-threatening emergency, Pollen was conscious of the police needing to speak to his patient and in between the various medical interventions, Rutland and Rees began the process of interviewing their only witness.

Rees would say at the end of a series of interviews in hospital that day that despite having received horrendous injuries, Valerie 'spoke rationally and only paused to wipe away secretions from her mouth, which were interrupting her speech. The conversation flowed from her naturally and it was unnecessary [*sic*] to ask only the minimum of questions.'[9] In fact, she had told Rutland that she thought she was going to die and wanted her to take down a full description of her attacker. Even at that point she felt adamant that she would know her assailant.[10]

Calmly and quietly, Valerie gave a comprehensive account, with considerable attention to detail from the moment she and Michael had been abducted in the cornfield to the moment the killer drove off in the Morris. On the journey along the A6, she told the two detectives, the man had said that he was going to tie them up against a tree and steal the car but he seemed to abandon the idea. After Michael had been shot 'from literally three inches firing range', she screamed for several minutes and stated the gunman had said, 'If you don't shut up, I will do the same to you.' She added, 'I thought he was slightly round the twist.' She stated that he had then said, 'I'll give you five seconds to get in the back of the car to be raped or shot in the back of the head.' Valerie said, 'I thought the first was the lesser of the two evils.'

When giving details of the moment she had been raped, Rees noticed that Valerie became very upset and it was obvious that she did not want to talk about it. The character of the killer became very apparent when Valerie told the detectives that when he took aim at her, she 'was looking at him pleadingly'. It had made no difference. She had never seen the man before. The only name she had, which she did not believe was real, was 'Jim'. Asked whether she would recognise him again, she said, 'I think I would be able to identify him. In fact, I'm sure I would.'

The description of her attacker was an important part of Valerie's account and she was clear in her responses. He had a young voice, could not pronounce 'th', and his hair was straight, well-greased and dark brown. His face was 'squarish', just broader at the forehead than at the chin, he had a pale complexion, and large eyes that were not deep set but at face level. He boasted that he wore gloves so that he did not leave any fingerprints, would disguise himself and although the police were looking for him he would evade them; he appeared very proud of that.

Finally, she spoke about Michael, outlined the background to their relationship and said, 'His wife was going to divorce him and then we were going to get married.'

It was now apparent that Valerie had been raped and Doctor Pollen was asked to take some samples from her. Pollen took a vaginal swab and sample of pubic hair from the patient and handed them to one of his colleagues, Doctor John Valentine. Valentine, a consultant pathologist at the hospital, examined the swab under a microscope and found that it contained a small quantity of mucoid material, which in turn contained a number of human spermatozoa. 'They were well preserved and there were tails. They were fairly fresh. I plugged the tube with a rubber bung and labelled it with Miss Storie's name and the date and time.' He placed the pubic hairs in an envelope that he sealed, labelled and signed. He then placed both items in the laboratory refrigerator.

Rees and Rutland had, over a period of five hours, obtained a very detailed account of the events from the night before. Rutland, in particular, had made copious notes and the information was passed to the incident post set up at the layby on the A6. Crucially, however, the colour of the killer's eyes had not been mentioned, only their size, but it was clear that they had been abducted from the cornfield at gun point. There had been no hitch-hiker. It was now shortly after 1.30 p.m. and the large eyes and brown hair of the abductor had been emphasised.

★★★

In 1961, it was still open to provincial police forces to call upon the expertise of the Metropolitan Police in cases that appeared complex or where the identity of the offender was not quickly established. Detective Superintendent Barron would have instantly realised that this was a case that was going to stretch beyond the county boundaries of Bedfordshire. The initial crime was committed in Buckinghamshire, its victims came from that area and potentially he could be searching for a madman who had been on the run for months. At least, that was the picture being presented to him. This was going to be a nationwide hunt. Bedfordshire Constabulary therefore took the decision to call upon Scotland Yard for their expertise. The crime remained the responsibility of the county force but the investigation was to be led by a metropolitan detective. He arrived at the scene shortly after half past two that afternoon, eight hours after the victims had been found and within an hour of Valerie's detailed description of her assailant being passed by telephone to the incident post.

Detective Superintendent Basil Montague Acott, known to his friends and colleagues as Bob, was 48 years old and had been a police officer for twenty-eight years. He had served in the Royal Air Force during the Second World War and had been awarded the Distinguished Flying Cross (DFC) in 1945. He had worked in the Criminal Investigation Department for most of his service and had received numerous awards and commendations for outstanding detective work and acts of courage. Only three months earlier, he had led the investigation of a murder committed in Sussex in the course of a bank robbery. A man was convicted and executed.[11] He was thus familiar with the investigation of capital cases of murder and the outcome that awaited those convicted. The murder of Michael Gregsten fell within that category since death had occurred through shooting.[12] Anyone convicted would hang.

One of the most dramatic events of that afternoon was the arrival of Janet Gregsten, Michael's wife, who had been visited at her home in Abbots Langley and had been told the tragic news. She informed the police that Michael had only left her at 3 p.m. the afternoon before to go and see Valerie and had given him some freshly laundered clothing, including a pair of pyjamas, which she had put in a duffel bag as she knew that he would soon be moving into his new accommodation in Maidenhead. Now, she arrived at the layby in Bedfordshire, accompanied by a female officer, Inspector Arnott, and was asked to see if she could identify the body of her dead husband, his freshly laundered, and now blood-soaked pyjamas draped over his head. The clothing was lifted to allow her to see the face and despite the upsetting nature of his appearance it was clear who it was and she identified him.

Formal identification was followed by the arrival of the Home Office pathologist, Dr Keith Simpson. In cases of murder, only approved pathologists are used to carry out post-mortem examinations, as cause of death is not the only issue to be determined but will likely require an interpretation of the injuries and an assessment of what possible scenarios may have led to the death. Simpson had been involved with police murder investigations for approaching thirty years and was widely known for his involvement in high-profile cases such as the acid bath murders in 1949 and the controversial Rillington Place killings in 1953.

In the layby, Simpson was concerned only with familiarising himself with the scene and taking a few hair and fibre samples from Michael's clothes. His main work was to be carried out at Bedford Borough mortuary, where he would carry out the post-mortem. This revealed that the victim had been shot twice in the side of the head, close to his left ear, and it was apparent that the shots had been fired one immediately after the other. The gun, he thought, would have only been a few inches away. The bullets had passed through the centre of the head and face wounds demonstrated that they had exited through the right cheek. He estimated that Michael was shot dead around four o'clock in the morning.

Meanwhile, on Charteris Ward at the hospital, Rees and Rutland had again been speaking to Valerie, this time to get information from her about the precise point where the initial abduction took place. As before, she was specific in her description and location of the cornfield and a new line of enquiry opened up for the police. Did anyone see or hear anything around half past nine last night?

Their interview was interrupted by the arrival of Valerie's parents, who had been told what had happened and had been driven to Bedford. Neither Rees nor Rutland would speak to Valerie again. According to an article in the *Daily Telegraph* the following day, although containing a number of factual inaccuracies, it stated that her parents had been in a state of shock as they prepared to travel to Bedford hospital to see their daughter. Both had been blissfully unaware that their daughter had not returned home the previous evening and it was only when Marjorie went to wake her at half past seven the next morning that she realised that her bed had not been slept in. She confirmed that Valerie had left the house the previous evening with Michael, taking their maps with them to plan a rally that weekend. Jack had telephoned the laboratory and he was told that neither Valerie nor Michael had turned up for work that morning. He rang the police, twice, who at that time had no knowledge of her whereabouts.

There is no official record of what their reaction was to the news that their daughter had been attacked while in the car with Michael, but Valerie's response to seeing them walk on to the hospital ward that afternoon was remarkable: 'What are you doing here?' she whispered.

Valerie later recollected, bizarrely, that she felt terribly guilty about being attacked that particular week as she knew her parents were due to go away on holiday to Scotland and it had been a break to which they had both been looking forward. Her father had Scottish blood in him, but had been born in Sussex and had never been to his homeland, as Valerie described it. If this had to happen to her then she would have preferred it could have been after they had been away.

She told them, 'I hope you're going to go on holiday. I'm alright. Don't stay because of me. I'll be alright. You go for your week's holiday.' Her parents' response: 'Oh no, we've cancelled it.'[13]

It was certainly not a family that flapped and panicked. They now had some private time without a police officer being there and Valerie could concentrate on talking to her parents. It was a tight-knit family, and she considered her parents to be honourable people with a strong sense of civic duty. Learning about the true nature of her relationship with Michael in these circumstances would not be easy for them.

In the meantime, Rees and Rutland had stepped out of the ward and were met by Detective Chief Inspector Harold Whiffen and Inspector Arnott. They had come to take over from the two officers who had been with her for five hours and the four of them now spent some time discussing the evidence already gleaned from Valerie. It was Whiffen and Arnott's job to write this down as an official statement. Gwendolyn Rutland took her notes with her and later said in her own statement that the notes, if necessary, could be produced.[14]

The two senior officers went through the same process as their juniors had done during the day, only this time writing it down on official paper that would become Valerie's first written witness statement. They observed the same protocol of being told by hospital staff when it was safe to speak to her. By quarter past seven in the evening they had only reached the point in the story where the victims had stopped for fuel and decided that was enough for Valerie to endure for one day. There had been no more conversation about the description of the attacker.

What they did not know was that while they had been speaking to Valerie, another police broadcast had been despatched. Transmitted at 5.40 pm, it read:

Man aged about 30, height 5 ft 6in, proportionate build, dark brown hair, clean shaven, brown eyes, fairly pale face, has a distinct East End of London accent, wearing dark lounge suit, and believed dark tie and shirt. The vehicle believed to be in his possession 847 BHN is a 1956 Morris Minor Deluxe, colour grey. He is still believed in possession of the .38 revolver.

The only time Valerie had, in fact, used the word brown was when she had described the colour of her attacker's hair. But, the word 'brown' had changed from it being the hair colour, to it probably being the killer's surname and now to the colour of his eyes. Even more inexplicably, the Metropolitan Police's Criminal Record Office issued a Special Notice headed 'Murder'. It gave scant details about the incident but the description of the attacker read:

MAN – BROWN. Born about 1936, smooth face and big eyes.

What 'BROWN' meant in this circular is not clear. Quite why the officer responsible for this publication did not challenge it and ask for clarity over what this colour referred to will never be known, but these errors, at a time when there were no clear leads as to the identity of the killer, would have a profound impact on the integrity of the investigation. But for now, the police were on the look-out for a man who had some connection to something brown.

Just over 50 miles away from the Bedfordshire layby, a man was taking his dog for a walk in Avondale Crescent in the Essex town of Ilford.[15] It was around quarter to seven in the evening. He was aware of the publicity associated with the A6 murder and that the police were looking for a man in his thirties, with an East End accent and who supposedly had brown eyes. He was probably in possession of a stolen Morris Minor, registration number 847 BHN and the murder weapon, a .38 calibre revolver.

Parked on the pavement in front of him, with its offside wheels in the gutter, was the stolen car; later enquiries would reveal that it had been there since at least 6.50 that morning.[16] All its windows were shut, and the front index plate had been completely bent underneath the bumper, so much so that it was necessary to get very low down to read it. Similarly, there was a dent in the rear bumper and the middle of the boot. He telephoned the police and by midnight the car had been photographed in situ before being taken away to the forensic science laboratory for examination.

The following day, newspapers, radio and television were full of the story and the misleading information was compounded. The *Daily Telegraph* led with one of its headlines stating 'Hitch-hiker murder car found'. Its first column said, 'All policemen in the Metropolitan area were searching last night for a hitch-hiking gunman who, having "thumbed" a lift in a car, killed its driver and wounded the woman passenger.' Further on it said, 'Police said they wished to interview a man about 5ft 6in tall, of medium build with dark hair and pale face. He has deep-set, brown eyes.'

The inaccurate information about the colour of the eyes clearly came from the police and the newspaper column revealed the source of the information about a hitch-hiker. Journalists had spoken to John Kerr, the man who had first spoken to Valerie, and he had told them that he 'went back to the woman who told me in whispers that about 9.30 the previous night as they drove through Slough a man thumbed a lift from them. She said they stopped and while they were driving he produced a revolver, saying it was a .38. The woman said she noticed he had staring eyes.'

It is more than likely that in those few minutes when a shocked and distressed gunshot victim was talking to an equally distressed and frightened 18-year-old, quiet whispers had been misheard or misinterpreted, and from that Kerr had understood that the man had been picked up by Valerie and Michael. But the reality was fundamentally different. The police knew that the couple had been abducted in a cornfield, there had been no hitch-hiker and that the killer had large eyes that were not deep set. As far as the public was concerned, though, the killer was a hitch-hiker with deep-set brown eyes.

The finding of the Morris on the extreme edge of east London brought some swift developments. John Skillett and Edward Blackhall had been driving to work in a Ford Consul along Eastern Avenue, Ilford, on the morning of Wednesday, 23 August, Skillett driving and Blackhall occupying the front passenger seat. Skillett knew the time as he was due in to work by half past seven and he had just passed the clock on the King George hospital, which showed it was shortly after seven o'clock. He was travelling in the outside lane of the dual carriageway and as he approached a set of red traffic lights, he left a gap between him and the car in front. Just as he was slowing, a grey Morris Minor cut in from the inside lane and skidded to a halt, narrowly missing both the front of his car and the vehicle in front, an Austin A40. The driving was dangerous and Skillett was annoyed. The lights turned green and immediately the Morris swerved back into the nearside lane and sped off. Wanting to 'give him a piece of my mind,' Skillett chased after him. At Gants Hill roundabout, the Morris was blocked by waiting traffic and Skillet managed to pull alongside it in the outside lane. He told his passenger to wind down the passenger window and he shouted across to the driver, 'Are you fucking mad or something? You ought to get off the fucking road.'[17]

Blackhall was rather more constrained and merely said, 'Get off the road.'

They both had a good look at the driver. Blackhall distinctly noticed his large, staring eyes and that he had a facial expression that was half smile, half sneer. He just laughed and drove off onto the roundabout. They both kept an eye on the car as it sped away, Blackhall noticing that it had what appeared to be three red strips on the rear bumper and a torn green label in the rear windscreen. Just as it approached Redbridge Station it suddenly, without any indication, branched off to the right and disappeared from view.

Moments later, just around the corner, James Trower was standing on the pavement between Avondale Crescent and Redbridge Station. He had just parked his Humber Super Snipe on the main road, got out and was waiting to collect his workmate. As he stood there, he heard the sound of a car, its engine racing, obviously changing down through the gears. He looked up and saw what he recognised as a 1956 split-screen Morris Minor travelling at about 20mph, slowing as it approached the nearby junction. As it passed him, he had a good 'full face' view of the driver and saw that he was wearing a dark jacket and white shirt. The car turned into Avondale Crescent and disappeared from his view. He could no longer hear the engine and he assumed it had drawn to a stop.

It was clear that the car Trower, Skillett and Blackhall had just seen had been the now abandoned stolen Morris with its distinctive red Scotch tape strips on the rear bumper, only four hours after it had left the murder scene. All of them had seen its driver.

★★★

Back at Bedford hospital, the day started badly. Suspecting that Valerie's life was beginning to ebb away, the matron and a sister from the ward went to fetch Marjorie and Jack, who had stayed overnight. They were told that if they wanted to see their daughter alive 'they should come quickly'.[18] It was their worst nightmare, but they knew that only slightly over twenty-fours earlier she had been shot several times and she still had two bullets lodged inside her chest. The day before, Jack had been with one of the police officers who held a file in his hand which bore the words 'Michael Gregsten' and 'murder'. It had only been at that point, when he had seen the words written down, that the gravity of the situation really dawned on him.[19] They went in and looked at their sleeping daughter, quite possibly, they thought, for the last time. Suddenly, Valerie opened her eyes and said, 'Have you had your breakfast?'

She was clearly unaware of the gravity of the situation and her parents indulged her. When they told her that they had not yet eaten, she said, 'Well, why not? Why haven't you had your breakfast? What are you doing here before breakfast?'

The medical team now ushered the parents from the ward and when Detective Chief Inspector Whiffen and Inspector Arnott returned that morning to continue the interview with their witness, they were refused access due to Valerie's volatile condition. Doctor Pollen monitored the patient for four hours and recorded that her health had deteriorated badly but after a while there was an improvement. Valerie's parents were told: 'Everything is going to be alright. There's been a miracle. She's going to live.'[20]

With Valerie's condition now more stable, Whiffen and Arnott returned to continue their interview with her. They finished at a quarter past eight that evening but nowhere in her now-completed statement did it contain the colour of her attacker's eyes.

At Rye Lane bus depot in Peckham, south London, over 11 miles away from where the stolen Morris Minor had been recovered, Edwin Cooke was busy at work. He was a cleaner, or as he preferred to be known, a pick-up man. It was his job each night to go through all the buses in the depot to collect any larger items that had been discarded by passengers that would be too large to go through the company's vacuum cleaners. He had been employed in this capacity for four years. Shortly before nine o'clock that night he checked the upstairs deck of the number 36A bus that routinely travelled the route from Peckham, across the River Thames, through Marble Arch, Paddington and up to Kilburn in north-west London. Cooke lifted the rear seat as he knew there was a cavity below it and immediately saw a handkerchief and a small box that contained some loose bullets. He picked up the handkerchief and saw a revolver and five further boxes of ammunition. In all the years he had been doing this job, the only thing he had ever found before under a seat 'was two dead rats', he would later tell a jury. He had checked the seat the night before, on 23 August, and they had not been there then. He had no idea whether any of this ammunition was live or spent but he carefully picked up the gun by its butt using his fingertips, took it to the office and immediately telephoned the police.[21] Within ten minutes, they turned up at the bus station and took possession of the find. It was sent to the forensic science laboratory, where Lewis Nickolls, its director, was already working on the Bedford shooting.

Nickolls was examining the Morris Minor that had been recovered in Ilford. He made some general observations about it such as the inability to open the boot due to the accident damage and that he had drained the petrol tank to reveal that it only contained three-quarters of a gallon of fuel. There were no fingerprints on the inside or outside of the vehicle that did not belong to either Michael or Valerie, and the blood was concentrated around the driver's area. The rug though, which had been draped over the seat, masked the blood that had soaked into it, indicating that whoever placed it there may well have been successful in preventing any blood from getting on to their own clothes. He had found two spent .38 bullets, one on the floor by the driver's seat, the other in the glove pocket situated in the dashboard to the right of the steering wheel. Examination of the bullets revealed that they each bore seven right-handed rifling markings, effectively a ballistic fingerprint, which was peculiar to an Enfield revolver. The type of gun was now known.

By now he had also received the spent bullets and cartridge cases that had been recovered from the layby by Chief Inspector Oliver and Inspector Milborrow. His examination of the bullets showed identical rifling patterns. The bullets in the car came from the same weapon that fired the bullets in the layby and Nickolls now had a number of items that were yielding vital evidence and which could be compared to any firearm submitted to him for analysis. The next morning, the gun and its ammunition from the number 36A bus were delivered.

It was an Enfield .38 calibre revolver loaded with spent cartridges. These types of weapon were relatively common and had been standard military issue during the Second World War, so there were plenty of them in circulation. It was, he said, in good condition and had a trigger pressure of between 13 and 14lb, meaning it could not have been fired accidentally. Anyone firing it would need to pull the trigger with some force. There was no safety catch fitted to it – this type of Enfield did not need one – and it had clearly been fired. He determined that the bullets found at the layby were from varying stock, some marked 1940, others 1943. One of the five boxes found on the bus was unsealed and contained a mixture of 1940 and 1943 bullets. The six bullets in the revolver itself were also of 1943 stock.

Testing to see whether a specific bullet comes from a particular gun is determined by firing a series of bullets, known as the control bullet, from the weapon being tested and examining the rifling marks and scratches on the discharged items. Nickolls carried out these tests and compared the marks against those on the bullets recovered from the layby and the Morris. They were identical, a perfect match. In addition, indentations to the cap of the cartridges on the control bullets caused by the firing of the weapon were also identical to those recovered from the scene in Bedfordshire.[22] The murder weapon had been found.

Bob Acott, the metropolitan detective, was now unequivocally in charge of the investigation. Not only did he have the resources of the Metropolitan

Police behind him, but the investigation was beginning to appear London-centric. The abduction had been to the west of the city, the Morris abandoned on its eastern fringes and the murder weapon found in south London. The Bedfordshire detective superintendent, Charles Barron, was overseeing local enquiries, and house-to-house enquiries in the Dorney Reach area were already being carried out by the police in Slough under the command of Detective Chief Inspector Harry Bowker.

Acott had an unusual request of Keith Simpson, the pathologist: he wanted him to examine Valerie's injuries. Simpson had vast experience in these matters and Acott needed a detailed account of her injuries from a criminal investigation perspective. Three days after the attack, on 26 August, Simpson paid a visit to Valerie while she recovered on her ward. Alongside Doctor Pollen who remained in charge of her care, and consulting his X-ray images, Simpson observed that Valerie had received four bullet wounds to her upper left arm and shoulder. One had exited by puncturing a hole through her chest and two, seen on the X-rays, were still lodged inside. The fourth could not be accounted for. A fifth had entered the left side of her neck and exited on the right. This wound, he said, 'had passed virtually through the middle of the neck and very close indeed to the main carotid arteries and jugular veins each side'. Not being able to perform his normal role as a pathologist and dissect the body, he had to engage in some guesswork, but he judged that the bullet had passed almost immediately in front of her main artery and vein vessels on the left side of her neck and probably within an inch of those on her right. They were, he said, 'dangerous wounds'.[23] Valerie had been shot five times and any slight variation to the trajectory of the bullet passing through the neck would almost certainly have been fatal.

In his later book, *Forty Years of Murder*, Simpson said, of Valerie:

> I was impressed by her intelligence and her very clear mental state so soon after her frightful experience. I was impressed too by her courage, for obviously she had to overcome great emotional stress to be able to talk about it as calmly as she did. She did not cry.[24]

The investigation was making progress but the press were still reporting that the killer had deep-set brown eyes. The only record from Valerie of her attacker's eyes had been her mumblings to Kerr in the layby when he first spoke to her and the rough notes written down by Detective Constable Rutland when speaking to her at her bedside. This was not satisfactory and Acott instructed that a further statement should be taken from her not only to clarify this point but also to answer some of the questions that were being asked by officers who were still trying to piece together events and reconstruct the journey from Dorney to Clophill. On 28 August, five days after the attack, Arnott and Whiffen took another statement from Valerie. It would take almost four hours to complete and it addressed all the points that needed clarifying. However, the first official, documented description now came from Valerie:

> The description of the man who was in the car on the night of 22nd/23rd August is aged between 25 and 30 years, about 5'6" in height, could be slightly less, is proportionately built, inclined to be slender, has brown hair, he was clean shaven, has a very smooth pale face, with icy-blue, large saucer-like eyes. The eyes were not sunken and appeared to be level with his face.

Finally, an accurate description had been documented.

Within a week of the murder, newspapers were starting to produce inaccurate stories, caused, in no small part, by the lack of accurate detail being passed from the police. A fine judgement has to be made about the amount of information that can be released to the public. On the one hand, the police want to get information from anyone who has something of importance to report, but on the other they do not wish to reveal what clues they have to the killer, who is likely to be reading the same newspaper articles and using the information to cover his tracks. For this reason, and one other, Acott only released partial details.

The fact that the couple had stopped at a petrol station at some point in the journey to refuel was made public, since the police were keen to trace the pump attendant who had served them. The repeated flashing of the reversing light by Michael as he drove along the route was released in the hope that someone might have seen it. Even if they were unable to describe the man in the back seat, it would go some way to help corroborate Valerie's story and to pinpoint key locations. A full description of the revolver and its ammunition, together with a photograph, was published and people who travelled regularly on the 36A bus route were asked to come forward.[25] An amnesty was even offered to anyone who may have had the revolver stolen in a burglary from their home but did not report it for fear of being prosecuted themselves. The police though chose to withhold the fact that Valerie had been raped, and that both she and Michael had had their valuables stolen.

There was another reason why the release of information was restricted. The story emerging from Valerie was incredible in the extreme. Michael had been shot dead and she had been shot by the same gun having already been robbed and raped. But how and why they had been abducted in Buckinghamshire and been forced to drive 60 miles was as yet unexplained. None of it seemed to make sense, especially as the attacker seemed to have inexplicably changed from abductor, to thief, to murderer and finally to rapist. The suggestion had come from Valerie that she thought they were dealing with a madman but even so, this account was extraordinary. Her account needed to be corroborated somehow, and this was firmly in Acott's mind in the weeks following the report of the attack. There was no doubt that the shootings had occurred but was anything being held back about the offender? By her own admission, Valerie was involved in an extra-marital relationship and jealousies could have been aroused. Typically, in any investigation, a good starting point is the victim, and speaking to neighbours, family members, friends and work colleagues can unearth vital clues. This was on Acott's list of enquiries but for now he remained guarded. In a report that in modern times would be deemed unacceptable, he later wrote:

> When the first account of her experiences during the night of the 22nd/23rd October 1961 was received from Valerie Storie, it sounded so fantastic that from the start it was treated as highly suspect – like the majority of accounts by women who have made allegations of rape.[26]

Yet slowly, her story was beginning to be corroborated. The cornfield had been identified, the Morris had been recovered with the murder weapon bullets inside and the revolver itself had been found in London. It was inconceivable that anyone would falsely manufacture such a dramatic scenario. The possibility that Valerie knew her attacker remained, but her story, on the face of it, appeared to be true. Even small detail, such as both her and Michael's watches being recovered from her wrist supported what she was saying.

In the days immediately following the finding of the car and the revolver, enquiries were concentrated on those people who could take the enquiry forward. Acott had four principal witnesses; Valerie Storie and the men who witnessed the Morris being driven dangerously: Skillett, Blackhall and Trower. Their descriptions of the man seen driving the Morris also needed to be made more public and it was to this that Acott turned his efforts.

By 1961, a new method was in place to track down suspects – the Identikit. An American development, Identikit allowed a witness to compile an image of a suspect through the careful construction of a face using a selection of hand-drawn facial features, which the person selected to reconstruct what they had seen.[27] It was cutting edge technology in August 1961 and had only been used once so far in Britain in a murder trial. In March that year, Elsie Batten had been stabbed to death in Charing Cross and the suspect, Edwin Bush, had been identified through the use of this new method. He had been hanged only a few weeks before in July.

Both Blackhall and Skillett were revisited by the police, this time by Detective Sergeant Jock Mackle, who was the Metropolitan Police's expert in Identikit technology. This resulted in two composite images being compiled. A few days later, with Valerie having now completed her witness statement, she too received Mackle at her bedside to carry out the same process. The three images were of varying quality in terms of the witnesses' abilities to recall detail but on 29 August, the police released not one, but two. The first had been compiled by Valerie, the second by Blackhall. Skillet's was not made public. The two images were shown on television screens and the following day they were front-page news. But the images, shown side by side, were very different. The *Daily Telegraph* reported:

> The one on the left has long straight hair brushed back with his right eyebrow a little higher than the other. The eyes appear hooded and the nose straight. The mouth has thin lips and ears are fairly large. In the second, which has more pronounced colouring and detail, the gunman is shown to have black, wavy hair and his eyes are more deeply set with bushier eyebrows. There is a slight hooding on the suspect's right eye and his nose appears wider and heavier. The lips are about the same though more strongly featured.

The description that accompanied the Identikits was now at least consistent with Valerie's account, including the killer's brown hair and icy blue, large, saucer-like eyes. However, two different Identikit images had been published and this aspect would conflate with earlier conflicting descriptions of the colour of the killer's eyes to produce a paradoxical and confusing picture.

The Identikit pictures nonetheless resulted in hundreds of sightings and suggestions from all over the country, though mainly from the Home Counties. They ranged from some being as simple as sightings of a man who

fitted the description, through to a 14-year-old girl who had been given a
lift in a car by a man fitting the description, and even one where a woman
reported being held up at gunpoint in her home at Knebworth. Some newspapers claimed that the police had lined up a number of suspects they now
wished to interview. There appears no basis in this statement, but certainly,
by the end of August the police had started to compile a list of people they
would research including, if necessary, a requirement to eliminate them
from the enquiry.

On the same day that the Identikits were issued, the Buckinghamshire
police were out in force at Dorney Reach. It was exactly a week since the
attack and they were keen to speak to anyone who may have been in the
area a week before. Motorists and local farmers were stopped and questioned
and shown copies of the newly compiled images. The village could not be
described as an isolated area but it was in the country and it was serviced by a
bus that ran through it on its way from Windsor to Maidenhead, towns only
a few miles away. Bowker asked people who travelled on this service to come
forward if they felt they had seen anyone on this route who fitted the description of the gunman. He carried out house-to-house enquiries in the area in
the hope that someone, somewhere had seen something. Yet little came from
the exercise.

Unhelpful rumours were now also spreading throughout the community
and the *Slough Express* reported that 'the murderer was known to either
Mr Gregsten or Miss Storie, and that he could be a local man'.[28] People
were starting to draw their own conclusions, some of which would gather
wider public support in the years that lay ahead. Suspects were not in short
supply, though. Apart from the numerous suggestions that were being telephoned daily into police stations including named individuals, the police
themselves were developing their own lines of enquiry and they did this in
two ways.

Firstly, their four key witnesses had seen the man who was suspected of the
killing and they wanted to show them albums of photographs of convicted
criminals in case any of them could see the man responsible.

Identification of suspects in criminal investigations has a chequered history. In 1896, Adolf Beck was sentenced to seven years' penal servitude for a
crime he did not commit. He was convicted on identification evidence from
a number of witnesses who, after his period of imprisonment, were proved to
be wrong. Unfortunately for Beck, there was no right of appeal at that time
and he spent his time in prison protesting his innocence.[29] There have been

many cases since that have hinged on witness identification and there have been many claims of a wrongful conviction due to genuine human error. Due to the growing concern, the law and police guidance from the Home Office ensured measures were put in place that were designed to protect against faulty witness testimony. Broadly, the position in 1961 was that where there was no known and available suspect, police officers were entitled to show photographs of convicted criminals to witnesses in the hope that a positive identification could be made. This had obvious weaknesses but if a positive identification was made this had to be followed up with an identification parade where the identified suspect was placed on a parade consisting of at least eight other similar people. Providing any future jury was made aware of this process, then it was for them to attach as much weight as they felt appropriate to the credibility of the witness and to decide whether they were sure or not about their identification. Clearly, if a known suspect was already available then no photographs should be shown and the suspect would be invited to stand on an identification parade as the first and only measure of the witness's ability to recognise the offender.

In this case, there was no known and available suspect for the attacks on 23 August and Valerie, as well as Skillet and Trower, were shown many albums of photographs, in an attempt to see if they could again see the face. None made any identification.

The second method the police employed to identify possible suspects was to trawl their own records to see if they could find anyone who not only matched the description but also whether their past criminal profile matched the behaviour of the attacker. Lists started to be compiled and each had to be assessed as to whether any of them should be actively pursued. By the end of August, the list had started to grow and files were created. The list of files comprised not only people of possible interest but key individuals who were central to the enquiry; for instance, Valerie Storie and Michael Gregsten. One file entry merely read 'two unknown men', presumably the result from someone ringing in to say that they had seen some suspicious behaviour. It was a manual system that today would be carried out far more effectively and quickly through the use of computers.

A judgement, however, needs to be made about the level of priority which needs to be attached to any information received into a police incident room. Such a significant investigation as the A6 murder was attracting a great deal of interest and members of the public were only too eager to suggest ideas and theories about what may have happened and what type of person could be responsible. It was an almost overwhelming situation in the days before computer technology made the management of vast amounts of information far more efficient. A manual card system was used, which in time would amount to thousands of handwritten entries giving details of the person contacting the police and the nature of their information. All of it needed to be recorded in case it later transpired to be of use to the investigation.

Identifying information that provides an obvious line of enquiry which could assist the investigation is a difficult task, but within a few weeks, such a development occurred. On Thursday, 7 September, just over two weeks after the shootings, a disturbing incident took place in East Sheen, south-west London. Twenty-three-year-old Meike Dalal, a Swedish national, was alone at her home in Upper Richmond Road West. She was expecting a man to call in response to an advertisement she had placed in several newspapers about a room she had to let. A man had telephoned earlier and made arrangements to visit the property to inspect the room. Around half past one in the afternoon, the man arrived and she allowed him into her house and showed him upstairs to view the available room, which was in the attic. As soon as the man entered, he closed the door and struck Dalal over the head with something heavy. With her wound bleeding, the man threw her on to the bed face down and started to tie her hands behind her back using a piece of flex. He said to Dalal, 'Listen. I am the A6 murderer and I want money.'

Dalal pretended to be unconscious but the man kept talking.

'Keep quiet. Don't scream or I'll kill you,' he said.

He hit her twice more and then ordered her to open her mouth, inserted a silk scarf into it and tied it loosely at the back of her head. She was now bleeding badly. He then tied her ankles together using a piece of blue ribbon before turning her on to her back and pulling up her skirt. At this point, Dalal started to struggle, pulled her hands free and managed to parry another blow aimed at her head. She screamed loudly, twice, and the man turned and ran out. The frightened woman freed herself and ran to the bedroom window screaming for help.

The description of the attacker she provided was a man aged 25–30 years, 5ft 8in tall and with dark, terribly scruffy hair that needed tidying around the neck. His face was oval in shape, pale complexion and clean shaven. His eyes 'may have been brown', he had a straight nose and was of medium build. With the mention of the A6 murder by the would-be sex attacker, Detective Sergeant Jock Mackle was at her bedside very quickly to compile yet another Identikit, which was passed to the press. There was little to compare between

Dalal's description of the offender and those given by the A6 witnesses but there were similarities between the two offences. In both cases there had been a sexual element and the victims had been tied up. If there was any suspicion that this was merely a copycat offender, it was striking that the fact that Valerie had been bound had not been made public. This new assault needed to be compared alongside the Bedfordshire offence in case the police were dealing with one offender responsible for both attacks. On the day that Dalal was attacked in her home, there were no real suspects for the A6 murder and possibly the attacker had struck twice.

Chapter Six

The Vienna Hotel

The Vienna hotel at 158 Sutherland Avenue, west London, catered for people seeking accommodation at the cheaper end of the market for which there was plenty of demand. It was part of a small group of hotels and on 11 September, its group manager, Robert Crocker, paid one of his infrequent visits to the property. Partly, he wanted to carry out an inspection of the rooms to check on maintenance issues and standards of cleanliness but more specifically, he had been contacted by the manageress of the hotel, a 22-year-old Spanish woman called Juliana Galves, who wanted to dismiss one of the employees.

Jack Glickberg was a man with many criminal convictions and he had stolen £5 from the hotel. He had only been working there, together with his wife Florence, for just over a week and already Galves had received complaints about his language and behaviour. Crocker's main concern was that the hotel was already under-staffed and losing two more was going to create a problem. That aside, while at the Vienna he decided to carry on with his routine inspection of the twenty-five rooms with Galves to check to see whether the right standards were being maintained.

Room 24 was a basement room with French doors leading out to a small garden. It was one of the few multi-occupancy rooms in the hotel suitable either for a family – it had two double beds and a single – or occasionally would be used by single travellers who were prepared to share. Towards the end of the morning, Crocker and Galves went in to carry out their checks. There was a small alcove on the left-hand side that housed the single bed with a small armchair at its foot. It was a tight squeeze but just about enough room for one person. Crocker noticed that the chair had a small piece of material dangling underneath and knowing that there was nothing that could be done immediately to repair it, he decided to simply move the cushion round to hide the damage. As he moved the seat cover, something fell to the floor and he saw it was a small cartridge case. Galves then found another on the seat cushion. Crocker, who had seen war service, recognised them as a pair of spent .38 calibre cartridge cases. He was aware of the A6 murder because of all the news coverage and knew that this was the calibre of the weapon used in the shooting. He telephoned the police, an officer quickly arrived and the find was immediately despatched to the forensic science laboratory for examination.

At the same time as the .38 cartridge cases were being transported across the city, Valerie was receiving further medical attention. She was seriously ill and a week or so earlier she had been transferred from Bedford to Guy's hospital in London. Doctor Pollen had given Valerie first-class care but now it was time for more specialised treatment and, if possible, the removal of the two bullets still lodged in her chest. Her care was taken over by neurological house physician Ian Rennie and upon admission to the hospital he made his own observations.

He re-examined the bullet wound through her neck and noted that there was complete loss of all sensation over her right ear. She was unable to open her mouth any more than a centimetre and although she was able to talk, her voice was soft. She had significant swelling on her neck and a further X-ray showed a chip off the left side of the angle of the lower jaw. The right side of her tongue had been paralysed but that appeared to be slowly recovering. Her left arm, which was broken at the top, was swollen and bruised and she could not move it without suffering considerable pain.

Her chest showed signs of fluid on the left side and there was complete anaesthesia to every modality of sensation below the level of the T4 thoracic vertebra, effectively from the chest down, together with complete paralysis of the muscles. Her abdomen was distended, her legs were completely flaccid and her bladder showed signs of a complete loss of function.

Rennie put a care plan into place that was the usual, he said, for 'a paraplegic patient': to be turned regularly and the bladder to be catheterised. She was given oral antibiotics and an injection of a radio-opaque solution into the fluid of the spinal canal at the back of the neck. Further X-rays were taken that showed a fracture of the fourth thoracic vertebra, the fourth bone of the spine in the chest region. The spinal cord was completely severed, irretrievably damaged and there was no useful purpose, Rennie decided, in performing an operation. Similarly, he felt that due to her condition, the bullets in her chest should, for the time being, be left alone but he set her left shoulder in plaster, which at least gave her some pain relief.

In a statement he made on 8 September he said,

Her future prospects are poor in that she shall very probably never regain any function such as voluntary movement below the level of her injury and whilst with physiotherapy, nursing care and rehabilitation she may be able to do a clerical job, it seems probable that she will have to go about in a wheelchair for the rest of her life.

It was, for Valerie, a devastating prognosis softened marginally by the fact that the attack upon her had not resulted in her becoming pregnant.

She remained at the centre of attention in one of Britain's biggest ever murder hunts and the police needed to speak to her again. Rennie said that Valerie was able to talk, and although she had found it hard sometimes to swallow, she seemed remarkably cheerful. He considered her an intelligent woman with no apparent loss of memory and gave permission for Bob Acott to speak to her.

With her voice being so faint, Acott placed a microphone just above her mouth to make sure everything she said would be recorded, and sitting next to a police officer with shorthand skills, Acott began going through his prepared list of questions.

The Metropolitan detective told Valerie that the purpose of the interview was to clarify a number of points so that enquiries could be channelled in the right direction. Acott's purpose was also to gently challenge Valerie's account, particularly where the story seemed so incredible. He wanted to explore in greater detail her relationship with the dead man to see whether there was any likely suggestion that it had been this that had sparked the whole sequence of events.

He began, though, on another tack. He had previously shown her photographs of criminals as a means of identifying a suspect and reminded her that this was merely an investigative measure and certainly did not mean that someone could be convicted as a consequence of her pointing someone out. He had with him more photographs, including some of those from the police files. Gradually he laid them before her, telling her to take her time. She set aside a few for a second viewing but made no identification. She tried to help Acott by indicating where some had similar features, but she was absolutely clear that none of the photographs shown to her was her attacker. This had been a good use of Acott's time but the identity of the killer remained unknown.

Acott then showed her the Identikit image produced by Meike Dalal of the man who had attacked her in her home in East Sheen just a few days before but Valerie could not see any resemblance. 'His face was too fat around the cheek and jawbone,' she said.

From Acott's perspective, while it was based largely on what Valerie was saying, it was looking unlikely that Man A was the man responsible or that Dalal's attacker had been the same as hers. In both their cases, neither of them had blue eyes and much of their descriptions did not match those provided by her; effectively, they were both eliminated from the enquiry.

With the showing of photographs unsuccessful, Acott turned to the main task at hand and began to ask questions about her relationship with Michael. She was able to add very little, only saying that it had not been 'all milk and honey', but they managed to get through the difficult times and remained close. She made the point that Michael had been very attached to his children. He was also attached to his wife but not in the way that he was to her. His relationship was not as it should be between man and wife; it had not been loving.

She was asked about their hobbies, their pastimes and Valerie only ventured that Michael had taught mathematics at a college. Acott continued to probe about whether Michael had become upset over whether she was seeing someone else. Indeed, he asked whether either of them was having an affair with anyone else at the laboratory. The answer was no. There had not been anyone else involved. Acott's motive for asking the questions was to establish whether there was any jealous third party, and he even asked whether she felt that Janet Gregsten could somehow be involved but she dismissed the idea out of hand. Janet knew of the relationship and had accepted it. Valerie was insistent in her answers and Acott moved on.

Next came the cornfield, the location of the abduction. Valerie explained that they had been there before, always after dark, and they had had intercourse there in the Morris two evenings before on the Sunday.

Acott probed.

'Have you ever been to that cornfield with any other man, Valerie?'

The response was indignant. 'Never.'

Valerie became rather frustrated with the repeated questions. She had explained before exactly what went on and in which part of the cornfield. Acott persisted, pointing out that the couple had been in the cornfield for nearly three hours. Valerie went through the story again. Acott was trying to establish whether they had been specifically targeted by someone who knew that they routinely went there but it was not going anywhere and he changed the subject.

The questioning was calm and Valerie was coping well, slowly whispering her responses. Acott asked about the journey itself – whether she was able to add any more detail about the location of the petrol station at which they had refuelled and which route exactly they had taken through London.

Valerie knew the roads well and was able to not just describe the route but could name roads and the junctions they passed. When asking about the journey north of London along the A5 and A6, Acott asked why she had not been able to see more of the gunman, given that many of the roads were well lit. Valerie told him that, in fact, much of the journey was in the 'de-restricted' speed limit areas and there had been no lighting. In any event, she was forced to face the front all the time; there had been no opportunity to have a good look.

Acott asked whether she was sure it was gloves the man had been wearing and not stockings and whether he smoked the cigarette given to him. She repeated the answers she had made when making her statement.

When discussing the shooting inside the car, and the time between that and the assault upon her, Acott openly expressed his doubts.

'Do you really think, Valerie, that it could have been as long as twenty minutes?'

Yes, she was sure. She was able to add a little more to the awkward moment when the rapist had crudely commented upon her sexual experience and she said that he seemingly based his comment on how he had found her body.

The awkward issue about the use of the word 'brown' in the various descriptions was discussed. Acott told her that:

One witness says that when he was speaking to you, you said, 'He's taken the car, he shot us' and when this witness asked you who he was, you said, 'He was brown.' Can you remember saying that?

Valerie was clear:

When I was lying there, I was thinking I was going to die. I was trying to gather little stones around me to write words. I was trying to think of the description of the man. I was trying to make the word brown with the stones, because he'd got brown hair and that's the only reason I can think of saying brown, was because I was thinking of his brown hair.

'The name Brown doesn't mean anything to you?'

'No.'

'Do you know anybody named Brown?'

'No.'

'Can you remember the name Brown coming up in the conversation?'

'No, it must have been a misunderstanding. It must have been me trying to describe the man.'

Valerie emphasised that she had never seen the man before and had absolutely no idea who he was. He was a stranger who had abducted her. She based her description of him as a madman on the fact that he kept on contradicting himself and could not seem to remember her name, nothing else.

Acott had a final question.

'Tell me in your own words, Valerie, just how you feel towards the man who shot you and Mike and exactly what you would like done to him?'

> I would like to see him hang. I believe in hanging people sometimes. One talks about these things when a case comes up in the newspapers and I have always believed in hanging and if a person wilfully kills somebody they should be made to hang. I would like to see him hang. I would like to see him thrashed and go through what Mike went through and what I've been through. On the other hand, I believe he is not mentally balanced and that in cases of people like this, people get away with murder, and people go to Broadmoor. I should hate to think a doctor might say that he's alright and let him go.

Acott walked away from her hospital bed believing that Valerie Storie was a decent, honest woman whose life had effectively been brought to an abrupt halt for which she was not to blame. He would later write: 'Her account was not only truthful but was most accurate in practically every detail.'

A few days later, news from the laboratory reached Acott. Lewis Nickolls had examined the two cartridge cases found in room 24 of the Vienna hotel and compared them to the control cartridges fired from the recovered revolver and those recovered from the layby in Bedford. They were identical. The hotel cartridge cases came from the murder weapon. A picture was emerging. The Morris had been abandoned in east London and cartridge cases from the murder weapon had been found in a hotel that was less than half a mile away from where the number 36A bus passed.

Nineteen days had passed between the shooting of Michael and Valerie on 23 August and the discovery of the cartridge cases on 11 September. Pinpointing when it had been possible to drop or mislay them in room 24 was now a priority for the investigation. The police needed to rely on those who ran the hotel and carried out the day-to-day task of booking clients in and out. Through examination of the records, the enquiry needed to establish who had been in the room between the murder and the day the cartridges were found. There were really only three people who could assist them; Juliana Galves, the Spanish manageress; Jack Glickberg, who had just been sacked for stealing; and his wife, Florence.

Galves was able to provide the police with the hotel records, which presented a clear picture. Room 24 had only been occupied once since the shooting and that was on 30 August, a week later. The client's name was Vigan Rapur,[2] an Indian man from Delhi, Galves recalled, though when asked about him being given room 24, she remembered that he had only been in it for a few minutes before she realised that a single room was available and moved him to it. Other than a brief visit, effectively he had not actually stayed there. His appearance certainly did not match the description of the person the police were looking for and attention turned to who had last stayed in the room. The records showed that on the night of Monday, 21 August, the night before the abduction in the cornfield, the room was taken by a J. Ryan, who had provided a home address of 72, Wood Lane, Kingsbury, an area about 6 miles away in north-west London. Galves stated that she had not personally been responsible for booking the man into the hotel – it had been Jack Glickberg.

An enquiry at the Wood Lane address revealed that the current occupier had lived there for the past twenty-five years and he knew no one by the name of Ryan.[3] He added, however, that he had received a letter at the property addressed to a Mr Ryan, which had been sent from Ryan Motors in Dublin.[4]

On 15 September, the police traced the Glickbergs and, armed with the hotel records, they interviewed them, though it was the husband who seemed to know the most. He recalled Ryan arriving at the hotel sometime between 9.30 p.m. and 11 p.m. He remembered it because Ryan had already tried to obtain accommodation at one of the sister hotels but found they were fully booked and arrived at the Vienna in transport supplied by the hotel. It was Ryan himself who had written his details in the register and signed it. Glickberg told him that breakfast would be served between 8 a.m. and 10 a.m. the following morning and had then taken him to room 24. The family room was otherwise unoccupied and Ryan was given the single bed in the alcove and was told that if other new customers turned up later in the night looking for accommodation, he might have to share.

The following morning, Glickberg continued, Ryan had breakfast early, after which he returned to his room to collect something he'd forgotten. He didn't know what it was he went to fetch but a few minutes later he returned. He was carrying what looked like a brown grip, which he thought contained a transistor radio. It measured about 12 × 9in. Before he left, which was around 8.30 a.m., he asked for directions to Queensway and Glickberg recommended he walked to Harrow Road where he could get a bus – the number 36. After Ryan had left, room 24 was cleaned by Glickberg's wife, Florence, and Juliana Galves, although they had not seen any cartridges.

Finally, Glickberg offered a description of Ryan, saying that he was aged between 24 and 30, 5ft 7in in height, slim build, thinnish face, round chin, medium-height forehead, clean shaven, and with dark brown to black hair, which was brushed straight back without a parting but with a wave or quiff at the front. He had 'wide-awake eyes but not what one would express as cod's eyes', but he couldn't remember their colour. He was wearing a dark suit, white shirt of the collar-attached type and a darkish tie.[5]

J. Ryan was becoming a person of interest. He was the right age and had distinctive eyes. He had used a false address when booking into the hotel the night before the murder and had stayed in room 24. He had also been advised to catch the number 36 bus from Harrow Road, a stop serviced by the number 36A in which the murder weapon had been found.

Other names and entries in the register were checked and one that featured was Frederick Durrant, who had given the address 7 Hurst Avenue, Horsham in Sussex. He had checked into the hotel between 11.30 p.m. and midnight on Tuesday, 22 August, the time that Valerie and Michael were being held captive in the cornfield and been allocated room 6. He had been booked in not by Glickberg, but by his wife, and it had been her that had showed him to his room. The only piece of information that Glickberg could usefully add was that the following morning, Durrant didn't come down for breakfast and so he went to his bedroom to check on him. Durrant told him that he didn't want breakfast and left the hotel around midday. He described Durrant as 30–32 years of age, 5ft 9in tall, slim build, clean shaven, with a thin face and dark hair, which was brushed straight back, was well greased and not wavy. He was carrying a brown suitcase and wearing a dark suit, a shirt but no tie. He did not fit the description of the killer and clearly had an alibi for the time of the abduction. The name was noted.

The Vienna hotel became the focus of attention and the name J. Ryan appeared significant. He was not known by the hotel staff and enquiries were initiated by the police to see if they could identify him. The name Durrant though, when checked, had already featured in police enquiries.

A week or so earlier, the police had launched an appeal in the newspapers asking for hoteliers to keep an eye out for anyone who was staying with them and was perhaps keeping a low profile. He may even be 'faking an illness to avoid going out,' detectives were quoted as saying.[6]

The manager at the Alexandra Court Hotel in Seven Sisters Road, north London, had identified such a person. A customer had checked in on the evening of 23 August, the night after the murder, and had kept himself locked in his room ever since. His name was Frederick Durrant and on

27 August he was visited by two detectives, who quickly established that his real name was Peter Louis Alphon. He held extreme right-wing views and was using a false name, and while that was not unusual or grounds to arouse any suspicion, it was his seemingly nomadic lifestyle and his evasiveness when answering questions that attracted the detectives' attention. In his suitcase he had a newspaper that featured the A6 murder, but so did every newspaper in London at that time. The detectives needed to establish, if they could, his whereabouts on the evening of the abduction and to see if anyone could alibi him.[7]

He confirmed that he had stayed in room 6 at the Vienna Hotel in Sutherland Avenue that night, as the records now showed, and prior to that he had met his mother around 9.30 p.m. in Streatham. The following morning, he left about a quarter to midday, and again met his mother. He did not match the description of the killer – he was 5ft 10in and was three days short of his 31st birthday – but his details were passed to the murder incident room, where a file was raised. Alphon's name, together with his alias, was fed into the police index card system, but he remained of marginal interest.

The position on 15 September was that room 24 in the Vienna Hotel was a strong line of enquiry. Cartridges had been found there, J. Ryan had occupied the room the night before the murder and Peter Alphon had stayed in the hotel the following night, albeit in room 6. Alphon was clearly of much less interest since he had an alibi and did not fit the description – too tall, too old and with brown eyes – but Detective Superintendent Bob Acott, interested by what he had read, wanted this individual thoroughly investigated and eliminated. And his starting position was to return to the hotel and to speak again to the man who was effectively his alibi, Jack Glickberg.

★★★

While the police were tracking down Glickberg, on 20 September something rather remarkable happened on Ruth Ward in Guy's hospital: Janet Gregsten, accompanied by her brother-in-law William Ewer, paid a visit to her husband's wounded girlfriend. No formal statements report why this meeting took place, but there are some conflicting explanations. Some newspaper reports suggest that it had been Janet who had requested the meeting but according to the *Daily Mirror*,[8] Valerie had specifically asked Janet to go to the hospital to speak with her and the newspaper reported the detailed conversation between the two women.

The *Mirror* claimed: 'For forty minutes, the two women who are united in one common cause – to bring a murderer to justice – talked quietly together.'

Janet told journalists afterwards that Valerie had told her that the gunman had tapped on the window, which had only been wound half down, and ordered them to 'open the door'. The attacker had blue and staring eyes and Valerie thought that perhaps he was a burglar and wanted a getaway car. She said that there had been a lot of talk about who should drive the car and the gunman went on about his criminal background. He said that he had not eaten for two days and needed to tie them up. He seemed nervous about the time and kept on looking at his watch. Valerie specifically said that the reason given by the gunman as to why he had shot Michael was because 'he frightened me. He moved too quickly.' In the layby, the killer had said, 'I'd better knock you on the head or something.' Janet even told journalists that the killer had wanted to tie them both up using washing from the laundry bag that she herself had freshly cleaned.[9]

The *Daily Mail* reported Janet as saying, 'The police have asked me to speak so that everyone will rack their brains again to see if they know anything they should tell. I appeal to them, whether they are mother, relative or friend to come forward if they can help. I don't want anyone else to have to go through my ordeal.'

Writing in 2001, when she was jotting down her notes in preparation of a book she wanted to write about her ordeal, Valerie reflected on this hospital episode and was quite clear in her recollections. She described it as 'the first betrayal'. Her handwritten notes record:

[It] came when I went in Guy's. Janet Gregsten visited me accompanied and supported by her brother-in-law. I told her what had happened – surely the very least I could do – but the following day, the police were horrified and I was totally appalled to find out most of what I had said reported in the press.

These comments need to be seen in the context of two issues. Firstly, by 2001 her thoughts towards Janet and her brother-in-law were probably tainted by events that were to occur the following year and this may have coloured her thoughts when jotting her notes down forty years later. Secondly, if the police were horrified, why had Acott authorised such a high-profile meeting and even agreed to a photograph of Janet sitting next to Valerie at her bedside? It is common practice in high-profile cases for events to be staged to be used to jog memories and encourage people to contact the police. It is conceivable that Acott had this in mind when allowing the meeting to take place, but it is highly unlikely that he would have wished Janet Gregsten to divulge all she heard from Valerie to the reporters; some of the withheld evidence had been divulged. Either Acott failed to properly brief Janet as to what she should and should not say or Janet simply ignored or did not understand the instruction.

But for now at least, the newspapers had a new angle and the police hoped that someone would make the vital call.

Having been dismissed, Jack Glickberg and his wife had already left the Vienna hotel by the time the police wanted to reinterview him, but he had heard that they wished to speak to him again about 'Durrant' and he made the assumption that he was now a suspect for the murder. When they did catch up with him, he was interviewed at the police station, a process that would last for eight hours because Glickberg now had a different story to tell. He was told that Durrant's real name was Peter Alphon, but that made no difference to him; he had a new story. Previously, he said, he had been confused and got the room numbers and times mixed up and he now wanted to clarify matters.

It was correct, he said, that Alphon had come to the hotel on 22 August but at one o'clock in the afternoon and not at half past eleven at night as he had previously said. Alphon's alibi was therefore no longer supported. When Alphon had arrived at the hotel, there was no single room and so he was allocated the family space, room 24, as it was company practice not to turn away guests. It was explained to him that if any other potential guests arrived, he would have to share the room but only pay a single person's rate. Both Glickberg and his wife accompanied Alphon to the room, where he chose the single bed in the alcove and placed his suitcase on the chair at its foot. He made some sort of comment about not liking the basement room and Glickberg assured him that if a single room became available he would be able to move. During the afternoon, Alphon left the hotel, telling the staff not to wait up as he would be back late. Glickberg reiterated that if another room became available he would leave a note for him to that effect on the door of his room and also in reception.

As luck would have it, a man who had been allocated room 6 for that evening cancelled and a single room became available.[10] By two o'clock in the morning, both Glickberg and his wife were still up and decided to go to bed. They noticed that Alphon was the only guest who had not returned and so left a note for him at reception telling him that room 6 had now been allocated to him. By 9.50 a.m. the following morning, Alphon had not come down for breakfast and Glickberg went to room 6 and knocked on the door. He got no reply and opened the door to see Alphon putting his trousers on. He asked him whether he wanted breakfast and Alphon said he did not. Glickberg noticed that Alphon appeared dishevelled, his hair was ruffled and he was in need of a shave. Alphon told him that he had only got in at eleven o'clock the previous evening. At 11.45 a.m. that morning, Alphon was still in his room and Glickberg told his wife to go and tell him he needed to leave otherwise he would be charged for another night. As far as he was aware, this is what she did and he never saw Alphon again.

Not only was Glickberg now withdrawing Alphon's alibi for the time of the abduction but he had placed Alphon in room 24, albeit temporarily, stated that he was out of the hotel until at least two o'clock the next morning and when he did see him again he was acting as if he had been out all night. This statement, taken on 21 September, significantly increased the possibility that Alphon could be the killer.

Glickberg's story, though, had inconsistencies that appear to have been ignored. If it were true that Alphon arrived back at the hotel at 11 p.m. that night, why was he not seen by both Glickberg and his wife, who were still up, and how did Alphon know to go to room 6 since the note written for him had only been left in reception at 2 a.m.? Someone, either Glickberg or Alphon, was lying but in any event, Glickberg's statement in isolation could not be taken at face value. However, a statement taken the following day from his wife backed up his story; they had both been confused.[11] Alphon was now a person of great interest to the police.

When Alphon had been spoken to on 27 August, he had said that he had visited his mother on the evening of the abduction.[12] That now needed to be checked and his parents were visited by detectives. His father, Felix, who ironically worked at Scotland Yard as a clerk, was unable to help since he had not seen his son for four years after they had had a major row. Gladys Alphon, though, provided some helpful information, including the fact that her son did not drive, was well-spoken and never wore a watch or a tie, but insofar as providing him with an alibi, she could not really help. Certainly, she saw him routinely without her husband's knowledge, and on the week of the attack they had met at the end of Gleneagle Road where they lived, but it could have been on the Tuesday, the Wednesday or the Thursday, she said – she just could not be sure.

Based only on his description, Alphon was unlikely to be responsible for the attacks, but Acott still preferred to speak to him himself since Glickberg and his wife had moved him much more towards 'suspect' status. With Alphon's whereabouts being currently unknown, Acott then took the rather unusual step of publicly naming him and asking all hotels and boarding house proprietors to check their records to see if he was staying with them. A full description was provided to the newspapers, including the clothes he could be wearing and where he was likely to be working and visiting, and invited people who knew where he was to telephone either the incident room at Bedford or Scotland Yard. Thus Alphon appeared to have 'suspect' status, even though his description varied significantly from that provided by Valerie. Acott's wording, however, was rather different. The *Daily Telegraph*[13] reported that the police had received information recently that stressed the importance of Alphon 'as a witness'. And when Acott appeared on television that night appealing for him to come forward, again he stressed the 'importance of finding this witness'.

Shortly before 11 p.m. that night, Peter Alphon telephoned the *Daily Mirror* to say that he intended to go to Scotland Yard 'to clear up this ghastly suspicion the police appear to have that I am the A6 killer'.[14] In truth, this was an attempt on his part to get some money out of the newspapers for his story.[15] Hugh Curnow, a journalist from the *Mirror*, met him outside the Metropolitan Police headquarters and Alphon told him that he had seen his name splashed across the front pages.

> How can I ever hold my head up again until this has been cleared up? I am an unmarried man. I live a decent, clean life. I do not live with my family. My father is employed at Scotland Yard and I know for a fact the police request to find me must have been a shock to them. I realised the only thing to do was to come along to the police and get them once and for all to stop looking for me and to announce publicly that I am unable to help them in their inquiries in any way at all.

And that was the line he maintained when he was interviewed by Bob Acott at Cannon Row police station between 2 a.m. and 5.15 a.m. on 23 September. It was an unusual interview.[16] Acott did not caution him, again indicating that he did not regard Alphon as a suspect, or if he did, he was flagrantly breaching the rules concerning the questioning of suspects. He was asked questions about his movements, exploring any potential motives he may have had for wanting to carry out the attacks and where he was at the relevant times.

Alphon denied any involvement and repeated what he had told police the previous month when he had been spoken to at the Alexandra Court Hotel: on the night of the abduction he had spent the evening with his mother and had gone to the Vienna hotel around 11 p.m. He confirmed he had not switched bedrooms at the hotel and had stayed only in room 6. Acott was very aware of what he had previously claimed but in view of the Glickbergs' second statements, and the fact that his mother could not now be sure of the day she had met him that week, he needed to probe further. When the latest evidence of Jack Glickberg and his wife from the Vienna hotel was put to him about his arrival time and his demeanour, Alphon said, 'You're trying to trap me; you couldn't have two witnesses to say that. They must be lying.'

He was most adamant that what the police had been told by Glickberg was wrong. He arrived at the hotel that night at 11 p.m. and had maintained that story from the very first time he had been spoken to.

It was a difficult interview and Acott did his best to reassure him that if he told him the truth, he would be in a position to clear him of the murder, a proposition to which Alphon seemed to respond. He apologised for accusing Acott of trying to trap him and said he realised that the detective was trying to get to the truth. In short, Alphon maintained his alibi of being with his mother and had gone to the Vienna hotel that night. Acott was satisfied that this man had nothing to do with the murder and he started to doubt what the Glickbergs had told him; but he needed to be sure.

Alphon was now available and was willing to stand on an identification parade, and on the same afternoon one was quickly arranged in the quadrangle at Scotland Yard. Officers were despatched to gather the array of witnesses who would be asked to attend and take part. Inspector Kenneth Nayer carried out the formalities and told Alphon that he would be standing in a line of ten other people all of similar age, appearance and class and that he was able to select exactly where he stood on the parade.[17] He was told he could have a friend or solicitor present but he declined. He chose to stand second from the left and the first witness was brought in. It was Edward Blackhall, the man who had been the passenger in Skillett's car when they were witness to the dangerous driving on the Eastern Avenue on the morning of 23 August, a month earlier. He looked along the line and selected a man fourth from the left. It was not Alphon.

The next witness was Jack Glickberg, the ex-hotel employee who was now saying that the man he knew as Durrant had temporarily stayed in room 24. He first selected the man on the extreme left but then picked out Alphon, standing immediately next to him. As a result of this selection, Alphon stepped forward and, being the only one who was not wearing a tie asked that the others be required to remove them. His request was carried out and the parade resumed.

The next witness was Florence Glickberg, who had seen the man she knew as Durrant at the Vienna hotel. She selected the man fifth from the right. Next was a man named Harold Hirons.

When publicity had been at its height after the events on the A6, Hirons stepped forward as possibly the man who had served petrol to the driver of the Morris Minor when it had stopped for fuel. That night he was working a shift at the 584 Garage at Kingsbury Circle, London NW9. He said that at around midnight an old grey Morris Minor had come into the garage from the Kenton direction and a man had got out of the back seat of the car and ordered 4 gallons of petrol. He then changed his order to 2 gallons, paid with a 10s note and then left. He described the man as between 32 and 38 years of age, 5ft 7½in in height and with long, tussled hair.[18] He had since been shown Gregsten's Morris and had thought it similar by virtue of its markings. His story varied in many ways from Valerie's, including a completely different description of the man and the banknotes used to pay for the fuel, but he needed to be tested. He went into the parade and selected a man third from the right.

Next was James Trower, who had heard the screaming engine of the car as it turned into Avondale Crescent and saw the face of its driver. He viewed the line and made no identification at all.[19]

Formally, this was the end of the identification parade relating to the murder of Gregsten and the attack upon Valerie. Other than Jack Glickberg, nobody had selected Alphon. There was, however, one other formality to complete. The parade remained assembled and Alphon was told that a second one would now take place involving an allegation of indecency committed on 7 September in East Sheen; the attack upon Meike Dalal. He was given the same opportunity to stand where he wished on the line and he elected to remain where he was.

The Swedish housewife walked into the quadrangle. She was obviously distressed and trembling.[20] She viewed the line and said, 'I think it's the second from the left,' which was Alphon. She was invited to go closer and she said, 'He didn't have such a crooked nose.' She seemed unsure and the inspector invited her to make a positive identification by touching the man on the shoulder but she simply turned away. Dalal's actions amounted to not making any identification.[21] Six other witnesses from the East Sheen incident went through the same process and none made any identification of Alphon.

The parade was over but there was one further witness: Valerie Storie. With no prospect of her being able to attend a parade, the parade would attend her, and did so the following day in Ruth Ward at Guy's hospital. Inspector Cyril Canham took charge of the proceedings this time and gathered together nine men of similar appearance to Alphon. This time Alphon elected to stand on the extreme left and since Valerie would not be able to walk along the line-up, each was made to hold a placard bearing a number. Alphon was number 10.

With the parade assembled, a set of screens was pulled away and behind was the bedridden Valerie accompanied by a nurse and Doctor Rennie, the physician who had been in charge of her care since her admission. He wanted to make sure that Valerie was psychologically capable of dealing with the prospect of facing her attacker at such close proximity again. She was, he said, 'very keyed-up, very tense, but not flustered and quite clear in her own mind'. However, only the day before he and another doctor had performed an operation on her, under a local anaesthetic, to remove the two bullets that had been lodged just under the skin near her right shoulder blade. He was happy for now that she was strong enough to go through with the identification and considered that she had not suffered any element of memory loss since her ordeal. Nevertheless, he wanted to make sure that consideration for her welfare was paramount. With the screen now rolled back, she faced the men paraded before her and was given the instruction by the inspector to view the line and select the man who was responsible for her attack. She looked up and down for five minutes, at least two of which she spent focusing on Alphon, before she said, 'Number 4 is the man.'

The screens were replaced and the men on the parade, including Alphon, were led away. Doctor Rennie noticed in Valerie that she was now a little tearful. 'She had been a little frightened and her emotions had suddenly been released,' he commented.[22] Acott, though, was annoyed with himself. Immediately before the parade, he had noticed that Valerie was upset and he had thought about postponing it, but he had Alphon in custody and could only hold him for a few more hours. He had decided to go ahead and was not surprised at all that Valerie had made an incorrect identification. Indeed, the man she had picked out was nothing like her description; he was 27 but was taller than she had described, 5ft 9in, had dark short-cropped hair and was heavily built. Acott told her that she had identified someone who was known not to have been involved and at this point she became very upset and distressed.[23] This wrongful identification would be used against her in the months and years ahead but for now it was significant that she had not identified Alphon.

The arrangements for the identification parades suggest that the instructions to the witnesses implied that the man they were looking for was actually present, hence the number of wrongful identifications. It would have been better if they had been told that the man they were looking for may not be there at all, as is now the practice. In any event, no one had selected Alphon as the attacker or the driver of the Morris, and on 24 September he was officially eliminated from the enquiry.

Chapter Seven

Enter James Hanratty

Lewis Nickolls at the forensic science laboratory confirmed that the two bullets removed from Valerie's chest came from the murder weapon found on the London bus. Valerie was transferred on 25 September to what would become her home for the next six and a half months, Stoke Mandeville hospital near Aylesbury in Buckinghamshire, where she was to receive intensive physiotherapy.

By this time the number of files created in the murder incident room had grown. Some were locations of interest, some were suspicious sightings but many were names put forward as people of interest either by the public or by the police themselves. J. Ryan was now the person of most interest.

Acott was suspicious of Jack Glickberg, so he did some checking and discovered that Glickberg was not his real name. Instead of challenging him directly, he sent his team out to fetch his wife, the so-called Florence Glickberg, and on 25 September he interviewed her.

It transpired that Florence, whose surname was actually Snell, was not Glickberg's wife.[1] She knew him as Dave, they did live together and they had been doing so for a couple of years. She now told Acott that after she had made her first statement, Glickberg had told her that he had made a second one altering his story to implicate Alphon, or Durrant as she then knew him. She had no idea why he had done that but she had gone along with the story. He had spent hours going over the detail with her, realising that the police would need another statement from her and when they did, she had repeated everything he had now told the police. Only when she was called to the identification parade had the seriousness of the situation dawned on her and she realised that she was helping to convict an innocent man. Snell had become frightened after she realised what she had done and was now terrified, but she confirmed that everything she had said in her first statement about Ryan occupying room 24 was all perfectly true.

'It's a most dreadful thing that we've done,' she said. 'I don't know what we can do about it. It's a wicked thing. He's [Glickberg] either mad or in some trouble. I have never been so frightened in all my life.'[2]

Glickberg was now brought to Scotland Yard and after initial denials about his true identity, he admitted his real name was William Nudds. He was using the other name because he had a chequered past and wanted to keep a low profile; Florence did not know anything about it. Acott confronted him with Snell's admission and as soon as he realised he had been caught out, Nudds admitted what he had done and that nothing in his second statement was true – Alphon had been nowhere near room 24.

Nudds, in fact, was a seasoned criminal.[3] He had spent most of his life behind bars but he had grown to be hated by fellow inmates. He would later say that while in prison he witnessed the slashing of a prisoner's face that needed fifty-six stitches. He had taken the view that the slashing was unwarranted and, against the unwritten prisoner's code of conduct, he had given evidence at court against the man who carried out the attack. It resulted in him being routinely attacked by prisoners, on one occasion so seriously he needed hospitalisation. Upon release, his reputation followed him around London and he got no support from other criminals that otherwise he may have received. He felt betrayed and sought to get some sort of revenge.

When he had been taken to Scotland Yard to make his last statement he felt he had also been poorly treated by the police but he also saw it as the opportunity he had been looking for to get his revenge. The police were clearly interested, he wrongly assumed, in charging Alphon for the murder, and he thought he would help them out by manufacturing a story that would convince them.

Acott would later describe this strange couple as 'liars and slanderers', whose statements had caused the police to concentrate on Alphon and even name him in the newspapers. However, following Nudds' latest statement, Acott refocused his efforts on J. Ryan.

The address written by him in the hotel register had been false and it was more than likely that the name was too. Correspondence had been sent there from a hire car company in Ireland and on 19 September a telephone call had been made to the police in Dublin passing details of the correspondence. A full description of Ryan was given together with the fact that he appeared to have hired a car in Dublin that had been found abandoned with some accident damage at the airport. The Irish police were asked:

> Please make all enquiries at Dublin airport and elsewhere to trace and iden-
> tify the man J Ryan. Obtain all known addresses and names he has or may
> have used, a copy of his signature and or handwriting, his full description,
> date of birth, height etc. Also mannerisms, peculiarities and associates.[4]

The Irish police established that on 5 September, a man presenting himself as J. Ryan walked into the Motor Registration Office in Dublin and applied for a driving licence. The man said he was 23 years of age, even though the date of birth provided suggested otherwise. The application form was signed J. Ryan and he was issued with a licence valid for one year. The same day, in Limerick, over 120 miles away, Ryan tried to rent a car but because one was not available he stayed at the Thomond hotel in the town. The next morning, Ryan, who gave his occupation as a window cleaner, paid £23 15s for a five-day hire of a Wolseley motor car, AZC 339, and signed the agreement form. The signature on this document matched that on the driving licence application form in Dublin. The man who served him said that Ryan had red tints in his hair, was unable to pronounce 'th' and was carrying a holdall/travelling bag.

That night, Gerard Leonard stayed at O'Flynn's hotel in Cork and he was required to share a room with another guest. It was J. Ryan. The two got on well together and Ryan explained that he had previously tried to get accommodation at a hotel called Hanratty in Limerick and the owner was somehow connected to his father. They later went out for a drink together and had gone on to a dance. Ryan drove and Leonard later remarked that Ryan was 'a very bad driver, possibly not bad, as more slightly reckless'. He overtook a lot, he said, and even saw some accident damage to the rear bumper, which Ryan said he had done while reversing. It was similar to that found on Gregsten's car.

The following morning after breakfast, Ryan explained that he was not a good writer and asked his new friend if he would write some postcards on his behalf. He agreed and wrote at Ryan's dictation. The first was to Mr D. France, Boundary Road in Finchley, the second to Miss L. Andrew at an address in Paddington and the third, which had started, 'Dear Mum,' to a Mrs Hanratty, 12 Sycamore Grove, Kingsbury, London, NW9. The last one was signed, 'Your loving son, Jim' with four kisses.[5]

Ryan's signature in the O'Flynn hotel register was the same as those on the other Irish documents and matched perfectly the one in the Vienna hotel in London. It was increasingly looking like J. Ryan's real name was Jim Hanratty and that he had an address just around the corner from Wood Lane and within 6 miles of the Vienna hotel.

The Irish police also established that Ryan was involved in a car accident in the hire car the same day he had dictated the writing of the postcards. He had been travelling at speed on the wrong side of the road as he negotiated a bend in the Cork town of Castlemartyr and crashed into an oncoming vehicle. He exchanged names and addresses with the other driver and went on his way.[6] Four days later he parked the car at Dublin airport and travelled to London on an Aer Lingus flight, which left at 6.40 p.m. that evening. All the indications were that Jim Hanratty was now back in London and Acott now had some clues as to where to start looking. The three people who had been sent postcards were top of the list to be visited.

A check with Scotland Yard's Criminal Record Bureau revealed Hanratty's past record. He had a number of convictions mainly for stealing cars but had, significantly, received three years' corrective training in 1958, something the A6 attacker had boasted. He was also a convicted housebreaker and was currently wanted for offences committed in north-west London; his fingerprints had been found in incriminating places. He had been released from prison in March, five months before the attack.

Acott visited the Hanratty family in Sycamore Grove on 26 September, although he suggested he wanted to talk about outstanding burglaries as he did not want to give Hanratty any advance warning of his interest in the A6 attack. Jimmy was not there and hadn't been for some time, his parents said. Acott asked them to let him know if he turned up and returned two days later to ask more questions. There was still no sign of him but it was an opportunity to learn more about this man.

The Hanrattys were a decent, law-abiding, working-class Irish family. James Hanratty senior and his wife, Mary, had four sons, the eldest being James, or Jimmy as they called him. The younger brothers were Michael, Peter and Richard. Jimmy had been evacuated during the war in 1944 partly because he had come close to being hit by a bomb that had landed in their back garden in Kingsbury, killing the next-door neighbour.[7] When he returned he went to St James' Catholic School in Burnt Oak where, after a medical examination, it was recommended he be sent to a special school, but his parents had refused to send him. At the age of 15, he left school with the classification of 'retarded'. Having been turned down by the army on medical grounds for National Service, he started work at Wembley Council as a dustman but very shortly afterwards he had fallen from his bicycle, broken his leg and injured his head. After the accident he stopped working.

He then disappeared from home but was later found in a road in Brighton lying in a state of unconsciousness. He appeared to be suffering from loss of memory and an operation was performed on his head to try to determine the cause. The doctor found nothing untoward, thought he had been feigning unconsciousness and endorsed him a 'mental defective'. He was still only 15 years old.

He returned to London, where he then embarked upon his criminal career, stealing cars and breaking into people's homes. After he had been released from prison in March, his father had left his job at the council to set up a window cleaning business for himself and Jimmy, but while he and his wife were away on holiday in Southsea, Jimmy disappeared again. That was in July, and the family had not seen him since, although he often sent flowers to his mother and they confirmed that they had received the postcard sent from Ireland. As much as they were disappointed in their son's wayward life, they had also seen the better side of him, a quiet, well-liked young man who never attempted to drag them into his more clandestine activities.

Acott once again let it be known that he needed to talk to Jimmy and asked them to get in contact if they heard from him. It was becoming apparent that the police interest in Hanratty was about the murder, and not some minor housebreaking. Acott had deliberately not given the name Ryan or Hanratty to the newspapers and he now travelled across to Ireland, with Detective Sergeant Ken Oxford, to progress the information that had been unearthed by his Irish colleagues; there was a remote possibility that Hanratty may still be there. The newspapers discovered Acott had travelled to Ireland, but not the reason why; he had no intention of creating another debacle like he had over the Peter Alphon affair. The Irish witnesses confirmed everything that had been said before but everything indicated that the hunted man was now back in London. Upon his return, Acott made sure that police informants were out looking for Hanratty and doubtless word would get to him before too long.

One of the places that James Hanratty frequented was the Rehearsal Club in Archer Street, in the capital's Soho district. One of his brothers, probably Michael, knowing that his brother was now wanted by Scotland Yard, visited there on 5 October and spoke to Ann Pryce. She knew Jimmy and had been out on dates with him; she would also later acknowledge that she had been given gifts of jewellery by him. He told her that Jimmy was wanted for the A6 murder. Two days later, Jimmy, now sporting dark auburn-coloured hair, came into the club and she told him what his brother had said. He appeared genuinely shocked by the news. She begged him to give himself up, he said he would, and simply left. She never saw him again.[8]

The second person sent a postcard was a Mr D. France at the Finchley address. He made a statement to the police on the same day that Hanratty's brother was asking around in the Soho club where France in fact worked as a manager. He would go on to make a number of statements that would help to tie Hanratty into the investigation.[9] He lived at the address on the postcard with his wife Charlotte and daughter Carol, but though his real name was Charles, his nickname was 'Dixie', hence the D in Hanratty's postcard. He knew Hanratty as Jimmy Ryan. They had known each other for around five years but became reacquainted in July after he came out of prison earlier that year. Ryan had nowhere to go that night so he allowed him to stay over at his house. He was always pleasant and friendly, the rest of the family liked him and over the next few weeks he was allowed occasionally to sleep over.

Dixie confirmed he had received a number of postcards from Hanratty, all from different locations in Ireland. Slowly, he began to provide background information about him. He knew he was a housebreaker and was always talking about going out to do some 'business' in the evenings. Occasionally, France would look at the jewellery Hanratty had stolen from people's houses as he was unable to 'tell paste from diamonds'. All this made sense. Hanratty was young and having an older mentor would have helped him as he built his career.

When interviewed by Acott, France recalled a conversation he had with Hanratty just a few weeks earlier on the early August bank holiday weekend when they had travelled back together from the Hendon greyhound track on a London bus. They had both gone to the upper deck and Hanratty insisted they went to the back. He pointed to the back seat and said, 'The finest place for hiding anything.'[10] He would later expand on that and claimed that Hanratty had said, 'This is the only seat that lifts up and it's a good hiding place.'

That same weekend, Hanratty asked France's daughter, an apprentice hairdresser, if she could dye his hair for him. He gave no reason but he was someone who always cared about his appearance and she was not surprised about being asked. She noticed that his hair was a kind of streaky mousy colour and she tinted it black.

On Sunday, 20 August, two days before the attack in the cornfield, Hanratty turned up at the France household again and asked if Charlotte could do some laundry for him as he was travelling the next day to Liverpool to see his aunt. She was happy to help Jimmy out and the following day, Monday, he came and collected it. He was wearing a chalk stripe suit and looked his usual smart self. Carol was able to specifically pinpoint the day as she was at home having had a tooth removed and was recovering.[11] Uncle Jim, as she called him, seemed in no hurry and actually stayed at the house until about 7 p.m. before leaving with his freshly laundered clothing. It was assumed that he was off to Liverpool but Dixie saw him later that evening in the Rehearsal Club and he had obviously not travelled that night.

France was beginning to build up a picture. If Hanratty was the man responsible he could be placed in Piccadilly on the Monday evening and again, if Nudds was now to be believed, at the Vienna hotel shortly before midnight. The next morning, Tuesday, 22 August, the day of the abduction, Hanratty had left the hotel with information about the number 36 bus.

France did not see Hanratty again until the following weekend but on the Friday he received a telegram from him timed and dated at 8.40 p.m. the previous day that read: 'Having a nice time, be home early Friday morning for business. Yours sincerely, Jim.' The sender was Mr J. Ryan, Imperial Hotel, Russell Square, London.

The following morning, around 9.30 a.m. he guessed, Hanratty turned up on his doorstep again saying he had just travelled down that morning from Liverpool on the overnight train. He had dispensed with his smart suit and was wearing more casual clothing. Dixie asked him when he had actually travelled to Liverpool as he had seen him in his club last Monday when earlier he had told him that he was going that day. He answered that he didn't go that night but had stayed at the Vienna hotel instead; he even showed him the receipt, remarking how expensive it was to stay in hotels. That Saturday, he spent the entire day there with Carol re-dyeing his hair. He left about 6.30 in the evening, his hair still wet with the dye.

In effect, the France family had shown that up until the night before the attack and the weekend afterwards, Hanratty had been in London. One matter the police were able to pursue was that Hanratty had told Charlotte that while he had been in Liverpool, he had visited his aunt and taken her out to the dogs one night. Christina Hanratty, who did live in Liverpool, was contacted and she told them that she had not seen or heard from her nephew in seven years. Hanratty's claim was a lie and where he had been that week remained unknown.

Over the next few days, Hanratty stayed the occasional night at the Frances' flat and on 3 September, he turned up dressed in a new suit he had just bought that day, he said, from Petticoat Lane. He asked Charlotte whether she would kindly do some laundry for him again as he was travelling the next day to

Ireland. He booked the flights by using the telephone in the house. The following day, he collected the laundry and left.

He returned a few days later with the driving licence he had obtained and within a few days he had bought himself a Sunbeam Alpine, of which he was very proud. He had always wanted to own a car, France said, and now he had one, a cream-coloured, two-seater sports version with red upholstery and white-walled tyres. Carol, who had gone out with him on one occasion, mentioned that he was a wild driver, 'zig-zagging' all over the road; 'He couldn't drive the car,' she said.[12] A few weeks later he would boast that he had taken it for a drive up the M1 and 'got 100mph out of it'.[13]

After that, France never saw Hanratty again.

Two of the recipients of the postcards had been traced and now the third one, Miss L. Andrew, needed to be found.

Shortly after midday on 6 October, however, Acott's telephone rang in Scotland Yard. It was James Hanratty, and he had a lot to say:

> I'm Jim Hanratty. I'm in a phone box but I can't tell you where. I want to talk to you and clear up this whole thing, but I can't come in there. I'm very worried and don't know what to do. I know you are the only one who can help me. I'd like to see you, but I've just come out from doing three and if I'm caught, I'll get at least five. I know I have left my fingerprints at different places and done different things and the police want me, but I tell you Mr Acott, that I didn't do that A6 murder. I am so upset I don't know what I'm doing and what I'm saying. I've got a very bad head and I suffer from blackouts and lose my memory.

The detective superintendent tried to convince him to meet or at least get in touch with his mother as she was worried, but it was met with refusals. He said he would call a newspaper to get some advice, and with that he hung up.

Hanratty now knew that he was being looked for by every London police officer, and he telephoned his friend, Dixie France. Dixie invited him to come round to his flat, but Hanratty was fearful the police would be watching his address. In fact, Dixie's phone was being monitored in the event that Hanratty called and the friendly fence did as he been instructed and kept him talking. Hanratty was clearly agitated and France told him to calm down. When he finally understood what Hanratty was trying to tell him, he tried to convince him to simply walk into Scotland Yard and clear the matter up. After all, he was a burglar not a murderer. Hanratty repeated to France what he had told Acott: that he knew he was wanted for burglaries and did not want to go back inside.

He said he was going to give the police a good run, had £250 stashed away and was going to ring the newspapers. He ended the call.

Later, he was back on the telephone to Scotland Yard. He seemed more relaxed this time and told Acott he had just been to the see a film at the cinema and boasted about being chased by two plain-clothed police officers, a claim that may have been true.[14] He told him that he had telephoned the *Daily Mirror*, who simply told him to give himself up.

During the call Acott managed to get Hanratty to acknowledge sending the postcard from Ireland to his mother and he said he had sent some flowers to her, which Acott knew she had received. He knew he had upset his mother, he said, a reference probably to his having spent his life committing crime. He seemed intent, though, on proving his innocence over the telephone and told Acott to get hold of a woman called Louise. She was a widow in her 50s, he said. He gave him her telephone number and said that she had a couple of his suitcases. Acott needed to look inside those; that would help him. Hanratty again hung up. This was probably the Miss L. Andrew on the third postcard.

Forty-eight-year-old Louise was not hard to find. Her full name was Louise Anderson and she had indeed been the recipient of the third postcard from Ireland. She lived in Sussex Gardens, near Paddington, and had an antiques shop in London's Soho, which she had operated successfully for the past fourteen years.

When the police arrived in the middle of the night, she was not surprised that they were looking for Hanratty's suitcases, which had been in her house since he had left them there two days ago. One was empty but the other contained some of his underclothes, a green suit and dark-coloured waistcoat and matching zip-up trousers that appeared to be part of another suit. The jacket, however, was missing.[15] At first, she said that he was just someone she had got to know and that she had first met him when he walked into her shop towards the end of July and had tried to sell her what she described as trinkets. She was not interested as they were paste and he had thrown them away in the wastepaper basket. Over the next few weeks she had seen him again, went out to dinner on one occasion and he had even stayed overnight in her flat once, sleeping on one of the chairs in her kitchen.

He had told her he was going to Ireland and she was not surprised when she got some postcards from him, three in all; she still had two of them. Her story did not seem to wholly ring true, particularly in view of what was written on one of the cards. It read:

Dear Louise, I have been thinking about you the last few days and I thought how nice it would be if you were only here with me. The food is really excellent. I hired a car on Monday and thought it very expensive. It is the best way to see Ireland. All my love, Jim.

Hanratty had signed it off with some kisses.

What was written on the postcard did not seem to match with what she was now telling the police; their relationship seemed a little closer than she was suggesting.

She finished her account of what she knew about Jimmy by saying that after he had come back from Ireland he had stayed over on a few other nights but on other occasions he had claimed to have stayed at one or two grand hotels in London, such as the Imperial in Russell Square.[16] She said he told her of a friend he had in St John's Wood by the name of Dixie, that she had unexpectedly received eighteen carnations from him and on another occasion she had noticed he had some scratches on his face that he said he had got from 'being in a scrap'.[17] The clothes in the suitcase were sent off to the laboratory, and it was noted that Anderson's house was on the route of the number 36A bus.

Over the next few weeks the antique dealer became increasingly nervous now that she was aware that Jimmy was wanted for the A6 murder, and she decided to tell the police more of what she knew. She knew he was a housebreaker and she had bought stolen property from him, handing over several hundred pounds in the process. Her shop was searched and forty-four pieces of jewellery and furs were found that Hanratty had sold to her.[18] She told the detectives that the reason she had done it was because she had become frightened of him, so much so, that she gave him money to make sure no harm would come to her.[19]

Hanratty was back on the phone to Acott on 7 October, and this time said he was calling from Liverpool. It was 5.26 p.m. and he claimed he had caught the overnight train from London:

I've come up to Liverpool to see some friends, but they can't help me. You see, it's very difficult for them. I asked them to say I couldn't have committed your murder, but they wouldn't listen and wouldn't let me stay with them as they said I'll bring the police down on them. You can't blame them. Because they are fences. You know what I mean, they receive jewellery. They're known to the police here and one of them is wanted now.

Hanratty told Acott that the three people he had come to see in Liverpool had been with him on the night of the murder. They could alibi him but, for fear of being arrested themselves for crimes they were wanted for, they refused to help him out. Acott was quite clear:

> Listen to me carefully, Jimmy. My duty is to investigate this murder and find out the truth. If you are innocent, it is my job to try to prove you are innocent. It is not my job just to charge you and get you convicted. If I can help you I will do my best for you. Is that clear, Jimmy?

Acott asked him to clarify exactly how these people could prove his innocence. Hanratty explained that he had stayed at the Vienna hotel on the Monday night and had travelled across to Paddington the following day to catch the train to Liverpool. Once he had got there he had realised that he was at the wrong station so he caught a cab to Euston, where he had caught either the 10.55 or 11.55 train. Acott could check that, he said. He then stayed in Liverpool with people whose house was full of stolen property, before returning to London on the Friday, where he stayed with different friends. Acott already knew that this was the France family.

He refused to divulge the most important piece of information about with whom and where he had stayed in Liverpool. All he had to do was name the people, and provided they backed up his story, he would be eliminated from the enquiry. Acott asked whether there was anyone else who could verify his movements in Liverpool:

> No. Those three are the only ones I can fink of who can say I was there.[20] I'm going to move now, Mr Acott, before you catch me. One day, you'll get the cuffs on me, but I'm alright now. I've got a lot of money which is fortunate isn't it? One day when all my money has gone you'll get the cuffs on me and I'll tell you the whole story then, but until then I'm going to give you a good run, Mr Acott. I stuck a few hundred away for a rainy day and it will last me a good few months. I am a bit fly, you know. Now, I must go.

Hanratty rang in again two days later. Acott was not available, though, and one of his detective constables took the call.[21] The caller said his name was Ryan, and he wanted to say how disgusted he was with Acott, probably because the police had been to his parents' house and his mother was upset.

He continued:

> Look, I've spoken to him before and I have tried to help him. You can tell him my luggage is at Louise's place. The green suit is blood-stained. It is my

blood. I cut my hand on some glass. It is nothing to do with the A6 murder. I thought I would explain before things get worse.

He ended the call.

★★★

Shortly after six o'clock in the evening on Sunday, 1 October, almost a week before Hanratty started calling Scotland Yard, the switchboard operator at Stoke Mandeville hospital answered the telephone. A gruff, male voice told her that he was the man who had shot Valerie Storie and he would be returning to the hospital at 11.30 p.m. that night to finish her off.

This was not the first time such a call had been made. Four days after the shooting, while Valerie had been under constant medical supervision at Bedford hospital, Hatfield police had received a call from a man who claimed another man had told him he was going to kill Valerie. Woman Police Sergeant Clapperton sat outside Valerie's ward for some time, and windows in the ward were closed.[22] Valerie was not made aware and no gunman arrived.

The phone call that was now received at Stoke Mandeville hospital five weeks later was traced to a telephone box in Sidney Place, Windsor, and doubtless sparked the same precautionary reaction from the police. But, ten minutes later, a further call was received, this time at Windsor police station. The caller identified himself as a Mr Butler and said, 'Look out for a Vauxhall Velox, registration number 527 AAA, which will be in Aylesbury at 11 p.m. with the A6 murderer.'

The call was traced to a telephone box in Clarence Road, Windsor, a mere 300 yards from where the earlier call had been made. A check with the registered keeper of the Vauxhall revealed that his car had been parked in Clarence Road at the time the call was made when he and his wife were making a social call. The police were satisfied that neither were involved and they were sure that the caller had simply seen the car number when making his call.

The following evening, another call was made. This time the voice said, 'I rang the hospital yesterday about Valerie Storie.' Almost apologetically, the man then said, 'I was unable to come to the hospital last night but will be there tonight.' The call, made by a man with a similar voice to the one made the day before, was traced to High Wycombe.

The following afternoon, the fourth call came. 'You know the call you had from Windsor? Tonight, may be the night.'[23]

Precautionary measures were put in place once more to ensure Valerie's protection, but no one ever materialised. It would not be the last of these calls, however.

★★★

Acott had still not established why the journey on 22 August had been in the direction of Bedford. Members of the extended Hanratty family were visited, who said that some of them lived in Bedford, and Hanratty himself had been there on a number of occasions, once for a period of three weeks, but that was eight years ago.[24]

On 10 October, 18-year-old Gladys Deacon spoke to Acott's team as she had known Hanratty for a number of years and had met him just before he was sent to prison in 1958. While he had been in custody, at the family's request, she had often written to him. She now told them that during the afternoon of 23 September, a month after the killing, Hanratty had unexpectedly turned up at her house, wearing a dark chalk stripe suit, in his Sunbeam and asked her whether she wanted to go for a drive to Bedford. She was dubious at first but decided to accept the offer. He drove at a terrific speed, she said, although she could not remember the route they had taken from her home in Langham Gardens. She recalled, however, that they had driven along some country lanes and at some point they passed Cardington aerodrome; Jimmy had pointed out a Spitfire as they drove past. Cardington is south-east of Bedford, about 8 miles away from Clophill.

When they got to Bedford, they walked around for a short time before having a meal somewhere above a cinema. Afterwards, Hanratty had wanted to find a friend who apparently lived in Ashburnham Road and they drove for a while before he stopped at the railway station. She was told to wait there for about ten minutes while Hanratty went to find his friend. He returned shortly afterwards, saying that he had not been at home. A quick check revealed that the railway station was immediately next to Ashburnham Road.

They returned to London, where they went out for a drink and on to Battersea Fun Fair, before he dropped her back at home at 1 a.m. the next morning. The following day they went out again, this time to Richmond, Edgware and Hendon, with Hanratty again dropping her back home in the early hours of the morning. She added that over the next week or so Hanratty would telephone her at work and repeatedly asked her to marry him, although she didn't take it seriously. In time, Hanratty would claim that this had been a full sexual relationship, but this was never confirmed by her.

Gladys' story gave the first real suggestion that Hanratty knew the Bedford area and the roads that he would need to travel along to get there from London.[25] She was asked by the police to let them know if Hanratty tried to contact her again and a plan was put in place to trace any call that she received. The following day at 10.30 he telephoned her saying that he was in Liverpool. While she spoke to him on the phone, Scotland Yard was contacted. It was a short, rather garbled call with Hanratty speaking about a rumour that he was seeing a girl called Mary, asking Gladys to contact his mum to tell her not to worry and to make sure she didn't believe everything she read about him in the newspapers.[26]

What happened next is not clear but within twelve hours of the call to Deacon, Hanratty was in custody; not in Liverpool, but Blackpool. Shortly after eleven o'clock in the evening, Detective Constable James Williams walked into the Stevonia café on the town's Central Drive with one of his colleagues. He saw a man he thought was Hanratty, though now with what he described as 'ginger coloured hair', but waited until he left the café. Once outside, Williams approached him, identified himself and told the man that he suspected he was James Hanratty and that he was wanted for housebreakings in the Metropolitan Police area. Williams cautioned the man that he need not say anything and the man responded by saying, 'You are making a big mistake. I am Peter Bates,' and told the two officers that he lived in Scotland Road, Liverpool.

Williams and his colleague searched him and then walked with him a short distance before their prisoner seemed to acknowledge that they knew who he really was and suggested they contact the Yard. Asked to explain what he meant by the comment, now admitting that he was James Hanratty, he said, 'I might as well get it all over with now. I will clear up the A6 job for you and the other jobs in the south.'

He was told that they would not be speaking to him as it was better left to the officers in charge of the investigation. At the police station, he was documented, further searched and his property taken from him. He continued to say that he had not wanted to give himself up as he had a record but he was urged by the officers not to continue speaking. His final words before he was put into his cell were, 'I am not worried too much. I am prepared to take a gamble and have got my solicitor fixed up.'

Exactly seven weeks after Michael Gregsten had been shot in his car in the layby in Bedfordshire, James Hanratty was under arrest in Blackpool.

Chapter Eight

Under Arrest

Acott and Oxford travelled overnight to Blackpool and were sitting in front of the arrested prisoner by 7.45 a.m. the next morning.[1] What followed would be subject to severe criticism in the trial the following year and it centred on the admissibility of evidence and the adoption of correct police procedures when dealing with complicated, sensitive and high-profile criminal investigations. As it turned out, the trial judge ruled that the police had acted properly and all the evidence was allowed to go before the jury.

Acott and Hanratty now met for the first time, the Scotland Yard detective noting the prisoner's 'clear blue eyes',[2] and after an exchange of words that satisfied each of them that the person sitting on the other side of the table was the person on the other end of the telephone a week earlier, the interview started, Sergeant Oxford taking down notes.

One of the first things asked by Hanratty was whether he could be referred to as Jimmy Ryan to save any further embarrassment to his parents. It was not in Acott's gift to do that and he quickly made the point that while he had been arrested for housebreakings in London, he wanted to talk to him about the A6 murder and cautioned him. Hanratty's reply was clear:

Yes, I understand that Mr Acott, but as I told you on the phone, I've got a perfect alibi for the murder. I'm not worried about the murder but as I promised you last weekend, I'd tell you the whole story when you caught me. Fire away and ask me any questions you like. I'll answer them and you'll see I had nothing to do with the murder.

Acott began and in reply to his first question about his movements on the day before the murder, Hanratty readily admitted that he had stayed in the

Vienna hotel, in room 24, had breakfast in the morning and then travelled to Liverpool. He described the inside of the bedroom and detailed exactly in which bed he had slept. He had walked from the hotel in Sutherland Avenue to Paddington railway station before realising that trains to Liverpool do not leave from there and so caught a taxi across to Euston, where he caught either the 10.55 or 12.55 train – although he had previously said 11.55 – arriving in Liverpool at 4.30 p.m. There, he stayed with friends until the Thursday. He returned to London the following day and eventually stayed with friends in Boundary Road, although he could not name them. The friends in Liverpool, he said, were people that he did business with: 'They buy my gear,' he claimed. Acott asked who these people were and there was a prolonged pause before Hanratty said:

> I can't involve them. How can I tell you who they are? They all have records and one of them is wanted by the police. They run me out of there [Liverpool] yesterday when I told them that I was the man wanted for the A6 murder.

Acott reinforced the point that without any names, his story could not be verified.

'I can't drop them,' Hanratty persisted. 'They are facing a lot of trouble. How can I tell you? They've looked after me since last Saturday.'

But then he added, 'I can prove it without them because I've got somefing else.'

Despite Acott asking for the names of his Liverpool friends again, Hanratty switched the subject to the luggage he had directed the police to in Louise Anderson's flat. When Acott confirmed he had taken possession of it, Hanratty said that the blue suit was the one he had worn at the Vienna hotel and in Liverpool and the green one had some blood on it, which was his. He had cut himself while breaking into someone's house. He finished off his explanation of the clothing in the suitcase by saying, 'There you are, Mr Acott. How could I have done the murder? I was wearing that suit all week.'

It seemed Hanratty felt he had explained that because the blue suit had been the one that he had been wearing, he could not have committed the murder. He was either not the killer or he knew there was no blood on it. Acott pointed out that the trouble with his story was that the jacket of the suit was missing. The waistcoat and trousers were there, but nothing else.

Hanratty had an explanation. He had dumped it, he said, in a children's playground in Stanmore after cutting it while committing a burglary on a house. He stole another jacket to make up for his torn one and then simply dumped the old one afterwards. He gave a detailed description of the property and where it could be found. Acott told him that he would try to find the report of the house being broken into, to which Hanratty replied with a series of boastful comments. He never left his fingerprints anywhere any more as he wiped them clean with a handkerchief. He said that he now used taxis, stayed in the best hotels and had made over £1,000 in the last two months. In fact, when he had come out of prison in March, someone he knew in Ealing, west London, had given him £25 as a start-up. He told this man that he wanted to give up 'the jewellery lark' and asked him to 'get a shooter to do some stick-ups'.[3]

'Are you trying to tell me that you tried to get a gun from a man at Ealing?' Acott asked, and Hanratty replied, perhaps reflecting on what he had just said, 'Yes. He wouldn't play and he never got me one. Oh, Mr Acott. I've never killed a man in my life.'

Again, Acott asked him for the names of the three friends in Liverpool who could provide him an alibi but once more it was met with a refusal. Hanratty said he had even paid them some money, £20 or £25, to come forward but they had refused. He went on to say that the flat they were living in had 'a load of jelly'. By 'jelly' he meant gelignite, the explosive used by safebreakers, and this appeared to be an attempt to demonstrate he was an associate of serious criminals.

He had something else, he said, which would prove his alibi. He told Acott that, not long after he had arrived in Liverpool, he had sent a telegram to his friend Dixie France in St John's Wood. This was about 6.30 p.m. on the Tuesday, the evening of the abduction, and he even explained how he had sent it from a telephone box outside the post office. Acott already knew from Dixie France that the telegram had been sent on the Thursday rather than the Tuesday, but he did not pursue the issue. That would come later.

Acott decided to break the interview with his prisoner as he wanted to check some of the information Hanratty had put forward, particularly about the burglary he claimed to have committed in Stanmore and whether any jacket had been recovered in a nearby children's park. Recovering his suit jacket was a pressing issue in case it yielded any of Michael Gregsten's blood.

Having been told that there was to be a break, Hanratty said, 'OK, I'll go to kip.'

Acott contacted his colleagues in London and enquiries were made that resulted in no record of any burglary being reported that matched Hanratty's description, nor had any jacket been found nearby. When the interrogation began again, six hours later, Acott told him what he had established, which was met with a change of story. He had destroyed the jacket, he said, but when asked when and how, his response was: 'I can't tell you that. You won't find out.'

When Acott tried to return to the question of the identity of the three men in Liverpool, the only progress he made was that Hanratty confirmed again that he had offered each of them £20 or £25 to come forward, but they had refused. Acott then changed his approach:

I can't make it too clear how desperate your position is. I must tell you now. After your leaving room 24 on the 22nd of August, and before it was occupied again, two empty cartridge cases were found at the end of the bed you tell me you slept in that night.

There was a long pause before Hanratty finally said, 'What size were the bullets, Mr Acott?'

'I can't tell you that.'

'Well, that's the end for me, isn't it,' said Hanratty. 'I tell you I've never had any bullets and never fired a gun.'[4]

Hanratty's response to being told that cartridges had been found in the room he had occupied at the Vienna hotel would be one of the points that would be criticised later at his trial. His defending counsel would argue that the whole of the interview should be inadmissible, although the judge overruled him. It is not difficult to see why his defence team adopted this position since Hanratty's response was not one that would be expected from an innocent man who had just been told that incriminating evidence could be linked to him.

Acott made one final attempt to obtain the names of the people in Liverpool who could support Hanratty's alibi, and while Hanratty described the area of the city in which the address was supposed to be and said he had met the people in prison some years before, he flatly refused to identify them:

They'll never come forward. They've got a lot to lose. I can't tell you Mr Acott. You don't do that sort of thing in our business or you're finished. I'm a very good gambler, Mr Acott. I've gambled all my life. I'm going to gamble now. I am not going to call the three men. I can get out of this without them. If I get the murder charge slung, I'll only get five years and that'll be slung too. If that doesn't pay off, I'm in trouble.

The interview was over. Hanratty had denied any involvement in the murder and he had provided what Acott considered to be an implausible alibi. Even if it was correct that he had been to Liverpool around the time of the attacks, by not providing the names of the people who could prove his innocence, he had set himself up to be disbelieved. Furthermore, he had said that he had disposed of the jacket he was wearing at the time and had come up with the story that he had stolen another one in a burglary to replace it.

Acott had also gained some useful information; Hanratty had distinctive blue eyes, was unable to pronounce 'th' and had used the word, 'kip', three key features of Valerie's story.

It had though, Acott would later say, been an unusual interview. There had been prolonged periods of silence as if Hanratty had been thinking about his answers before he gave them. The answers had not been spontaneous and the pauses were sometimes so long that Oxford wrote on his contemporaneous notes, several times, the word 'pause'. His reaction to some of the questions had also been odd. At times there had been 'great flushing up the face and the back of the neck, the Adam's apple seemed to jump up and down a good bit and the mouth twisted in an attempt to control it. But the most outstanding feature was the eyes. 'At times,' he said, 'they literally came out, and when they did, they looked almost transparent blue.'[5]

The following morning, Detective Superintendent Barron arrived, formally arrested Hanratty for the murder of Michael Gregsten and conveyed him to Bedford, where the investigation would continue. The law in 1961 precluded the police from any further interrogation of Hanratty but all other matters could be pursued, including the most pressing issue of whether the witnesses who had been found could identify the prisoner.

While identification parades can provide important evidence as part of an investigation, much research has shown that they come at some risk, for instance if a witness has previously seen photographs of suspects or if a witness is under the impression that the guilty individual is definitely present. Acott had further concerns: some of his witnesses had already attended an identification parade when Peter Alphon was being investigated and some had picked out innocent people. One of those witnesses was Valerie Storie and now she would be asked again to go through the same process.

Shortly after 4 p.m. on the day that Hanratty travelled to Bedford, an identification parade was formed at Bedfordshire County Police headquarters. By now, Hanratty had had time to consult with his solicitor, Emmanuel Kleinman, who had stepped in to represent his interests.

Hanratty was wearing a dark blue suit, a white shirt and a yellow tie and he was paraded with eight other men. He was 25 years of age and 5ft 7in tall. His hair, as described by the arresting officer, was ginger. The men on the parade ranged between 19 and 29 years and between 5ft 7½in and 5ft 10½in in height. Four had auburn-coloured hair, one was described as dark auburn, two were ginger and one was fair. Hanratty was specifically asked, as was required, whether he was happy with the arrangements for the parade and both he and Kleinman said that they were. He was allowed to choose where he stood in the line and he selected a position third from the right.

The first witness was John Skillett, the man who had the driving altercation on the Eastern Avenue on 23 August. He did not attend the Alphon parade as he was away at the time but now he positively identified Hanratty by touching him on the chest. He was escorted from the parade and Hanratty elected to remain where he was for the next witness.

It was Edward Blackhall, Skillett's passenger. He had previously attended the Alphon parade where he had selected a man unconnected to the investigation. He touched the chest of the man immediately to the left of Hanratty, an unconnected volunteer. He too was led from the parade and again Hanratty chose to remain where he was.

Next was James Trower. He had attended the Alphon parade but had made no selection at all. This time, however, he touched Hanratty on the chest.

Acott now produced his fourth witness: Harry Hirons, the petrol pump attendant who thought he had served the driver of the Morris Minor. He had already attended the parade in which Alphon had stood and selected one of the volunteers. Once more, he promptly identified one of the volunteers.

With all the witnesses now gone, Hanratty was asked whether he wanted to object to any aspects of the parade and he said, 'I was going to ask how many more people there were to come as I wanted to change my coat, because they know I wear a dark suit.'[6]

His comments were noted on the official form, as indeed was the fact that six of the eight volunteers had also been wearing suits. He was led away.

The police now had a man in custody who they were confident was Valerie's attacker. That would have been conveyed to Valerie, and she would have to take part in a second identification parade. The parade, as before, was held in hospital.

Chief Inspector Reginald Ballinger was in charge of its arrangements and conduct. He was required, in law, to ensure that all aspects of it complied with the guidance that had been laid down by the courts. Part of those arrangements required him to select eight or more volunteers who were as similar as possible to the suspect in size, build, age and station in life.

He turned to the nearby airbases at RAF Halton and RAF High Wycombe, where twelve volunteers were selected to take part. All were asked to wear suits since Hanratty would be wearing one. They were all aged between 20 and 30 and between 5ft 6in and 5ft 9in in height. Six had fair hair, three were auburn, two were ginger and one had brown hair.

When Hanratty arrived at the hospital, he was dressed in his dark blue suit and Ballinger informed him about the arrangements. Hanratty did not want to proceed at that point since he wanted his lawyer to be present. Three-quarters of an hour later, Ballinger returned and saw that the solicitor had now arrived, but noted that Hanratty had changed from his blue suit and was wearing a greenish-brown and grey check sports jacket. They were taken through to the medical room where the parade was to take place. The rules were quite clear about the suspect's rights and in accordance with those rules Hanratty and his solicitor were given the opportunity to object to any member of the parade. Once again, no objections were made.

Hanratty was asked to select where he wanted to stand and opted to position himself sixth from the right, at the same time asking one of the volunteers to stand immediately next to him. His request was granted and each of the men was required to hold a numbered card since Valerie would be unable to touch the chest as the normal means of identification. Hanratty held card number six. A phone call was made and at 11.14 a.m., an orderly wheeled the witness in her bed into the medical room accompanied by medical staff.[7]

Ballinger gave Valerie detailed instructions about what she was required to do. He emphasised that she could take her time in trying to identify the man who was in the car with her and her companion on the night of 22 August and if she could see him, she should say so out loud by calling out the number on his card. She was then wheeled up and down the line, twice. She looked at the man holding card number six, Hanratty, and recognised him.[8] But, instead of pointing him out, she said to Ballinger, 'I would like to hear them speak.'

When asked what she wanted them all to say, she said, 'Be quiet will you, I'm thinking,' the phrase the gunman had used so many times on that night.

The line of volunteers was instructed to say the words as Valerie was wheeled past them and their number was called out. She went from left to right as they spoke. Afterwards, she was asked whether she wished to see them all again and she said that she did. Again, she was pushed up and down the line before she said, 'Can I hear them speak again?'

The same process followed after which Ballinger said, 'Do you want to see them again?'

Valerie was silent.

Ballinger then said,

'Do you see the man?'

'Number six,' she said confidently.[9]

Hanratty, Acott observed, 'was shaken almost to the point of collapse'.[10] Valerie was taken back to her ward and the prisoner led away by police officers. The whole process had taken just eleven minutes,[11] and Valerie had identified her attacker.

Chapter Nine

Liverpool

Once Hanratty had been identified by three key witnesses, together with all the other evidence that had been gathered, there were sufficient grounds to charge him with the murder of Michael Gregsten. There were a number of other formalities, but he made his first appearance at Ampthill Magistrates' Court on 16 October.

Emmanuel Kleinman, Hanratty's solicitor, had been busy taking instructions from his client. The information he gathered would be subject to a great deal of challenge over who said what to whom and when, but in essence, Hanratty furnished him with much more information than he had offered in his interview with Bob Acott. All of it was to support his alibi that he had spent the night with three of his friends in Liverpool, but he still refused to divulge their names, even to his solicitor. Kleinman could have investigated this information himself since it was crucial to the defence of his client, but he chose to pass it directly to Acott, who would have a duty to investigate the claim.

The solicitor told the detective that on the day that his client had arrived in Liverpool, Tuesday, 22 August, he had gone to a sweet shop in Scotland Road to ask for directions. He was looking for either Carlton Road or Talbot Road but the woman serving, who was accompanied by a child behind the counter, had been unable to help. If the woman in the sweet shop could be found, it would be a major step forward to supporting the alibi. If it was true, it would make it inconceivable that he could have been in a Buckinghamshire cornfield later that evening.

Scotland Road would soon become a major feature of the investigation but for now it fitted in with something else that had already been established. A woman who ran a flower shop in Scotland Road told the police that on 9 October, a man with auburn-coloured hair, who had a cockney accent and had with him a large bunch of rolled-up £5 and £1 notes, had come into her shop and had sent 35s-worth of artificial carnations to his mother in Sycamore Grove, London. He had asked for a message to be sent with the flowers that read:

I hope you will like this token. I am sorry to have caused you this trouble. You must have faith in me and I will work it out in my own time. I phoned you a few times the other evening and I spoke to Mrs T. I won't phone you again. If I do, it will only upset you and me. Give my love to Dad and the boys. Your loving son, Jim.

This piece of information demonstrated that Hanratty had, for certain, been in Scotland Road on 9 October, two days before his arrest, but now he was claiming he had been there on the day of the abduction. This would need to be checked.

In addition, he claimed that when he arrived in the city, he deposited his suitcase at Lime Street railway station and the man who took it from him had a withered arm. Hanratty had given him his name and address and he could easily verify his claim. He added that when he collected the case later, it had been a different member of staff who had returned it. He also said that at some stage he had gone to the New Brighton area of Liverpool, had seen the film *The Guns of Navarone* at the Gaumont cinema and had watched a boxing match at a stadium 'between a man named Winton and a coloured man'.

He added some other detail about the description of the house he had stayed in, somewhere near the Bull Ring, he said, and clarified that the time of the train he had eventually caught to travel back to London had been shortly after midnight on the Thursday. All of this was additional information but none of it addressed the fundamental question of who the people were with whom he claimed to have stayed.

Acott needed to follow up this additional information, but whereas earlier in the investigation he had travelled to Ireland himself to follow up the postcards and the car rental, now he decided not to go to Liverpool himself to explore Hanratty's alibi, nor did he despatch any of the Scotland Yard or Bedfordshire detectives. Instead, he wrote a letter to the Liverpool force on 16 October asking them to carry out the enquiries.

Detective Chief Inspector Thomas Elliott was Liverpool born and bred and had more than thirty-one years' police service. He was the perfect person for identifying locations, people, road names, junctions and making sense of local colloquialisms, plus his knowledge of the criminal fraternity was vast. Liverpool police had already been involved in the A6 investigation before the receipt of Acott's letter. Ever since the wanted man had telephoned Scotland Yard on 7 October saying that he was in the city, enquiries were being covertly carried out in an effort to identify potential addresses at which he could be hiding. The list had been growing, mainly with names of people with whom Hanratty had been in prison. When he was eventually arrested in Blackpool late in the evening of 11 October, within the hour, twenty-three addresses were visited and searched in the hope that evidence connecting him to the offence would be found. It had yielded nothing but it meant that Elliott already had some information to help find the address that Hanratty was claiming he had visited.

His first observation though was that the description of the area given by Hanratty made little sense. The Bull Ring, or to give its proper title, St Andrew's Road, was a mile away from Scotland Road and the few people who lived there did not match the description given by Hanratty. Elliott established that *The Guns of Navarone* was a long-running feature at the Odeon cinema, opposite the Gaumont that Hanratty had named, and was showing from 16 July through to 7 October. Similarly, there was a well-advertised boxing match on 24 August between Howard Winstone, holder of the British Featherweight title, and a Black man by the name of Aryee Jackson. The bout began at 8.50 p.m. Hanratty may well have attended these events, but there was no way of establishing that he had actually done so, and even if it could be proved that he went to the boxing match, it was outside of the times needed to alibi him for the murder.

Attention turned to the date and time of the telegram sent by Hanratty from Liverpool. Originally, he claimed that he had sent this late in the evening on the Tuesday, the day he had arrived, but later changed his account to either the Wednesday or the Thursday, something that Dixie France had already clarified. However, this needed to be independently corroborated. William Robinson of the General Post Office was interviewed and said that it was not possible to send a telegram from a post office after seven o'clock in the evening as they were closed. However, a correspondent could telephone the telegraph office, which would take the message down and send it by wire. At 8.40 p.m. on Thursday, 24 August, he was on duty in the telegraph office when a male caller rang from the telephone box at St George's Hall directly opposite Lime Street railway station. The man told him that the telegram was for his business partner and he would like it delivered that night. He told the caller that would not be possible but it would be delivered the following morning. Robinson sent the message, which was addressed to Mr Frances, 8 Theering House, Boundary Road, Finchley Road, London. It confirmed the timing of the telegram to

Dixie France; it was some forty-eight hours after the attack in the cornfield. It did not help Hanratty in his alibi and, if it was true that he had sent it the evening he had arrived in Liverpool, it suggested he had travelled to Liverpool the day after the murder. Furthermore, Hanratty had stated in the text that he would 'be home early Friday morning for business'. He had sent it late on the Thursday evening and had been told by the operator that it would not be delivered until the following day. There was therefore no point in sending such a message as he could be back with Dixie France before he would have received the telegram.

Across the road from where Hanratty had made his telephone call was the city's main station, Lime Street. This featured heavily in Hanratty's story due to the number of times he said he had travelled by train to and from the city. He had claimed that he deposited his suitcase there, on the day of the abduction, to a man with a withered arm.

Given that Hanratty said that he thought it was either 10.55, 11.55, or possibly even 12.55, the only two trains that he could have taken in that approximate time period were the 10.35, which arrived in Liverpool at 3.25 p.m., or the later one at 12.15, which arrived at 4.45 p.m. The earliest he could have been in Liverpool that day was therefore 3.25 p.m.

No member of the regular cloakroom staff fitted the description of a man with a withered arm, but Peter Stringer, who worked in the toilets at the station, occasionally helped out in the cloakroom. He had an artificial left arm and wore a glove over his left hand. Moreover, on the week commencing Monday, 21 August he worked a 2–10 p.m. shift in the toilets and sometimes, he said, he helped out in the cloakroom. If it was him who had taken luggage from Hanratty, it could only have been after 8.45 p.m. in the evening since he only helped out at that particular time and then for only between thirty and forty-five minutes. He returned to his toilet duties at 9.30 p.m. before going off duty at 10 p.m. The earliest Hanratty could have arrived at Lime Street was 3.25 p.m. and the latest 4.45 p.m. Neither of these times fitted with Stringer's movements as he was not in the cloakroom until much later in the evening.

The Liverpool police now investigated Hanratty's claim to have visited a sweet shop, and there were no fewer than twenty-nine such shops in Scotland Road. Hanratty said he called in one of them to ask for directions to Carlton Road or Talbot Road, but no such road name existed in the city. Finding the right sweet shop, if indeed the visit took place, was going to be the only way forward and Elliott briefed a number of police officers to start checking. On the first day of enquiries, when a police officer[1] armed with a single photograph of Hanratty went into Cowley's sweet shop at 408 Scotland Road, he met Olive Dinwoodie. She occasionally helped out behind the counter and when asked about a man visiting her shop and asking for directions, she remembered the occasion. He showed her the photograph he was carrying and she thought it 'resembled a chap that came in',[2] although she only had a fleeting glimpse of him. He had not asked for Carlton or Talbot Road, she said, but Tarleton Road and she had pointed out to him that there was a Tarleton Street but no Tarleton Road. She was unable to help further and pointed him towards a customer in the shop who may have been better able to help him. She had paid no further attention to the man and carried on serving in the shop. It was, she said, very busy.

The officer asked Dinwoodie when this incident took place and if it helped, apparently when the man had asked her for directions, he had said there was also a child serving behind the counter. This extra piece of information enabled Dinwoodie to narrow down the event and now she was quite clear in her recollection. The shop's owner's wife had gone away on holiday on Saturday, 19 August and on the following Monday, the 21st, her husband, David Cowley, had sent a note round to her asking her if she could come in and cover the shop for a few days. The note suggested that if she wanted to, she could bring her granddaughter with her. She thought that was a good idea and they both arrived at the shop at 12.30 p.m.

Cowley needed to go to the hospital that particular afternoon and left Dinwoodie and her 13-year-old granddaughter, Barbara Ford, alone in the shop, where they remained until around six o'clock that evening. She knew that this was the Monday immediately after Mrs Cowley had gone away on holiday and this was the only time that Barbara had accompanied her. Her recollections were reinforced by two other events. That evening, one of the regular drivers, Albert Harding, visited the shop and she remembered asking him whether he knew the location of Tarleton Road. He only knew of such a road outside of the city. She also remembered that she worked the following day, on the Tuesday, but had been taken very ill by half past six, visited a doctor, and did not return the following day at all. When asked about the time that the man asking for directions had visited, she said it was somewhere between 3.30 p.m. and 4 p.m.[3]

Hanratty had told his solicitor, who in turn had passed the information on to the police, that he had visited the sweet shop in Scotland Road on the afternoon of Tuesday, 22 August. He had gone there after having arrived by train, deposited his luggage in the station cloakroom and then made his way to Scotland Road. It was the very essence of his alibi; he was 200 miles away at the time. Yet Dinwoodie was absolutely clear that the man, if it was Hanratty, had gone into the shop the day before.

Even if it was true that the event did actually occur on the Tuesday, and Dinwoodie was wrong, the times of the trains arriving in Liverpool made it unlikely, though not impossible, for Hanratty to have been in Scotland Road between 3.30 p.m. and 4 p.m. The earliest train arriving in Liverpool had been 3.25 p.m. and if it was true that he had deposited his luggage and then made his way to Scotland Road, a distance of about a mile, before going into the sweet shop, then his arrival time there just about fitted. If Hanratty had caught the later train, he most certainly could not have been in the sweet shop at the relevant time.

Dinwoodie, placing the man who resembled Hanratty in Liverpool on Monday, 21 August, contradicted what was already known about his movements in London. The France family had all stated that he had been with them at their address in Boundary Road during the afternoon on the Monday and Charles France had even seen him at the Rehearsal Club that night. If the Frances were lying or simply wrong, it was most unlikely that Hanratty could have been in the sweet shop at 4 p.m. and been back in London in time to check into the Vienna hotel around 11.30 p.m. A train had left Liverpool at 5.15 p.m. that evening and arrived at 9.10 p.m., plenty of time to get to his hotel.[4] But if Louise Anderson, the Soho antique dealer, was correct, and Hanratty had stayed in her flat on the Sunday evening, he must have travelled to Liverpool during the day, gone to the sweet shop to find an address that did not exist and then returned immediately to London.

A week later, in an effort to firm up on Dinwoodie's identification of Hanratty, the police showed her an album of sixteen photographs, one of which was of Hanratty. Dinwoodie pointed to his photograph and said, 'He was more like the man than any of the remainder.'[5]

A further week later, on 2 November, Dinwoodie's granddaughter was interviewed by the police, and confirmed everything her grandmother had said about it being on the Monday, although she could not recall the name of the road the man had asked for.

For now, all aspects of Hanratty's alibi had been explored and a confusing picture had emerged. There was no evidence that Hanratty had been in Liverpool on Tuesday, 22 August, the day of the abduction, nor indeed Wednesday, 23 August, the day of the murder. There was, though, conflicting evidence as to his whereabouts the day before. There was a possibility, albeit remote, that on Monday, 21 August, the day before the attack in the cornfield, Hanratty had been in London and in Liverpool.

Back in London, enquiries were continuing. The missing suit jacket was a key line of enquiry. The other suit found in his suitcase and which he had been keen for the detectives to find, had according to him been sent for cleaning before the murder and only collected some time afterwards. Burtol Cleaners in Swiss Cottage were able to confirm that it had been dropped off by a Mr Ryan of 72 Boundary Road for cleaning and some alterations. This had been on the morning of Monday, 21 August and the man had collected it two weeks later on 4 September, the day Hanratty had gone to Ireland; it most certainly was not being worn at the time of the murder. Perhaps the most significant part of this find though, was that another witness could now put Hanratty in London on the morning of 21 August.

However, the missing jacket remained the focus and earlier enquiries had already led the police to a tailor's, Hepworths, in Burnt Cottage. One of the assistants there, William Clapp, was shown the recovered pair of trousers and waistcoat and was able to track the order. On 8 July, a Mr James Hanratty of 12 Sycamore Grove, Kingsbury, had placed an order for a black, chalk stripe suit and it had been Clapp who had measured him for it. It was collected by him six weeks later on 18 August, four days before the attack. Clapp noticed that the Hepworth labels had been ripped out of the trousers and waistcoat, but he could positively identify them as Hanratty had asked for it to be made in a particular way – he recognised the cut. The missing garment, he said, was a double-breasted continental-style jacket, with a box fitting, although tapered down over the hips, and it would have a Hepworth label sewn into the inside breast pocket.

Hanratty had collected a brand new suit four days before the attack in the cornfield and, to a degree, this fitted with the description given by Valerie that the gunman had been immaculately dressed.

★★★

Late in the afternoon of Sunday, 22 October, as the police were busy continuing to take statements from their witnesses in London and Liverpool, the telephone rang once more at Stoke Mandeville hospital. A male caller asked whether Valerie Storie was still there or whether she had been moved. The operator told the caller to contact the police and the call was ended.[6] Later that evening, two national newspapers received calls from a man talking about Valerie Storie who said that 'friends of Hanratty were going to "do her up" if she gave evidence against him'. They both passed the messages to Scotland Yard. An hour later, the news desk at the *Daily Mirror* took a further call from a man who said, 'You remember me. I called you before. If anything happens to Jim Hanratty his mates will be up at Stoke Mandeville hospital to do her up.' The caller said his name was 'Tim'. Two days later, another call was received, this time by the *Daily Herald*. 'Tell Bob Traini,' the caller said, 'I am going to kill Valerie Storie tonight.' Traini was one of the crime reporters working for the newspaper.[7]

As with the earlier threatening messages, there is no evidence that Valerie was made aware of these calls. Hanratty's senior defence counsel, Michael Sherrard, would later express the view that the caller was someone with an 'unhinged mentality'.[8] He was probably more concerned about the wider public turning against his client if they felt that Hanratty in any way orchestrated these calls, but in some ways these anonymous calls set the tone for Valerie to be cast in a rather more negative light. The messages had now become public knowledge, and given that Valerie was willingly engaged in, as many people saw it, immoral behaviour at the time of the attack, public sympathy may well have begun to fade.

On 30 October, as the Liverpool police were tidying up the loose ends of Hanratty's alibi enquiries, a man walked into Rhyl police station in North Wales. Arthur Webber said he worked at the Foryd Amusement Park on the town's Ocean Beach where, among its attractions, were the dodgems or 'bumper cars'. He handed the officers a Ministry of Pensions National Insurance card issued on 24 July 1961 in the name of James Hanratty, which he had just found in the 'pay box' at the park. The address on it was 240 Bute Street, Cardiff. The name James Hanratty was now on all the front pages of newspapers and he decided to immediately inform the police of what he had found. Webber told them that on 25 July, a man had applied for a job on the dodgems. He took him on and that night he worked between 7 p.m. and 10 p.m. At the end of the shift he had gone home with another of his employees, a man called Terry Evans, who was going to put him up for the night. That was as much as he could say.

The Rhyl police showed Webber a series of photographs and he immediately picked out James Hanratty. They immediately set to work to see if they could find Evans to establish whether he could provide any useful information. It took a week to find him but when they did, he confirmed that a man called 'Jimmy' had turned up at the dodgems in July and he had offered him, and another employee, a bed for the night at his house. The next morning, Evans made arrangements to meet them both at the fairground. He too was shown a photograph of Hanratty and he confirmed it was the same man. He remembered 'Jimmy' well as his shoes had 'bursted'[9] and he lent him a pair of his own. Not a cheap pair, he said, almost new; they had cost £3 15s. He gave them to 'Jimmy' on the understanding he returned them once he had earned some wages but he never saw him again; nor his shoes.

The statements provided an insight into Hanratty's nomadic lifestyle and how he had occasionally needed to live hand to mouth, which may have fitted with the gunman's claim in the cornfield that he had not eaten for two days. But other than that, it all happened a month before the attack and the statements were filed.

Chapter Ten

Committal

The primary purpose of committal proceedings is for the magistrates to satisfy themselves that there is a prima facie case upon which the prosecution can rely and is designed to filter out cases where there is no evidence upon which a jury could be reasonably expected to make a judgement.[1] Serious charges such as murder could only be tried at the assize courts and the case against Hanratty would now need to be publicly aired at the committal. Evidence needed to be given by witnesses in the magistrates' courts before the matter could be sent to the assizes.

The hearing began at Ampthill Magistrates' Court on 22 November 1961, with Hanratty charged not only with the murder of Michael Gregsten but also the rape and attempted murder of Valerie Storie.

Acting on behalf of the prosecution was solicitor Mr MacDermott from the office of the Director of Public Prosecutions (DPP). Hanratty was represented by Michael Sherrard, a barrister who would later represent him at his trial. He was a formidable advocate and he took full advantage of the opportunity to cross-examine the sixty-nine witnesses produced by the prosecution during the eight-day hearing.

It was to be expected that certain witnesses would be subject to strong cross-examination. William Nudds, the man who had fabricated the story about who had occupied room 24 in the Vienna hotel, was exposed for what he was: a convicted, unreliable witness. At one point Sherrard implied that it had been Nudds who had planted the cartridges in the room.

Bob Acott was accused of carrying out interviews with the defendant that were in flagrant breach of the rules. More significantly, he was accused of withholding evidence that could show Hanratty's innocence, specifically matters concerning the Liverpool alibi. This particular aspect must have been a genuine source of frustration for Sherrard, since it had been Hanratty's solicitor, Kleinman, who had put forward details of Hanratty's alibi and yet the defence had not been furnished with the outcome of the police enquiries. The main witness, Olive Dinwoodie, did not alibi Hanratty and the prosecution chose not to admit this evidence at the proceedings. Sherrard had to acknowledge that it had not been Acott who had taken this decision but the prosecuting solicitor, but it felt like they had put forward a legitimate alibi and were now being kept in the dark. The law did not require the prosecution to divulge all such matters but it nevertheless sowed the seed of allegations of police corruption for years to come.[2]

When John Kerr, the man who had first spoken to Valerie in the layby, gave his evidence, he was asked about the description given to him by Valerie, and he said that he had written the details on the back of one of his census forms he was using that morning. This was the first time the prosecuting solicitor had heard of such contemporaneous notes made by a witness. When the statement was taken from Kerr by the police, if he had mentioned it, the forms should have been seized and produced as an important exhibit. It would have the potential to show exactly what Valerie had said and resolve the question of the colour of the eyes of the attacker, which the police had originally said were brown, but later changed to blue.

Police officers searched the papers in the courtroom but since Kerr had not mentioned this before, the census form was not there. Sherrard demanded that the witness should not be allowed to continue with his evidence without this important document but he was overruled. Kerr finished his evidence, but another question had been raised about the competence of the police investigation.

The third day of the proceedings was Friday, 24 November, the day set aside for Valerie to give her evidence and coincidentally her 23rd birthday. Sherrard made an application that her evidence should be held 'in camera', not in public, since he felt there may be legal issues about the admissibility of some of her evidence.[3] MacDermott had no objections and magistrates and court officials made their way to Stoke Mandeville hospital, some 30 miles away.

The court was held in the hospital's Archery Ward, usually reserved for physiotherapy treatment. The room was laid out with chairs and, due to the threats that had been recently made against Valerie's life, a police guard was placed outside. With lawyers, magistrates and court officials in place, Valerie took her position in a wheelchair, flanked by a nurse and a doctor, ready to give her evidence. Twenty yards in front of her, between two police officers, sat Hanratty. For the third time, she came face to face with the man she had identified as her attacker.

Valerie gave her evidence in a firm voice and was resolute in what she said. She had no doubt Hanratty was her attacker: 'I am quite clear he is the man. Having talked to him for six hours, it is very hard to forget a voice or face,' she said.

She was accused of making a mistake over her identification, as she had on the previous parade with Peter Alphon when she had picked out an innocent man. She accepted that she had made an error on that occasion, but now she had no doubt that Hanratty was her attacker. Sherrard suggested that upon seeing Alphon, she had been 'staggered' by his presence, implying that he was the real killer. Valerie quickly dismissed his assertion.

She cleared up the issue around the mix-up over the colour of her attacker's eyes. She had never said they were brown – she had always maintained they were blue. In fact, she had tried while lying paralysed on the side of the road to use stones to try to write the words 'brown hair' and 'blue eyes'. She had no idea about how the error occurred, but it certainly did not come from her.

Valerie was examined for nearly five hours before being wheeled back to her ward, where her birthday celebrations could begin.[4] Her latest ordeal over, and with her parents by her side, she cut the cake that had been made for her by the hospital chef with the words 'Greetings to Valerie' iced on the top. Two of her friends from the laboratory were there to give her a yellow jumper they had bought for her.[5] She read dozens of cards from well-wishers across the country plus telegrams she had received from relatives.

The proceedings now continued back at Ampthill Magistrates' Court. Under cross-examination by Sherrard, Acott admitted that he had now found a record of a break-in in the area where Hanratty had said he had stolen the jacket he needed to replace the one that he had torn. No jacket had been stolen but everything else matched the description given by the prisoner: the method of entry and that it was obvious the owners were away on holiday. It appeared Hanratty was telling the truth about this break-in, but any positive impact disappeared when MacDermott told the court that a close relative of Hanratty had made an approach to the witness Louise Anderson and told her that if she ever came across the lost jacket she should hand it over to him, rather than the police. That relative had been James Hanratty senior, who had turned up at Anderson's shop on 2 December having that same day been to see his son in prison. Jimmy had told him that she had the missing garment and he wanted it back because it had some money in it.[6] This appeared to be an attempt to interfere with the investigation by recovering an incriminating piece of evidence.

Janet Gregsten gave evidence of identifying her husband's body and she spoke about how she had last seen him the afternoon before as he set off to meet with Valerie Storie. Sherrard chose not to ask her any questions in cross-examination but took the opportunity to present himself in a different light: 'You have the fullest sympathy of everybody in the court and I shall ask you no questions,' he said.

His comments were almost certainly genuine but it probably reinforced the message that it was with Janet on whom public sympathy should rest, not Valerie.

At the end of the eight days of evidence, Sherrard addressed the Bench for ninety-three minutes, arguing that the case should not proceed to trial.

'It may have crossed your mind,' he said, 'that this has been a case which might fairly be described as very flimsy and one in which [the prosecution] have indeed attempted to scrape even the underside of the bottom of the barrel.'

His comments about Valerie were unequivocal: 'She was honest, but wrong absolutely,' in her identification.

The magistrates retired for thirty minutes before their chairman delivered their decision:[7] 'We rule there is a case to answer,' and the case was sent for trial.

A significant milestone had been achieved. The prosecution had shown that its case was suitable for trial but damage had been done. The investigation had been tainted with the idea that it was built on unreliable evidence and that the police had employed underhand techniques to get it this far. Clearly, it indicated that problems lay ahead, but something rather interesting had taken place about which neither the police nor the defence had any knowledge. Before going into court, two of the prosecution witnesses had been sitting in the waiting area when a chance conversation started. It was between Louise Anderson and Dixie's wife Charlotte; Anderson did not know who Charlotte was or what her involvement had been.

Both were nervous about giving evidence and Louise told Charlotte that she felt sorry for the people who Hanratty had been staying with as he had kept the gun at their home. Realising that she was referring to her house, Charlotte asked what she meant. Louise explained that Hanratty had told her that he had secreted the weapon in a cupboard at the top of the stairs where the people kept their blankets. She described a carrier bag in which the gun had been placed and the colour of the bedding in the cupboard. Both descriptions matched exactly what she had in her house. Even more worrying was that Hanratty had claimed that he had made his own bed with the blankets when staying there and returned them to the cupboard the following morning himself. Charlotte was deeply shocked about what she had just heard and when she finally gave evidence herself that day, she collapsed in court and needed to be taken outside. She probably assumed the police were already aware of this piece of rather important information and did not tell them what she had learned. Not until 12 January, ten days before the trial would start, did she finally do so.

The incident at the committal hearing when John Kerr announced that he had passed some notes to the police was of considerable concern. MacDermott immediately recognised the implications, as had Detective Superintendent Barron, who was sitting in court when the drama unfolded. The position was made even worse when Kerr told the court that he handed the piece of paper to a uniformed, senior officer who had pips on his shoulder and was wearing brown gloves. The three uniformed officers who had been at the scene in August – Chief Inspector Oliver and Inspectors Edward Milborrow and Robert Webster – were paraded before Kerr and he identified Webster. Webster had no knowledge of such an incident and said so.

Kerr's new evidence raised a number of issues quite apart from whether he was correct or mistaken in his identification. If it was shown that such a valuable piece of evidence had gone missing, it tended to undermine even further the integrity of police enquiries and a separate mini-investigation was carried out by Barron.

Kerr's supervisor, John Carrington, and another colleague, Jeffrey Claughton, reported that it was obvious that Kerr had been understandably extremely distressed when they arrived on the scene, and he was attempting to give his clipboard to anyone who would take it so that he could leave the scene as quickly as possible. One witness thought he had seen Kerr writing notes when he was talking to Valerie as she lay in the road, so it was imperative to trace the clipboard. However, rather than Kerr having handed it to a police officer, as he had testified, Barron established that he had in fact given it to his supervisor, but had said nothing about making any notes. The clipboard had been taken back to the County Council offices in Bedford. Barron's investigation report concluded that any notes that Kerr may have made had been mislaid there, and a letter on which Kerr had incorrectly noted the registration number of the Morris Minor was found in Claughton's desk drawer: he had written the number the wrong way round, BHN 847. Claughton had subsequently used it as scrap paper to make some calculations. Barron further concluded that if there had been any further notes, they too would have been used as scrap in the Council Office and probably later discarded.

At the same time as the committal hearing was being heard, another witness had come to notice, though it was too late to give his evidence. Roy Langdale was a 24-year-old man with a long criminal record including prison sentences for stealing, assault and forgery. He had been held on remand at Brixton prison since 5 November, but perhaps surprisingly released on probation on 23 November, rather than having another prison sentence imposed. During his stay in Brixton, he claimed he had become acquainted with James Hanratty, who initially denied he was responsible for the A6 killing, but as the days passed, Hanratty started to talk more about the murder. After some discussion about his own and Gregsten's blood types, Hanratty had told Langdale that he had carried out the attack on the woman, and that the man had been 'in the way'. He said he had shot Gregsten after a struggle and then raped the woman in the back of the car. He then told her to lie down, and 'shot her in cold blood'. The attack on Valerie had not been made public at the time.

On 22 November, the day before he was released from prison, Langdale travelled in a prison van with some other inmates, escorted by prison officer Alfred Eatwell. On the way back to the prison, Eatwell heard Langdale telling the others what Hanratty had told him, and he made a formal report, which Acott received a week later. Sergeant Ken Oxford was sent to Langdale's address and the former prisoner agreed to make a statement the following day, as he said 'the truth needed to be known'.

Langdale's alleged conversations with Hanratty had all been before 22 November, the day committal proceedings had begun, but he was yet to be interviewed by the police.

Emmanuel Kleinman had also been busy. At the committal hearing, Acott had admitted that he had established there had been a burglary in Stanmore in the area where Hanratty claimed he had stolen a jacket. Hanratty's solicitor now followed this up and spoke to Annie Mills, the owner of the property. She had told the police that no jacket had been stolen, but at Kleinman's insistence she checked with her husband. He looked in his wardrobe and confirmed that a jacket was in fact missing.

In essence, it looked as though the police had been provided with specific details about the burglaries, yet had not investigated them sufficiently thoroughly. At the committal hearing, Sherrard had made it clear that the integrity of the police investigation would be subjected to close scrutiny at the trial and this latest discovery reinforced the point.

As the date for the trial got closer, communication between the prosecution and defence legal teams increased, as the Crown was required to provide details of people who had made statements to the police but who they did not intend to call as witnesses. The defence followed up on dozens of convicted criminals who had spent time in prison with Hanratty and who could possibly identify the three alibi witnesses in Liverpool. They also interviewed anyone connected to the Liverpool sweet shop, including a young girl[8] who was a friend of Barbara Ford, and the possibility remained, however remote and contrary to all the other evidence, that Hanratty did go into the shop on Tuesday, 22 August.

PART 3 — THE TRIAL

Chapter Eleven

Valerie's Evidence

On Monday, 22 January, five months after the attack in Dorney Reach, the trial began at Bedford Assizes. It was presided over by Sir William Gorman QC, who had more than forty years' judicial experience. The man selected to prosecute the case was Graham Swanwick QC. He had been called to the bar in 1930 and was described as a quiet but forceful barrister.[1] He took silk in 1956 and was appointed as Recorder of the City of London the following year before being appointed to the City of Leicester. The role of defending Hanratty remained with 33-year-old junior barrister Michael Sherrard. Called to the bar in 1950, he had been briefed by Emanuel Kleinman very early on in the investigation and represented Hanratty's interests at the committal proceedings in spite of there being a Queen's Counsel available.[2]

Hanratty pleaded not guilty to the only charge that had been brought to trial: the murder of Michael Gregsten.[3] This was the normal procedure at the time in cases involving capital murder but which allowed for the evidence relating to Valerie's attack to be placed before the jury.

Swanwick opened the case, as was normal practice, by summarising the evidence that would be presented to them. He made it abundantly clear at the outset that the motive for the crimes that were to be presented to them was lust and that what Hanratty did was motivated by his desire to have sex with Valerie Storie. But he also made it clear that it was for them, and them alone, to decide what weight they should attach to each of the witnesses and they should only convict if they were satisfied beyond all reasonable doubt that the prosecution had proved its case.

The evidence could be broken down into a number of discrete areas, all of which he knew would be challenged vigorously by Sherrard and his team. The case centred on the evidence of identification of Hanratty not only by Valerie but also by the witnesses who saw the Morris being driven recklessly. However, Valerie had previously picked out an innocent man on another parade and other witnesses such as Edward Blackhall and Harry Hirons had not identified Hanratty as the driver of the car. The supporting evidence would therefore be of major importance.

The finding of the murder weapon and two spent cartridges in the Vienna hotel in the room where, by Hanratty's own admission, he had stayed the night before the murder was an important part of the prosecution case but it was based upon the evidence of William Nudds, a self-confessed liar, and his credibility as a witness was going to be tested severely. He had crucially said that when Hanratty had left the hotel on that vital morning he had given him directions to catch a number 36 bus, on which the revolver had been found. Dixie France, quite apart from being able to demonstrate that Hanratty appeared not to be in London over the important dates of 22 and 23 August, would say that Hanratty used the underneath of seats to get rid of his unwanted stolen jewellery. A third witness, Louise Anderson, not only demonstrated how Hanratty used to sell jewellery in her shop but also how he had abandoned his clothing, with the potentially incriminating jacket missing, while he disappeared for a few days. Her home address where Hanratty often stayed was on the route of the number 36A bus.

Roy Langdale, to whom Hanratty had allegedly made a practically complete confession in Brixton prison, was going to face allegations of lying and his credibility as a witness was going to be tested severely. Swanwick ensured that the prosecution was not hiding this man's lengthy criminal record and told the jury to exercise 'extreme caution'[4] when considering what he had to say.

The alibi that had been put forward by Hanratty was going to feature heavily in the defence case and so it was made clear to the jury that the prosecution had not only made extensive enquiries about the claim but they had concluded that it was dubious in the extreme. Swanwick told them that it was, of course, important for anyone accused of a crime to put forward their alibi, if indeed that was their defence, at the earliest opportunity but in this case not only was it 'studiously vague' but also bore the 'imprint of falsity'.[5]

There were many aspects of the case not touched upon by prosecuting counsel as he addressed the jury as this would be covered in great detail by the eighty-four prosecution witnesses that would appear before them, but it was important to give them a broad summary of the amount of supporting, circumstantial evidence that was going to be presented.

The man who had abducted the couple in the field at Dorney Reach had talked a lot about his supposed past, in particular his criminal record. With the agreement of defence counsel, Swanwick outlined what was known about the defendant. He matched much, though not all, of what Hanratty had said of himself including his periods of imprisonment, his time serving corrective training, and that he had been on the run for four months. Hanratty had committed a burglary in April for which he strongly suspected he was wanted because he knew he had left his fingerprints at the scene, exactly four months beforehand.

He was a poor driver, which appeared to explain the damage found on the recovered Morris, he did not like smoking and routinely wore gloves. He knew Bedford and the Middlesex area – Hayes, Stanmore, Harrow – through which they had driven that night; he would do, as this was where he had lived, and carried on his business of housebreaking. He always wore suits and the recovered trousers from his suitcase had zip-up flies, comparatively unusual at the time.

He matched in great part the description given by Valerie of her attacker. He was 25 years old, 5ft 7in in height, had a young-sounding cockney voice with the inability to pronounce 'th', used the word 'kip', had brown hair when it was natural, had distinctive blue eyes and, notably, was called Jim.

During his address to the jury, Swanwick needed to refer routinely to bloodstained items and where they had been found. Before he had finished, one of the members of the jury became ill each time the word blood was mentioned and after some deliberation, it was agreed that the trial should continue without him. The outcome of A6 murder trial would be decided by a jury of eleven, not twelve people.

After the crime scene had been explained to the jury by a number of police officers producing plans and photographs, Valerie was pushed into court in a wheelchair, flanked by a nurse, a therapist and a woman police officer holding her hand. After she had been told that she could take as many rests as she wished to during the course of giving her evidence, she told the court her name and address in a loud, clear voice. With the formalities over, her name and address confirmed, Valerie calmly answered questions from Swanwick as he guided her through the events of the night some five months earlier.

The prosecution needed to adduce only that evidence that would allow the jury to determine whether or not the man in the dock was guilty of murder, and Swanwick slowly brought out all the relevant points that were necessary to help prove the prosecution case. Valerie relived the story from the moment she and Michael had left her home, had gone to the pub in Taplow and driven to the cornfield. She described the moment the gunman tapped on the window of their car and the hours of terror they had endured as they were held up at gunpoint and robbed. She told of how the gunman had wanted to put Michael in the boot but had been persuaded otherwise.

The journey through Slough, Middlesex and on to the A6 was recalled in great detail, the stopping for cigarettes and petrol and how on numerous occasions she had tried to frustrate the gunman in his endeavours. She described how they had tried to attract attention by switching the car's reversing light on and off, how they made obvious attempts to convince him to leave and their questions about what it was he wanted.

Valerie emphasised how their captor clearly did not have a plan and told the jury of his continual orders to face the front and to keep quiet while he was thinking. In graphic detail she spoke of the moment Michael was shot twice in the head at point-blank range and became very emotional as she told the part of the story where all she could hear was the sound of blood pouring from her boyfriend's head. She said that this was the first time she screamed out. She turned and looked directly at Hanratty in the dock, now the fourth time they had faced each other, and said angrily: 'You shot him, you bastard.'

Then the moment came of being forced under threat of death to move into the back of the car, glimpsing the ice-blue eyes as they were caught in the passing headlights of a car. She had helped him remove his glove, was ordered to undo her bra, remove her knickers and take off her glasses. Then he had raped her. She told of the sexual taunts afterwards about her being sexually inexperienced and then the callousness of making her drag Michael's blood-stained body from the car and pull it to the edge of the layby. She recounted how she begged him to let her to go before he aimed his gun at her and shot her five times.

After the detailed description of the attack, Swanwick then asked her to explain how she had picked out an innocent man on the first identification parade but on the second, when Hanratty was then present, she had been absolutely sure.

'Had you any doubt at the time?' asked Swanwick.

'I had no doubt at all that this was the man who shot Mike and myself.'

'Have you any doubt now?'

'I have no doubt whatsoever.'

It was then the turn of Michael Sherrard to challenge what Valerie had just told the court. His duty was to test the evidence of the prosecution insofar as his instructions from Hanratty allowed him to do so. His client's defence was that he was not the man in the back of the car that night, and therefore, Valerie Storie was wrong in her identification. His plan was to try to demonstrate that not only was she wrong about that, but also that she was an unreliable witness in many other regards. He intended to ask her questions that would expose her weaknesses but needed to do that in a way that appeared sufficiently caring.

He began:

Miss Storie, I want you to understand quite clearly that I am in no way attempting to belittle the horrifying experience you underwent or the magnitude of the tragedy which overtook you. I am sure your courage must be admired by everyone, but you will appreciate, on the other hand, my plain duty to my client is to attempt to save his life and indeed to see that he is not imperilled on anything other than the basis of objective evidence and objective evidence alone.

Valerie's response was a simple 'yes'.

Sherrard put it to Valerie that the Morris they had been in that night, the one that both she and Michael lived for, had somehow been 'hotted up' because of its use in rallying and that, coupled with the fact that the car had a leaky exhaust, made it much noisier than otherwise would have been the case. If the noise in the car was so loud, wasn't it just likely that much of what was said between the three of them was only part heard or perhaps misunderstood. Valerie quashed the suggestion immediately; the car had not been adapted in any way and the leaking exhaust made no difference to the sound of its engine at all.

Despite making no progress with this line of questioning, Sherrard developed it. He had cross-examined her at the magistrates' court proceedings when she was in Stoke Mandeville hospital the year before and made full use of any word or words that varied in the slightest detail between what she had said then and what she was now saying in court. Today, she had told the jury that the gunman had seemed reluctant to want to go to London but at the committal proceedings she had said he seemed not to want to go to Slough or Maidenhead. Valerie replied it was both, and despite Sherrard pursuing the point, Valerie maintained her position.

He next challenged her over where the cigarettes had been purchased that night; at first she said Harrow, now it was Stanmore. To Valerie they were the same place; they were simply urbanised areas that bordered each other. He questioned her description about the roadworks Hanratty had warned them of, the clear inference being that the gunman knew the area well. Sherrard suggested that there had been an advanced warning sign of the roadworks and that was how they knew there would be some just around the corner. Again, Valerie told him his suggestion was wrong.

He continued to probe her ability to accurately recall conversations on the night. He was particularly interested in her use of the word 'institutions' when she described what the gunman had said about his criminal history. At one stage she used the word and then she referred to it directly as 'borstal training'. Which had been correct? Once more, she said she had used both terms to describe what she had been told; they were interchangeable as far as she was concerned.

When Sherrard turned his attention to the witness John Kerr, who had spoken to her in the layby that morning and who was yet to give his evidence, Valerie strongly denied that she had told him that they had given the man a lift: 'Hardly that,' she said. Further she had never said the attacker's hair was light in colour; she had told him it was dark brown. Again, Sherrard referred back to the evidence she had given at the magistrates' hearing when she had used the term 'medium brown'. If she had used that phrase, she said, she could not recall but she was telling the court now that it was dark brown.

Notably, despite the errors made early on in the police investigation about the colour of the offender's eyes, Sherrard made no mention of it; that line of questioning would come much later. He was making little headway with Valerie in his attempt to weaken her credibility as a witness but he was leading up to the most crucial part of the trial: her identification of James Hanratty. He had already questioned her about this at the committal hearing and once more got her to acknowledge that throughout the entire ordeal, she had only a momentary glimpse of her attacker's face when the passing car's headlights had lit it up just as he was building up to his sexual advance.

'This was the only real, proper glimpse of him that I had,' she told the court.

This was an important point for the defence team. If a witness only has a fleeting look, a second or two in a dark environment and under such stressful conditions, their evidence must be viewed with caution. The suggestion Sherrard was making was that here was a witness who had been in such an extreme state of terror that her evidence about the identity of the attacker must be viewed by the jury as of no value.

Much was made about Hanratty's height. Sherrard told the court that his client was 5ft 8in and that Valerie had described her assailant as slightly taller than herself; she was 5ft 3½in in flat shoes. For the majority of the five hours that Valerie had been held captive, the gunman had been sitting in the back of the car. The only time when she saw him standing up was when he got out of the car to force her into the back seat before he raped her – she knew by that time exactly what misfortune lay ahead of her – and the other was when she was pulling her boyfriend's dead body from the car with the gunman standing over her.

Sherrard was most exercised about the Identikit picture that Valerie had helped to prepare and he asked her to examine it. It was clear, and indeed the press had made much of it, that the right eyebrow of the suspect was markedly raised and bushier than the left. Asked whether this had been part of her description, she said that at no time did she ever mention this feature and could not explain why it appeared that way. At one point, Sherrard was rebuked by Mr Justice Gorman for purposely trying to confuse and mislead the witness, but he now turned to the identity parades.

The first one in which Peter Alphon had taken his place was dealt with directly. She had made a mistake, although she added that she did not realise that the men were allowed to speak, something that had been made available to her at the second in which Hanratty had been present. The point had been made, though, that Valerie was human and fallible. Matters for the defence were helped by the fact that after the Alphon parade, she had seen a photograph of him in the national newspapers and had commented to a doctor that he did 'resemble' her attacker. The defence strategy was developing: not only was Hanratty innocent but the police had released the real killer.

The defence's position on the second identification parade was straightforward: she had made a genuine mistake. But two points would emerge that would feature for years to come. When Hanratty had been arrested his hair was dyed ginger. A police officer had commented on it and so too had Hanratty when he had exclaimed that it had not 'done him any favours'.[6] He was, by any standards, noticeable. When he had taken his place on the parade, he was distinctive and stood out among the others. As Sherrard suggested to Valerie when she was giving her evidence, Hanratty must have 'stood out like a carrot in a bunch of bananas'. The implication was clear. Hanratty may as well have invited the witnesses to pick him out.[7]

Understandably, Sherrard chose not to point out that if Hanratty or his solicitor felt he had been at a disadvantage in any way at the identification parade he could have refused to take part. Nor were the witnesses actually looking for a man with ginger hair.

The second point Michael Sherrard laboured was that Valerie had taken twenty minutes to make her identification. Quite apart from the logistical arrangements of needing to push her in a bed up and down a line of men three times and then asking them twice to speak the phrase, 'Be quiet will you, I'm thinking,' Sherrard was wrong. Valerie told him that she didn't remember that it had taken that long, although prosecuting counsel Graham Swanwick did nothing to rebut the suggestion. In fact, the parade had taken only eleven minutes, a detail recorded on the identification forms by Chief Inspector Ballinger.

Sherrard was trying to make the point that because she had taken so long in her identification, she surely must have been uncertain. In fact, Valerie had been sure about Hanratty's identification almost as soon as she had seen him but she wanted to hear them all speak first. Prosecution counsel did not rebut this allegation immediately, as he could have done, an omission that would contribute to growing public doubt on the reliability of the identification in the years following the trial.

Sherrard then adopted a different approach to suggest to the jury that Hanratty was not the attacker. Part of the prosecution case was that the gunman was a bad driver and a nervous passenger. Throughout the journey, he had asked Gregsten to show him how the gears worked and wrongly commented on the gear in which he should be driving. At the layby, before he shot Valerie he had asked for the gear positions to be shown as well as the location of the light switch. When the car was recovered in Ilford, it had minor accident damage, suggesting that the driver had been careless. Sherrard pointed out that his client was a convicted car thief and had openly boasted about the range of cars he had driven. If it was the case that the gunman was a poor and inexperienced driver, that description certainly did not fit Hanratty. Experienced as he was, there would be no need for anyone to show him how the gears operated and he would not have left the car in a damaged state. He intimated as much to Valerie when she spoke of the moment she had told the gunman how the gears worked and had needed to start the car engine for him. Valerie was quite clear.

'He got in and drove it off quick enough,' she said. 'He asked what positions the gears were.'

It was entirely appropriate for Sherrard, as defence counsel, not to inform the jury that Hanratty had never taken a driving test and had only secured a provisional driving licence in Ireland in order to hire a car, which had been recovered damaged. Other witnesses had made statements to the police about his careless driving, but that too was omitted.

Sherrard now drew his questioning to an end: 'Miss Storie, one appreciates your position of course, but it is my plain duty to suggest to you, that although you may be convinced in your own mind, you are nevertheless absolutely honest, but absolutely wrong. I must make that quite plain to you.'

Valerie's reply was short and to the point: 'I do not agree with that suggestion.'

Graham Swanwick had a few further questions for her but finished his re-examination by asking, 'Have you any doubt whatever about your identification?'

'I have no doubt at all,' she replied.

Examination and cross-examination complete, Valerie had been in the witness box for almost three hours spread over two days. In November the previous year when Acott had been writing his concluding report, he said of Valerie, 'Whatever success the defence may have with some of the many witnesses in this case, I feel certain that they have no hope of gaining any ground with Valerie Storie.'[8]

Chapter Twelve

Prosecution Witnesses

Witness number eleven for the prosecution was John Kerr, the Oxford undergraduate who had spoken to Valerie in the layby that morning and now said he had made notes on a piece of paper that he subsequently handed to a senior, uniformed police officer. Detective Superintendent Barron's investigation into the claim had concluded that he probably had written some details down but had not handed them to a police officer; they had instead been returned to the County Council offices where the rest of his paperwork had been found.

Kerr went through his story again, saying that he had been told by Valerie that they had been held up by a gunman around 9.30 the previous evening. He had written down her name and address and the man's description as having large staring eyes and light-fairish hair. Swanwick handed to him the document that had been recovered from Bedford County Council and asked him to confirm that it was the piece of paper he had with him that morning. He was able to confirm it, but when he was asked to comment on the incorrect registration number written on the rear of the form he said that it was not his writing. This was a considerable surprise. Kerr had been shown this form before when he had been interviewed by Inspector Milborrow and he had not said then that this was not his writing. He had maintained that he had written more, which appeared to have gone missing, but there was no suggestion that the erroneous registration number was not his writing.

In cross-examination, Sherrard picked up on the issue of a piece of paper that Kerr said he had handed to a police officer. It contained the first description of the assailant as given to him by Storie and it had gone missing. However, he did not pursue the point that Kerr thought the writing on the form was not his, nor did he probe him about the actual description given to him. Specifically, he did not question him on the colour of the attacker's hair nor the colour of his eyes.

After a number of medical witnesses had given their evidence about Michael Gregsten's injuries and cause of death and Valerie's early treatment in Bedford hospital, three more crucial witnesses went into the witness box: John Skillett, Edward Blackhall and James Trower, the three men who had witnessed the erratic driving of the Morris Minor in Ilford just a few hours after the murder.

They each gave their evidence, Skillett that he had seen the car being driven badly and had positively identified Hanratty as the driver and Trower, that he too had seen the car being driven at speed and had subsequently picked out the defendant on a parade. Sherrard adopted the same approach to these witnesses as he had to Valerie in that they were simply mistaken.

He asked Skillett, who only ever attended Hanratty's parade, whether Hanratty's ginger-coloured hair had been a distraction and he told the jury that it had not been an issue. He was looking at the faces of the men and that ever since he had been told by the police that the man may be responsible for the A6 killing, he had worried about it and it was a face he would never forget.

Sherrard made the observation that Skillett had not noticed the distinctive red strips on the rear bumper of the car in the same way as his passenger had: 'It is my duty to put it to you that in fact you made a most serious mistake in your identification.'

Skillett simply said, 'No.'

Trower was also asked about Hanratty's distinctive coloured hair at the parade, but he dismissed it out of hand. He hadn't even thought about it. It was the face he was interested in. In the same way that Valerie had only had a fleeting glimpse of Hanratty's face, Trower had only seen the driver of the car for a matter of seconds and at a time when it was travelling at about 20mph. Sherrard made much of this but the witness stood firm. He told the court that he knew a man's life was at stake, but he had no doubt that he had made a correct identification. His position was supported by the fact that he had attended the earlier parade when Alphon was present and he had not selected anyone. He had only picked out one man and that was Hanratty.

The last of the three witnesses was Edward Blackhall. He had seen the red strips and the green sticker on the back of the car as it raced along Eastern Avenue that morning but on each of the identification parades, he had picked out someone unconnected to the investigation. He had done little to implicate Hanratty – other than later identifying the abandoned Morris – but Sherrard was hugely critical of him. He questioned him over the issue of the raised, bushy eyebrow in the Identikit he had compiled but he said he knew nothing about it and he had not given that as part of his description. Sherrard's main point was that Blackhall was a man who, in a case of capital murder, appeared to have casually walked into two parades and picked out innocent people.

'You are not saying are you that you regarded this a children's party game or anything like that?' Sherrard suggested.

Blackhall immediately rejected the suggestion and said that the police should have told him that there was a possibility that the man he had seen that morning may not be on the parade at all. He hadn't been told that and had he done so he may not have picked someone out on each occasion. Sherrard's questioning had been intended to cast doubt in the jurors' minds on the witnesses' ability to identify Hanratty accurately, but each had confirmed their observations.

For the rest of the day, the jury heard about the finding of the revolver on the number 36A bus, the trail of suits owned by Hanratty being bought or being put into dry cleaners and his visit to Ireland, including his episodes of bad driving and the postcards he had sent back to various people in London.

The following day, the fifth of the trial, was taken up mainly by the evidence of William Nudds, the man who would effectively place Hanratty in room 24 of the Vienna hotel in which the cartridges from the murder weapon were found. Swanwick made it clear immediately that Nudds was a convicted criminal who had made three statements to the police, the second of which was not true. The reasons for that would become apparent. For the sake of brevity, Nudds was invited to tell the jury that Hanratty, or J. Ryan as he knew him then, had booked into the Vienna hotel on the evening of Monday, 21 August and had occupied room 24. The following morning, after breakfast he had asked for directions and was told to walk to Queensway and there get the number 36 bus. His evidence given, Michael Sherrard began to cross-examine him.

He would make much of Nudds' deception and the lies he had told to the police. A man's life was at stake and he had deliberately misled them. He now told the court exactly why he had embarked upon this reckless course of action; to get revenge on the criminal fraternity who had let him down. He emphasised that he was now telling the truth and at one point he picked up the Bible, held it in his hand and said, 'I repeat to you that I am a Christian, but not a religious man, but when I hold that thing in my hand I know I have a maker and I tell the truth as I am telling you the truth now.'

Sherrard's questioning adopted the position of not only trying to show that what Nudds was now telling the court was completely untrue but also to demonstrate that documentary evidence could prove that Peter Alphon could have occupied room 24.

Relying on him to confirm certain entries made in the hotel register, Sherrard showed that it was theoretically possible, at least according to the records, that when Alphon had checked into the hotel on 22 August, he could have been allocated room 24. The room had been unoccupied at the time and the room he eventually stayed in only became available later in the day when another guest had cancelled. His arguments were all based around certain annotations made in the register and Nudds was simply unable to provide any alternative explanation, other than what was now being suggested by Sherrard simply did not take place.

There was to be no argument that Hanratty had occupied the room with the cartridges on the day before the murder, but Sherrard had ably demonstrated that so too could Alphon the following day and therefore, it showed that it was possibly him, and not Hanratty, who had carelessly left the cartridges lying around on the chair at the end of the bed.

Graham Swanwick, in his re-examination, led Nudds through his second statement line by line and he affirmed it had been Hanratty alone who had occupied room 24 and Alphon had gone nowhere near it. Defence counsel, though, merely had to introduce doubt, and Sherrard had done that in his questioning of Nudds. As a result of Nudds' lies early in the investigation, Superintendent Acott had publicly suggested that Peter Alphon was a suspect, and Sherrard had successfully done so as well, this time in front of the jury.

The following two days were taken up with a number of different witnesses giving their evidence. Perhaps the most significant of those were the France family, who were able to detail the movements of Hanratty immediately before and after the murder. 'Dixie' France told of the occasion when Hanratty had pointed out to him where he hid his unwanted jewellery underneath the seat of a bus and although the exact date and words used were challenged, his story remained as he had told it when he was first spoken to by the police.

He was followed by his wife, Charlotte, and it was at this point it could have been expected that she may have been asked about the conversation she had had with Louise Anderson in the court waiting room concerning the hiding of the gun in her airing cupboard. She had made a statement to the police a couple of weeks earlier and Swanwick was aware of it. But the subject never came up and she merely supported what her husband had already said. During the giving of her evidence, as she had at the committal proceedings, she collapsed and needed to withdraw from the courtroom.

When Louise Anderson gave her evidence about her knowledge of Hanratty, it could have been anticipated that her supposed knowledge about Hanratty's gun being secreted in a cupboard would have been revealed, but it was not. Furthermore, she had made a further witness statement after the trial had started[1] in which she indicated that a pair of black nylon gloves had gone missing from her home, but this too was not mentioned in court. Quite why either of these seemingly important aspects were omitted from her evidence is unclear, but it is likely that she was perceived as a somewhat unreliable witness given that she had failed to mention such critical evidence in her earlier statements.

She admitted though, that over a period of time, she had paid Hanratty around £600 and was well aware he was a housebreaker. She spoke of his movements either side of the important days and at one point, though she readily admitted that she was not good with dates, said that Hanratty had visited her on the morning of the 22nd, the morning of the abduction, dressed in his suit. She also confirmed that he had left his suitcase containing his clothes at her flat in Sussex Gardens, an address, it had already been emphasised, which was on the 36A bus route. So too did she remember seeing him on the Saturday, the 26th, and he had cuts to his face, but there was no mention of a gun.

The prosecution's sixtieth witness, on day seven of the trial, was the Director of the Forensic Science Laboratory, Lewis Nickolls. He had been responsible for all forensic aspects of the case since the investigation started. It was he who had examined the recovered revolver and compared it with all the bullets and cartridges found in the layby, room 24 at the Vienna hotel and in each of Michael and Valerie's bodies. It was he that proved that the gun on the number 36A bus was the murder weapon. When he was explaining how it was not possible for the gun to have been set off accidentally, the weapon was passed among the jurymen for each of them to squeeze the trigger and to feel the pressure required to make it fire.[2]

He had also examined the Morris and he described how the blood was distributed on its inside as well as describing blood marks on the boot. He had examined blood recovered from the scene and the clothing taken from the two victims, and his analysis supported everything Valerie had said in terms of where he had found traces of their blood.

To do this, he had tested each of the victims' blood and was able to group them, a scientific procedure that had been operative in the criminal courts since the 1930s. Blood could be categorised as either group O, the most common, A, B or AB. Identifying a person's group is usually determined by examining their blood, samples of which had been obtained from both Valerie and Michael, but in the majority of cases a person's blood group could be determined by examining other bodily fluids such as saliva, mucus or semen. If this can be done, the person is a secretor; quite simply, their blood group is secreted in their other fluids. When Valerie's saliva was tested, it had not been possible to determine her blood group and she was therefore a blood group O, non-secretor.

When Nickolls had examined her petticoat, he told the jury that he detected some staining that upon closer examination was a mixture of vaginal and seminal fluids. This substantiated Valerie's story that she had been raped. When he tested the staining it demonstrated that it was group O secretor. Since Valerie was a non-secretor, it was the semen that was producing the O secretor reading and since Michael was blood group AB, the semen could not have been his. Hanratty was a group O secretor, but since blood group O was the most common group in Britain, as many as 17 million people in the country could have the same blood group as him. It took the case no further other than demonstrating that he could not be eliminated.

Like Nudds before him, the prosecution's seventy-second witness, Roy Langdale, was going to experience a testing time. He too had a long criminal record for a man of only 24 years and his evidence, which effectively amounted to a full confession by Hanratty, meant that he was going to be very closely cross-examined by Sherrard.

Questioned by Swanwick, Langdale recounted his conversations in the exercise yard at Brixton prison while he had been on remand. Hanratty had told him about what he had done to Valerie in the back of the car and how concerned he was about blood that had been on his suit.

Sherrard now suggested that the only reason Langdale had made his statement to the police was for money. It had become apparent in the past few weeks that Langdale had sold his story to the newspapers and he now admitted being paid £25 by the *Sunday Pictorial*. Sherrard suggested to Langdale that all of his evidence was exaggerated or simply lies. Langdale denied the suggestion and at one point even blurted out that Hanratty had told him that he hated Acott and had wanted to shoot him.

Hanratty had allegedly said that there had been a struggle in the car, which was not what had happened, and Sherrard suggested to Langdale that he was getting his information partly from newspapers, which he readily admitted reading, and partly from his fellow inmates. Sherrard made a particularly valid observation that tended to suggest that this information would not have come from Hanratty himself. According to Langdale, Hanratty had told him that he was concerned that Valerie had survived as she would be able to identify him. That was an extraordinary thing for Hanratty to have said as by that time, weeks after he had been charged with the offence, he had already been picked out on an identification parade not only by Valerie but by two other witnesses as well. Surely, Sherrard asserted, Hanratty would have mentioned that rather than merely saying that Valerie *would* be able to pick him out. It supported the idea that Langdale was dramatising his already fantasised account.

When Hanratty had allegedly told Langdale that he had raped Valerie, the sexual attack had not been made public; the prosecution had pointed out that only she and the gunman knew about it. However, Sherrard was able to show that Langdale had made his witness statement to the police at Scotland Yard on 30 November, eight days after the committal proceedings at Ampthill Magistrates' Court had started and by which time Valerie's rape ordeal was public knowledge. Langdale could have gleaned that from the newspaper and simply added it to his already-embellished pack of lies.

As he had with Nudds, Sherrard's strategy had been to question the honesty and reliability of this key witness, all the while knowing the defence simply had to establish sufficient doubt about Hanratty's guilt for the trial to result in an acquittal.

Detective Superintendent Bob Acott was the eightieth prosecution witness. Graham Swanwick established that he was in charge of the investigation, asked some questions about his interview with the defendant and some further questions about his investigation into the Liverpool alibi. He knew that he would get to sweep up any major issues after he had been cross-examined by his opposition colleague.

Sherrard was to probe meticulously the detail behind every aspect of the investigation. He started with the defendant's occupation of room 24 at the Vienna hotel; it was a vital link to the murderer. Acott had told Hanratty in his interview with him that no one had occupied the room between the time he had stayed there and the time the revolver had been found. This was now no longer the case since the hotel manager, Juliana Galves, had changed her story since she had made her statement to the police. When she had given evidence at the committal proceedings she told the magistrates that in fact the Indian guest, Rapur, had stayed in the room for one night in between the two important dates, a point that Acott had to acknowledge. Sherrard suggested Acott had not carefully investigated this particular aspect as even a superficial examination of the hotel records would have shown that to be the case. Acott defended his approach but the fact remained that had Rapur and another resident of the hotel been traced and interviewed, this detail would have been resolved well ahead of Hanratty being interviewed.

At one point, Acott was unable to answer whether one of these important witnesses had even been traced. Sherrard was suggesting that Acott's investigation had been substandard.

Once Hanratty had become aware he was wanted for the A6 murder, he telephoned Acott on several occasions and Sherrard challenged him over the accuracy of his notes he had made about the conversation he claimed to have had with him. He argued about the exact wording used and suggested he had left out important features, which Acott strongly denied.

Once Hanratty had been arrested in Blackpool, Acott and Ken Oxford had travelled there to interview him. Sherrard spent a great deal of time challenging both the legality and the content of this 'interrogation', as it was called at the time, attempting to discredit Acott by suggesting he was being less than truthful in his account, perhaps demonstrated by the fact that the prisoner had not been afforded the opportunity to sign the interview notes as being accurate. He challenged the length of time it had taken to carry out the interview, questioned the long pauses in between the questions and suggested much had been left out. On all of these points, Acott asserted that his account was truthful, lawful and accurate.

As expected, Sherrard made much of the fact that on the day his client had been arrested, he told the police, in response to why the jacket of his chalk stripe suit was missing, that he had committed a burglary in Stanmore and stolen another jacket to replace his, which had become torn. It had taken two months for the police to prove that what Hanratty was saying was true. It helped very little to show that Hanratty was innocent of the murder but it made the valid point that Acott's investigation had not been thorough. In the same way that he had been careless around establishing who the occupants of room 24 had been at the Vienna hotel, he had been equally casual in pursuing Hanratty's explanations of why he had thrown away his jacket. At one point, Acott had suggested that any questions relating to the burglary aspect of the investigation should be directed towards his sergeant, Ken Oxford. This was an unacceptable position to adopt. Acott could not pick and choose which parts of the investigation he wanted to be in charge of; he was responsible for everything and should have known everything.

Given that Liverpool was going to be a key part of the defence case, Sherrard made relatively little reference to the police enquiries that had been carried out, arguing over minor matters such as whether it had been Hanratty or his solicitor Kleinman who had passed on to him certain information. He laboured the points in an attempt to again discredit Acott, but no real progress was made. At one point, Mr Justice Gorman intervened to once more rebuke Sherrard for making an unwarranted suggestion to Acott without any evidence to support his claim and on another occasion both Acott and Sherrard were wrong in their recollection of the timings provided by the Liverpool sweet shop assistant, Olive Dinwoodie, but the matter passed without it being corrected.

Sherrard continued along the lines of seeking to undermine the detective. The more he could imply about this man's competence, the more chance there was of the jury ignoring much of the evidence. He accused him of posing for photographs for the newspapers during one of the lunch breaks but realised the error of his ways when the photograph showed Acott being caught unawares. He accused him of colluding with witnesses during the trial and he was proved wrong and had to withdraw his comments, making what almost amounted to a full public apology.

Undermining the police investigation was a key element of the defence strategy: the intention was to place doubt in the minds of the jury about whether the police interviews were accurate, and it had demonstrated that some aspects of the investigation had been careless and selective in their manner. Now Sherrard wanted to demonstrate that the real killer was still at large.

Meike Dalal, the 24-year-old Swede who had been sexually assaulted in her home, was brought into the defence case. So too was a Mrs Audrey Willis, who on the day after the killing of Michael Gregsten had been attacked in her home at Knebworth, some 20 miles away from the scene at Deadman's Hill. In both cases there were similarities. Dalal had been tied up, hit over the head and would have been raped had the attacker not been disturbed. He had claimed to be the A6 killer. Willis had been held up by a man brandishing a revolver and claiming to be hungry; he had drunk a glass of milk while in the house. She had been required to remove one of his gloves and she too may have been raped had he not been disturbed. Both crimes, admitted Acott, remained unsolved.

Having established that similar attacks had been committed, the inference was made that the A6 killer remained at large. One of the suspects in the A6 case, Peter Alphon, had been identified by Dalal as the man responsible for her attack and at a time when Hanratty had been in Ireland. In fairness, Sherrard pointed out that Alphon had subsequently been released from this charge by virtue of some diligent police work that confirmed Alphon's alibi.[3] In fact, Dalal had made no such positive identification, but nevertheless Sherrard wanted to show that Peter Alphon could have been the killer.

Sherrard referred back to the events of the previous September. Acott had effectively claimed in the newspapers and on television that Alphon was a suspect, even though he referred to him as a witness. If Valerie Storie was such a reliable witness, as Acott had claimed when he was examined by prosecuting counsel, the killer had icy-blue, saucer-like eyes. Alphon had hazel eyes, so why was he a suspect? Acott's answer was simple. At the time there were two people of interest; one was J. Ryan, the other was Alphon. In September, he had no idea as to the identity of Ryan. As for Alphon, he had the wrong colour of eyes – in fact, he had nothing in common with the killer's description – but Acott was also in possession of a statement from Nudds claiming that it had been Alphon who had occupied room 24. He had little doubt that he was not the man responsible for the murder but he needed him to be properly eliminated. For sure, had he not adopted that position, Sherrard would have criticised him for not doing so.

This was an extremely important part of the trial; so important that Swanwick in his re-examination of Acott, ensured the jury were quite clear about why Alphon could not have been responsible. In answering Swanwick's question as to why he had officially eliminated Alphon, after rather bizarrely suggesting he had a 'seventh sense' about it, he detailed twelve points:

Alphon's name was Peter. The suspect had called himself 'Jim'.
Alphon was 31 years old. The suspect was in his mid-20s.
Alphon was 5ft 9in. The suspect was 5ft 6in.
Alphon had hazel eyes. The suspect had blue eyes.
Alphon did not mis-pronounce 'th'. The suspect did.
Alphon was well spoken. The suspect had a cockney accent.
Alphon was an educated man. The suspect appeared not.
Alphon displayed no tendency to be hesitant. The suspect had been.
Alphon never used the word 'kip'. The suspect did.
Alphon had shown no inclination to sleep during the prolonged period that he was in Scotland Yard the night he was being questioned. The suspect had expressed the need to sleep.
Alphon could not drive. The suspect could.
Alphon was shabbily dressed. The suspect was immaculately dressed.

Sherrard finished his cross-examination with a summary of his accusations, which focused solely on his dealings with Hanratty:

Mr Acott, I have to suggest to you in the respects I have put to you in some detail – and I apologise for going through it at such laborious length – that your note is not accurate, your enquiries were not thorough or careful in the respects I have specified, and that as a whole your recollection as well as your note is at fault and you have not told my Lord and the jury the truth about what was said to you by this man.[4]

Acott replied, 'I deny all those suggestions, my Lord.'

Acott had spent more than thirteen hours in the witness box presenting his case and defending his actions. He had occasionally shown that he lacked care in certain areas of the investigation and could, and should, have done better. At times he had demonstrated intransigence in ceding any ground to Sherrard over minor points that might perhaps have been better viewed by a jury had he been more conciliatory. But he had given answers to all of Sherrard's accusations. There was no evidence whatsoever that he had done anything illegal or corrupt. Perhaps most importantly though, these challenges had, quite rightly, been put to Acott in front of the jury and they would be in a position to take all of it into account when considering their verdict.

A number of police officers followed the senior detective into the witness box to give their evidence, including Sergeant Oxford, who was more able to answer the questions relating to the Stanmore burglary. It remained an unsatisfactory part of the investigation but otherwise Oxford merely corroborated everything his superintendent had said.

After eighty-four witnesses, the prosecution closed its case.

Entrance to the cornfield in Dorney Reach where the abduction took place on 22 August 1961. (Reproduced with kind permission of Bedfordshire Police)

The A6 just north of Clophill, Bedfordshire, where the shootings took place. The RAC box where John Kerr was working can be seen in the foreground. (Reproduced with kind permission of Bedfordshire Police)

A police officer indicates the position where Michael Gregsten's body was found. (Reproduced with kind permission of Bedfordshire Police)

Redbridge Lane East, Ilford. Beyond the shops on the left is the entrance to Avondale Crescent where the stolen Morris Minor was abandoned. The identification witness James Trower was standing on this pavement when he saw Hanratty drive past. (Reproduced with kind permission of Bedfordshire Police)

The abandoned Morris Minor in Avondale Crescent. (Reproduced with kind permission of Bedfordshire Police)

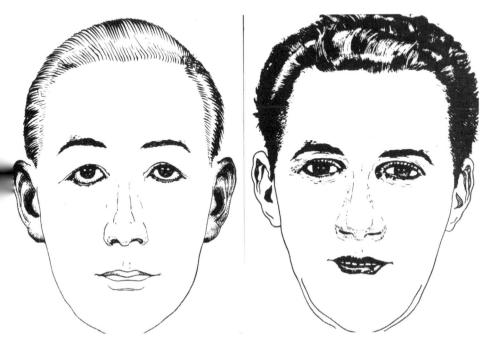

dentikits of suspect issued on 29 August 1961. (Reproduced with kind permission of Bedfordshire Police)

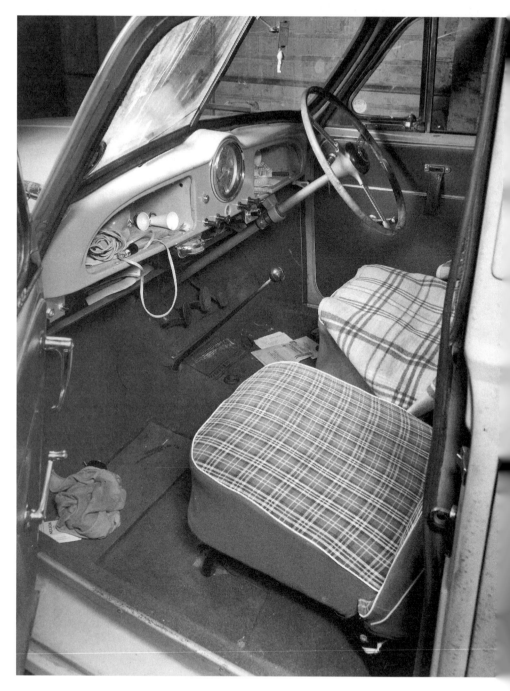

Inside the Morris Minor. Michael Gregsten was shot dead in the driver's seat. Valerie Storie was tied up in the passenger seat. (Reproduced with kind permission of Bedfordshire Police)

rear seat of the Morris Minor where Valerie Storie was raped. (Reproduced with kind
mission of Bedfordshire Police)

The lifted seat on the number 36A bus under which the murder weapon was found. (Reproduced with kind permission of Bedfordshire Police)

The Royal Enfield .38 calibre murder weapon. (Reproduced with kind permission of Bedfordshire Police)

Room 24, Vienna Hotel. The bed in the alcove was occupied by Hanratty on the night before the abduction. The two spent cartridges from the murder weapon were found on the chair at the end of the bed. (Reproduced with kind permission of Bedfordshire Police)

Peter Alphon, who repeatedly admitted and denied the rape of Valerie Storie and the murder of Michael Gregsten. (Author's collection)

James Hanratty. Convicted and hanged for the murder of Michael Gregsten. (Author's collecti

Glengarriff, from Cobduff Mountain, Co. Cork, Ireland.

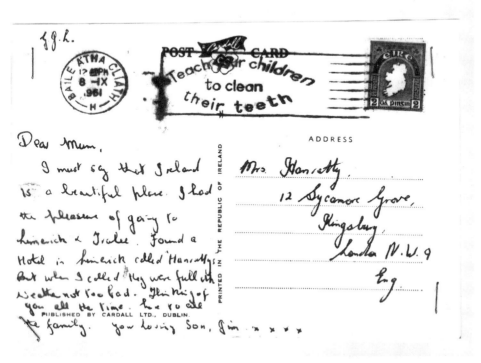

POST CARD

Teach your children to clean their teeth

Dear Mum,

I must say that Ireland is a beautiful place. I had the pleasure of going to Limerick & Tralee. Found a Hotel in Limerick called 'Hanrattys' But when I called they were full up. Weather not too bad. Thinking of you all the time. Love to all the family. Your loving Son, Jim x x x x

ADDRESS

Mrs. Hanratty,
12 Sycamore Grove,
Kingsbury,
London N.W.9
Eng.

PRINTED IN THE REPUBLIC OF IRELAND

PUBLISHED BY CARDALL LTD., DUBLIN.

One of the postcards sent by Hanratty from Ireland to his mother. (Reproduced with kind permission of Bedfordshire Police)

Bedroom inside Ingledene guest house in which Hanratty claimed to have stayed on the night of the murder. On the right can be seen a green bath, which became a significant feature in his trial. (Reproduced with kind permission of Bedfordshire Police)

Valerie in the years before the attack with unknown male. (Not annotated)

Michael Gregsten. (Not annotated)

...rie with her parents in January 1962.

Valerie outside gates of Stoke Mandeville hospital, December 1961. (*Daily Express*)

rie arriving home in Anthony Way, Slough, with her parents. (*Daily Express*)

Valerie in December 1961.
(*Daily Express*)

Valerie in summer 1962.
(Today)

Valerie back at work at Road Research Laboratories. (R.G. McFarlane, Today)

ie Storie around 2001. She remained about her ordeal for thirty-five years. annotated)

Celebrating the life of

VALERIE JEAN STORIE

24 November 1938 – 26 March 2C

Valerie in the summer of 1992 with Cookham WI Institute president and committee. (Not annotated)

The front page of the service order for Valerie's funeral in April 2016.

Slough Crematorium

Tuesday, 19 April 2016 at 2.30

Chapter Thirteen

The Case for the Defence

It was Tuesday, 6 February 1962 and Michael Sherrard rose to address the jury with his opening speech. In the same way as the prosecution had opened its case just over two weeks ago, the defence were to take their opportunity to outline the nature of the evidence the jury was about to hear. But what was going to be said would come as a major surprise. What Sherrard outlined was a result of some work his defence team had desperately been carrying out over the previous fourteen days.

After Hanratty had instructed his solicitor in October about his Liverpool alibi, and as a result of learning that witnesses, particularly Olive Dinwoodie, were unlikely to be able to help him, the defence had preferred to rely on their own resources to explore his defence. Until that point, Kleinman had been happy for the police to investigate the claim and hopefully demonstrate that Hanratty could not possibly have committed the murder. That was not the outcome and Hanratty was remaining most insistent that what he was saying was true. Kleinman, therefore, decided to employ someone to go to Liverpool to carry out the enquiries more diligently.

That someone was Joseph Gillbanks, a retired detective sergeant from Liverpool City Police, who with thirty-three years' police service was the ideal man for the job. Retired detectives are often appointed to such tasks since they are recognised to be competent and practised in interviewing witnesses and taking statements. People in Liverpool needed to be traced and interviewed in some of the most challenging parts of the city and Gillbanks would be able to complete the job fairly quickly.

He was first approached on 11 December and he was set the task of going to Liverpool and proving Hanratty's alibi. His efforts though, despite all his experience, proved fruitless. He could find no one in the Bull Ring area who would have known Hanratty and the most he could achieve was casting doubt around Dinwoodie's recollection of the days when it was thought she had tried to help out Hanratty by giving directions to Carlton Road. Even this had resulted in her husband complaining about the defence team's behaviour. Having done as much as he could, he was withdrawn and not required to be at court when the trial started on 22 January.

Three days later, something extraordinary happened. In a private consultation, Hanratty told Kleinman that while it was true he had gone to Liverpool on 22 August, to find a man called Aspinall, and he had gone to the sweet shop in Scotland Road, he had not then stayed in Liverpool with three of his friends. He had made that up. In fact, what he had done was to catch a bus to Rhyl in North Wales, where he hoped to find a man called 'John'.

Having got to Rhyl he asked around, and he provided details of a café he had gone into to ask if anyone knew John; he knew he owned an old taxicab. At one point he had gone into a chemist as he was suffering from a toothache. He had stayed for two nights, 22 and 23 August, and had stayed in a boarding house that was terraced, had a B&B card in its window, and had no front garden. It was near a railway, had a hallstand with flowers and the woman who ran the place was about 50 years old, 'stoutish' and on her own. He had slept in an upstairs bedroom at the back of the property that had a sink and there was a green bath in the house. He paid 12s 6d for each night.

This brand new, detailed alibi was being presented to his legal team about the same time that Sherrard had been challenging Valerie in the witness box. For months, the defence had been preparing their case based on his visit to Liverpool and this was a wholesale change of direction and one that would need to convince the jury. So concerned was Sherrard that he made Hanratty sign a declaration stating that it was his decision alone to change direction.[1] Hanratty was adamant and Kleinman contacted Gillbanks again.

The following day, Gillbanks set off for Rhyl armed with a photograph of Hanratty plus all the information he had provided. For the next week or so he knocked on doors of boarding houses showing people the photograph and trying to get any sort of lead on what he had been told. He even went into the local police station to see if they could help.

In the meantime, the trial was moving on at a pace and by 2 February, when Acott was being cross-examined by Sherrard, Gillbanks had made no progress. On the Sunday, he and Kleinman visited Hanratty in Bedford prison in the hope that he could add more clarity but nothing was forthcoming. What was needed, they thought, was a better, current photograph of Hanratty to show the residents of Rhyl and with that in mind, Sherrard made an application to the judge at the first opportunity. On the Monday, during a convenient break in Acott giving his evidence, Sherrard asked the judge if it would be possible to take some photographs of the defendant as 'from the point of view of the defence enquiries in this case it becomes necessary to have available some photographs of this defendant'. Gorman was a little surprised but granted permission for them to be taken.

Now in possession of a fresh photograph, Gillbanks returned to Rhyl the next day for some more door-to-door enquiries, although given what Hanratty had described in the new alibi, he was reasonably confident that the house he was looking for was in Kinmel Street.

At eleven o'clock in the morning, Gillbanks knocked on the door of 19 Kimel Street and spoke to the landlady, Grace Jones, who was there with her daughter, Brenda Smith. Gillbanks felt that Jones did not look much like the description Hanratty had given, plus she was not 'on her own', but nevertheless, he showed them the photograph. Jones said that she 'felt like she recognised him'. He looked familiar but she couldn't be absolutely sure. She would later say that she said to Gillbanks, 'I am not sure whether I know him or not.' Gillbanks asked her whether the man could have stayed at her lodgings in the last week of August but again she could not be sure. Her lodging house, Ingledene, did have a hallstand with some flowers on it and she confirmed that the house had a green bath. Gillbanks thought that Jones seemed a genuine enough person but he was not convinced about her identification and continued to knock on more doors, finding nothing that could help.

The former Liverpool police officer reported what he had found out to Kleinman and very quickly an instruction came back: bring Grace Jones to court.

Sherrard's opening speech was powerful and incisive. Firstly, he appealed to the jury's sense of responsibility in arriving at the proper conclusion and how equally a similar responsibility rested on his shoulders to do the best he could for the defendant by ensuring he was properly acquitted. He told them that they must extinguish all prejudices they might have and dismiss the notion that the man in the dock is somehow the man of violence who committed the atrocious crimes in August of last year. There can be no doubt that everyone must harbour bad feeling towards Valerie Storie's assailant, he said, but the decision they had to make is whether Hanratty was that man. He then reminded them that the burden of proof rested with the prosecution and the prisoner had to prove nothing.

He turned his attention to the prosecution case, which they had listened to for the last twelve days, and dismissed it as a lost cause. They had assembled evidence that had not withstood scrutiny and he was particularly critical not only of Nudds and Langdale as credible witnesses but the prosecution's reliance upon them. Their case, he said, had two major weaknesses; identification by witnesses who were honest, but wrong, and Superintendent Acott's selectiveness in relying on evidence that suited him and ignoring that which did not. He had fallen far short of the care required when investigating the case and cited specifically the events at the Vienna hotel, the examination of the Liverpool alibi and the carelessness with which he had examined Hanratty's claims about burglaries he had committed in Stanmore. Hanratty did not fit the profile of the killer – and he detailed exactly where Hanratty differed in his background from that proffered by the assailant – and then made sure the jury had not forgotten the name Peter Alphon and the fact that Audrey Willis had been attacked in her home the day after the A6 attack and before the revolver had been recovered on the number 36 bus. It was a legitimate attempt to deflect the jury away from Hanratty and to keep Alphon always in the back of their minds.

Sherrard had given the briefest of overviews but had emphasised what he considered the inherent weaknesses of the prosecution case. Now he needed to turn his attention to what only the defence team knew: Hanratty was to introduce a new alibi, one that had had no opportunity of being investigated by the prosecution.

He told the jury that the defendant was not obliged to give evidence and could sit in the dock and make the prosecution prove its case. But they would hear from him and they would be able to make their own assessment of him. They would see his mannerisms, hear him talk and judge his truthfulness or otherwise. He would be frightened and for that they should make allowances.

He then refocused the minds of the jurors on some of the prosecution witnesses who had changed their stories, Nudds in particular, before turning his attention to the three men in Liverpool whom Hanratty had refused to name.

'There are no such men so far as this man is concerned,' he told them. 'The trip to Liverpool, the visit to Mrs Dinwoodie's shop, the telegram from Liverpool; all that is true, but the three men in Liverpool is a lie.'

The prosecution team must have been astonished. For four months Hanratty had maintained that he had stayed with the three criminals and for four months they had spent many hours trying to substantiate the claim, but now, at the last minute, his story was to change. Sherrard outlined the account provided by Hanratty of his visit to Rhyl, preferring not to go into too much detail as they would soon hear it from him. He made the point that the reason he had not said anything until this point was because he knew he was unable to provide any detail, unable to pinpoint the exact address where he had stayed and therefore unable to prove his new claim.

'What is happening now,' he told them, 'and what has been happening for some days past is that Rhyl is being combed for some trace of the boarding house. Whether they will remember a casual visit in August in the holiday season is very, very speculative. We must wait and see as this case goes on whether somebody comes forward.'

The next day, Hanratty took his place in the witness box. So far, the jury had heard only from the prosecution that he was the killer. Sherrard eased him through his introduction, the prisoner telling the jury that he was a convicted thief who had lived with his parents until July last year when he had left home. He had been committing break-ins throughout the summer and had adopted the name Jimmy Ryan as a means of attempting a change of identity and had dyed his hair to make him less obvious; he had natural auburn hair, he said. He admitted his friendship with Louise Anderson, the antique shop owner to whom he sold stolen jewellery, and the France family. While he did not accept the fine detail, he acknowledged that he had told Charles France that he hid his unwanted jewellery under the seats of buses, and since coming out of prison in March he had stayed with both of them on a number of occasions. Effectively, these people were his means of disposing of some of his stolen property.

He detailed his movements on the days leading up to the killing, saying that on Sunday, 20 August he had told the France family that he intended to go to Liverpool to sell the property he had stolen in a Stanmore break-in. He told the court that the name of the man he was hoping to find was called Aspinall, someone he had met in prison some years ago, and whom he thought lived in Carlton or Tarleton Road. This was the first time he had mentioned the name Tarleton and had presumably learned of it through his solicitor's dealings with Olive Dinwoodie.

On the Monday night he had stayed in the basement room of the Vienna hotel, had indeed occupied the single bed in the alcove of the room and left the hotel the following morning, after breakfast, around 9.30 a.m. He had had no conversation about the number 36 or 36A bus. He then walked to Paddington railway station to catch the train to Liverpool before realising his error and so took a taxi to Euston. It was some time before there was a train, so he bought a return ticket and some toothpaste and a toothbrush and then went for a cup of tea in the station buffet. There was a rough sleeper in the eating area and the woman behind the counter moved him on.

When he eventually boarded the train around midday, he shared a compartment with a gentleman who he was able to describe in some detail. The word 'gentleman' was a word frequently used by Hanratty and was a feature of the way he spoke. While it was true he had a cockney accent and his grammar and diction was poor, he always maintained an air of politeness about him. Acott had earlier commented that Hanratty was 'always polite and never swore'.

The man in the compartment was making notes on a pad with a binding ring that allowed him to flick the pages over. He was using a gold biro – he noticed that specifically, he boasted, as it was his line of business – and cuf-flinks that had the letters 'H E' initialled on them – he could see them because the man wore his cuffs short. He was right-handed but he wore his watch on his right wrist, which struck him as odd. He had a briefcase with him on the floor. He had a black barathea coat, was wearing a pair of trousers and jacket and had a pair of glasses that he overlaid with a second pair, presumably for reading. He noticed his black shoes were particularly shiny at the toe and his socks were black.

All this was more detail that had never been imparted to Acott, and Sherrard made a great theatrical display of hoping that someone would rec-ognise himself from the description and come forward to support his client's version of events.

He arrived at Liverpool around 4.30 p.m., had a wash and brush-up at the station and had a cup of tea in the station buffet before depositing his case in the left luggage office with a man whose hand was deformed in some way, though not withered, he emphasised. This was the first time anything had been mentioned about his having a wash and a cup of tea at the station.

Outside the station, he asked for directions to Carlton or Tarleton Place, or as he put it, 'I made for directions to Carlton Place,' a phrase the judge asked him to clarify. A woman suggested he catch a bus, which he did, but the con-ductor who had never heard of the address advised him to get off. He then told the story of going into a sweet shop and asking the lady behind the counter, who was with a little girl, for directions but she was unable to help. He even managed to remember some detail about railings designed to prevent children from running into the road that he had to walk around as they were too high to climb over.

He then walked back into town and had a cup of tea in Lyon's café in Lime Street before trying to sell a stolen watch to a man standing at the bottom of some stairs leading up to a billiard hall. He recalled this in detail. In an awk-ward style of speaking he said, 'I had some talkings to another gentleman who was standing on some stairs.'[2]

The watch was a gold Omega, inscribed 'To Tony with love from mum', he said, and he had stolen it from a house in Harrow. The man refused to buy it and he started to make his way up the stairs, or as he said, 'I was making grounds to go upstairs,' when the man called him back and told him not to go in as he didn't want stolen property being sold inside the premises.

Hanratty's story so far fitted with much of what he had told Acott during his interviews, although much more detail had come to the surface, seven points in fact, which could have been tested by Detective Chief Inspector Thomas Elliott when he had carried out his enquiries in Liverpool. But now Hanratty elaborated on his trip to Rhyl and Sherrard instructed him to tell the jury in a loud voice all the detail he could remember, no matter how unimportant it may seem to him. For the first time, the prosecution heard his new alibi.

He caught a bus there, he said. 'I went there on one purpose only. That was to interview a man called Terry Evans.'

He arrived when it was dark and having got there he asked five or six people for directions to a bed and breakfast. He eventually found one. The house had a B&B sign in the window and the woman who answered the door was middle-aged, about 50, average build, was wearing glasses and had greyish hair. There was a large coat rack with a mirror in the hallway and there was a green plant in a bowl. He had gone up a flight of stairs and had stayed in a room on the second floor at the back of the house. Once in his room he didn't draw the curtains as it was at the back and he could hear trains shunting. He said that he had seen a green bath in the top part of the property, which he presumed had been the attic. There had been no register to sign but he paid 25*s* for two nights' stay.

Sherrard now announced that he was hoping that someone would recognise themselves from this description and come forward. In fact, Grace Jones, the Rhyl landlady, was already being prepared to travel to Bedford.

Sherrard now asked Hanratty to expand on what he did once he had got to Rhyl, arriving, he said, just about the same time as Michael Gregsten and Valerie Storie were pulling into their cornfield over 200 miles away in Dorney Reach.

It was Terry Evans he had come to find, a man he had met in July when he had worked with him on the bumper cars at the fairground and who might be able to help him with his 'business'. This was not new to the police since Arthur Webber had come forward back in October having found Hanratty's national insurance card and had employed him for a few hours. Hanratty went on to say that he had stayed the night at Evans' house but only knew him as 'John' at the time – Gillbanks' enquiries in Rhyl had in the meantime identified 'John' as Terry Evans – but was aware he owned an old black taxi.

Hanratty said that having stayed the night in the bed and breakfast on the night of 22/23 August, he spent the next day trying to find Evans. He had no luck, stayed another night in the boarding house and returned the following day to Liverpool, still with his stolen jewellery unsold. He deposited his case in the left luggage office again, had a meal and then went to see the film *The Guns of Navarone*. Sherrard asked him to tell the jury of anything else he could remember about his activities in Liverpool that day and in a manner that really started to emphasise his poor diction, he said, 'Well, I have studied this very hardly and the most important factors of what I can remember was a boxing match.'

He was very interested in boxing, he told the court, but he had been unable to get tickets for the bout as it had sold out. Instead, he had gone to the Exchange, near Lime Street station, where he had seen a night porter dressed in a blue uniform with brass buttons and had sent the telegram to Dixie France before going to New Brighton for the evening. Later that night, he travelled back to London by train, arriving in London around five or six in the morning. On the journey, he had seen a lady with two young girls, aged about 12 to 15 years of age, who said they were going on holiday. The train stopped at Stafford, where two workmen got on board and during a conversation he had with them, they told him about the work they were doing and how one of them had got an upset stomach because of something he had eaten. This was information that he could have furnished to the police even when he had been maintaining his Liverpool alibi. He had not, but that did not stop Sherrard openly asking for the people on the train to come forward.

Having emphasised how being in Rhyl made it impossible for him to have committed the murder, Sherrard asked Hanratty to talk about events after his return to London but it was only a matter of time before he returned to the Rhyl issue. He knew there were some obvious questions that were going to be put to Hanratty when Swanwick began his cross-examination and he preempted them. He asked the man in the witness box why he had not told the police the truth about his visit to Rhyl and Hanratty said:

> I didn't tell Superintendent Acott, because at that point I didn't know the name of the street, the number of the house or even the name of the people living in the house. At that stage I knew that I was only wanted for interviewing, not for the actual A6 murder trial, which I eventually found out later, or the truth would have been told straight away. I know I made a terrible mistake by telling Superintendent Acott about these three men but I

have been advised that the truth only counts in this matter and what I have said here, every word of it, is the truth.[3]

I am a man with a prison record and I know in such a trial of this degree that it is very vital for a man once to change his evidence in such a serious trial, but I know inside of me somewhere, in Rhyl this house does exist, and by telling the truth these people will come to my assistance.[4]

Sherrard then asked if what he was saying about Rhyl was the truth then why, in the time between becoming aware that he was wanted for the murder and his arrest in Blackpool, a period of five days, did he not go to Rhyl to find the people who could support his story instead of staying in Liverpool?

Hanratty answered, 'Because when I went to Liverpool I didn't have the right bearings of Rhyl as I had only been there on two occasions. Though I did stay there two nights, I have some idea of the house I stayed in and some description.'

With Rhyl dealt with, Sherrard tidied up the loose ends. Hanratty admitted travelling to Ireland, buying his Sunbeam, a dalliance with a young woman called Mary Meaden, who had been introduced to him by Louise Anderson, and his trip to Bedford with Gladys Deacon. He admitted the burglaries in Stanmore and the stealing of the jacket that had apparently evaded the notice of the police.

Once he had learned that he was wanted by the police and had spoken to Acott on the telephone, he stole a Mk VII Jaguar from Portland Place in London and drove it to Oldham, where he abandoned it and caught the train to Liverpool. This had been one of the many enquiries from the defence to the prosecution ahead of the trial and the police were able to confirm the theft.

He acknowledged most of what Superintendent Acott had told the court was accurate, but he said some of the answers he had allegedly given were simply not true. He did not say that he suffered from blackouts, as Acott alleged, and told the court that at one stage Acott even suggested to him that he may be suffering from some sort of mental illness, clearly an attempt to get him to admit the killing while mentally affected. He also denied saying anything about Acott 'getting the cuffs on him'.

'I wasn't brought up to be cocky like that,' he said.

He denied using the word 'kip', but accepted that he had asked Acott about the size of the bullets found in the Vienna hotel, something that Sherrard had earlier suggested was never said by his client. Finally, he was adamant that Roy Langdale had never had any conversations with him in Brixton prison. There had been no confession made by him and in fact he did not exercise with him as he had claimed. Langdale's evidence, he said, was a total fabrication.

Hanratty had been in the witness box for most of the day and Sherrard had completed his examination.

Chapter Fourteen

Cross-Examination

Graham Swanwick had a host of questions for the man in the witness box and he would concentrate on the revelations from the day before. He would also probe Hanratty about all other aspects of the evidence against him that would test his memory and truthfulness, but he started on an unexpected note.

During the prosecution case, Sherrard had made great play of the two Identikit pictures prepared by Valerie Storie and Edward Blackhall and made the observation, as did the newspapers at the time, that in each one the right eyebrow of the suspect appeared raised and bushier than the one on the left. This was a significant feature of the published images and Sherrard had wanted to know which witness had made this observation. He had cross-examined Valerie, Blackhall, Skillett and Acott, none of whom knew. The Identikit pictures had been compiled in the days immediately following the attack and many weeks before Hanratty's name was known, but the source of the images remained a valid observation and it seems strange that the one person who perhaps could have answered the question, the man who had built the images, Detective Sergeant Mackle, was never called as a witness.

Swanwick opened his cross-examination of Hanratty: 'Hanratty, do you always hold your right eyebrow higher than your left?' which was met with an equally bizarre response.

'I don't know, Sir, because I can't see it.'

Swanwick said no more about it. It was true that Hanratty's right eyebrow did appear somewhat higher than his left, but no witness had ever mentioned it and it was not an issue to which the prosecution wished to bring undue attention. It was a subtle point to make to the jury.

He then moved to getting Hanratty to admit that he had sent the police on a wild goose chase around Liverpool trying to prove his false alibi and suggested that he had gone back to Liverpool himself in October in an attempt to either fake an alibi or buy one. Hanratty admitted his lies but said that his solicitor had now impressed upon him the importance of speaking the truth since his life was at stake.

'I had already told a lie,' he said, 'and I had started on one and I had to cover up and cover up and cover up until eventually I made things a lot worser for myself.'

He knew full well the importance of giving details of an alibi as soon as possible in order for the police to investigate the claim but Hanratty said that Sherrard had had the same amount of time as Swanwick to now investigate it. This was obviously not true as he had made his initial disclosure to his defence team thirteen days earlier, after which they despatched Gillbanks to Rhyl to start his enquiries. To prove the point, Swanwick asked Hanratty why it was that he had had his photograph taken outside the court two days earlier if it was not for the purpose of showing it around various boarding houses in Rhyl to see if they could find a witness who would say he had been there. Hanratty denied any knowledge of why the photograph had been taken and said, 'What Mr Sherrard does is of no concern of mine. He is my barrister and if he wishes to take a photograph he does so. I don't ask him.'

Probably recognising the weakness in what he had just told the court, he shifted to a position of accepting that he had some idea why it had been taken, although he left everything, he said, to his defence counsel.

Swanwick then turned his attention specifically to the Rhyl story and Hanratty told the court he had travelled there by bus from Liverpool, leaving, he thought, around 7.30 p.m. It had been a double-decker bus and he had paid for his ticket on board.

By the time he had found the boarding house, it was dark, but he had now remembered some more detail about the property that he had not said when he was being examined by his counsel. It had no front garden and a small courtyard out the back. Asked who else was staying there he said there had been no one, at least no one he saw. He could not remember any detail of the wallpaper in his room, the colour of the carpet or the name of the street where the property was. The lady who 'entered me into the house',[1] served him with breakfast the next morning, which he ate in a room that contained two tables. He didn't see anybody else, didn't sign the register, didn't give his name and he didn't get a receipt.

Hanratty stood by his story that he had travelled the 40-mile journey from Liverpool at the time Valerie and Michael were having a drink at the Station Inn at Taplow. He had given a description of the house he had stayed in and the lady who ran it, but he also knew that Grace Jones was on her way to court. He was confident. Swanwick wanted some independent corroboration of his story and he moved his questioning towards the following day, Wednesday, 23 August. This was important since the murderer had abandoned the stolen Morris in Ilford at 7 a.m. that morning and if Hanratty had been in Rhyl, then he could not be the killer.

Asked to describe what he did that day, Hanratty said that he had gone out to look for Evans, a man he thought he could do 'business' with. He had met him a few weeks earlier when he had gone to Rhyl for the first time after he had stolen a car with a friend of his and abandoned it after a bit of a police chase. He had then hitched a lift in a lorry from Cardiff and ended up in Rhyl. He had then gone to the front to look for work and stumbled across Evans, who worked on the dodgems. He only knew him as John but also knew about the old black taxi he had, a 1935/36 model, he thought, and he set off on his search for him.

He left the boarding house around 9.30 a.m. after having eaten his breakfast but didn't head for the fairground, the obvious place to start looking. He had 'left a man short' there once, he said, and didn't want a confrontation. This man was clearly Arthur Webber, who had employed him on 25 July, with Hanratty walking off after just one shift. Instead, he went to Dixie's café in the town about 200 yards from the fairground, and had a meal. There was no sign of Evans, but he didn't leave any message for him and went and 'messed about a bit', playing on the pintables. He also had a shave in a barber's saloon in the town centre. He didn't know the address but it had three or four barbers, with chairs and sinks.

He finished by saying that he eventually went to the fairground in the evening, failed to find Evans and had gone back to Dixie's for a cup of tea and then returned to the boarding house. In effect, Hanratty said he had spent the day doing virtually nothing and did not meet anyone he could name to verify his movements.

Swanwick handed Hanratty a street map of Rhyl and together they studied it and identified various locations; the railway line, the river, the street where Dixie's café was located and the fairground. Having eliminated various parts of the town, including areas where houses did not fit the description of the boarding house, Swanwick pointed out how easy it would have been to have instructed either the police or his solicitor on where to look for the guest house. It was not a big town and by his own admission the boarding house was no more than half a mile from the fairground and Hanratty said he had been able to find it easily enough when walking back from Dixie's. Asked how he had done that, he said, 'When I had come out in the morning, when I come out …'

He then paused and said, 'Let me put it this way. I know what you are going to get at. You're going to say, "You could remember it then but you can't remember it now."'

Swanwick pushed him for an answer.

'I found my way back to the boarding house as I normally would, just my own direction, and I went to the boarding house.'

Swanwick observed that if he was struggling now to tell the court how to find the street, it would have been much simpler back in October when he was arrested, when the events would have been fresher, not only in his mind, but in the minds of the barber, the café staff and the bus driver.

Hanratty had earlier said that he had stayed in Evans' house in July and Swanwick now suggested to him that his description of the mysterious boarding house was in fact nothing more than a description of Evans' house transposed onto a fictional property that now suited his purpose. The description of the landlady was similarly a description of Evans' mother, who indeed bore a closer resemblance to Hanratty's description than did Jones.[2] Hanratty denied the suggestions.

Hanratty had, of course, finished his Rhyl alibi story by recounting how he had bought another single ticket for his bus journey back to Liverpool the following day, deposited his luggage at Lime Street station and sent the telegram to Dixie France in the evening before leaving on a midnight train to Euston. He recalled in some detail the men who had boarded at Stafford and the woman and her family going on holiday, all people who would be able to verify his story if they had been found. After his revelations in the witness box the day before, the newspapers had publicised their descriptions, something the defence had hoped would happen. Asked why the information about these people had not been publicised much earlier, Hanratty adopted his earlier stance and said, 'Well, that is entirely up to my counsel. That is not up to me. I am here to answer questions. I cannot speak for Mr Sherrard.'

Swanwick had an alternative answer and that was because the entire story about the people he had seen on the train was a complete invention. He suggested it was incredible that Hanratty had recalled so much detail about people he had met only once, even down to the detail of initials on cuff links and on which wrist a watch was being worn, yet his recall about the most important part, the boarding house in Rhyl, was somewhat lacking. Hanratty denied he was inventing anything.

There was an interesting link between Hanratty's alleged activities in Rhyl and Dixie France, his criminal friend in London. It was France to whom Hanratty had sent a telegram from Liverpool on 24 August just before he claimed to have travelled south, and it was disputed between them whether he arrived on the Friday or Saturday morning. It was, in the scheme of things, a small, almost unimportant point, but it laid the ground for suggesting that the France family were prone to getting their dates mixed up. Hanratty disagreed about the date that he had had the conversation with Dixie about hiding jewellery under the seats of buses and the date he had had his hair dyed by Carol. They were, according to Hanratty at least, to that extent unreliable.

Swanwick shifted the emphasis to Liverpool and the whole episode of how and when he got there and what he did and who he spoke to once he had arrived.

Peter Stringer, the man with the artificial arm at Lime Street station, had already given evidence and other than demonstrating that he could not have been the person Hanratty claimed to have seen, it did show that at least he had some problem with his arm, as suggested by Hanratty. He now claimed that he had never mentioned the word 'arm' – his solicitor must have written it down incorrectly – but instead he had said 'hand'. Quite simply, Hanratty implied, the police had found the wrong man.

Swanwick suggested that the man outside the billiard hall was also a fabrication. Hanratty had described in detail the Omega watch he had been trying to sell, including its inscription, and which he claimed to have stolen from a burglary in Harrow, yet there was no record of one being stolen. The prosecution was not on a steady footing here given their poor track record in finding the burglary where the jacket had gone missing but nevertheless, Swanwick pressed home his point. He suggested to Hanratty that he had again transposed the story from someone else who had tried to sell the watch. It was not him, suggested Swanwick, but Hanratty stood his ground.

The whole purpose, according to Hanratty, of going to Liverpool on 22 August was to sell a stolen diamond ring worth £350 to a man named Aspinall, someone he had met in prison four or five years ago and with no idea about where he lived. He had made great effort to make the 200-mile journey with the intention of 'doing some business'. Yet, not once did he ask a policeman for directions, nor a postman, nor a taxi driver, something that would have been reasonable to have done given the great distance and time involved in getting there.

It was all just a big lie, said Swanwick. He suggested that Hanratty had laid low for a while after the shooting and once he had discovered that Valerie

Storie was still alive, he dumped the gun on a bus and made his way to Liverpool in a desperate attempt to build an alibi. The alleged visit to the sweet shop and the sending of the telegram were all part of that poorly thought through lie. If he had ever been to Dinwoodie's sweet shop in Scotland Road, it had been on the Monday, not the Tuesday. Swanwick was suggesting that Hanratty had simply shifted events from the Monday to the following day. He continued. There was a train, he said, which left Liverpool at 5.15 that day and he could easily have been back in London by 9.15 with plenty of time for booking into the Vienna hotel.

Hanratty reacted to the suggestion and said, 'How about Mrs France? I didn't leave them until seven o'clock. I thought you had more intelligence, Sir.'

Quite apart from receiving a rebuke from the judge about his impoliteness, Hanratty's argument that he was in the company of the France family during the day and evening of the Monday showed that he had seemingly forgotten that he had earlier implied that the family could not be relied upon when it came to dates and times.

To conclude his cross-examination, Swanwick summarised his theory about what Hanratty had actually done. He left the Vienna hotel on that Tuesday morning, armed with his gun, intent on carrying out some sort of stick-up. He had indeed gone to Paddington railway station, where he deposited his case, and then caught the train for Maidenhead and Slough. Once there he scoured the area looking for places to break into or someone to hold up and by chance he had stumbled across the unfortunate couple in their Morris. He wanted the woman. In fact, his predominant motive was now sex, not theft, but Gregsten stood in his way. After an aborted attempt to bundle him into the boot, to give himself time to think he forced them to drive for hours while he considered his options.

'If I wanted a woman,' Hanratty boasted, 'I could have gone in the West End and had a woman for a fortnight.'

Swanwick continued. After he had shot them both, he stole the car, abandoned it in Ilford and then hid up for twenty-four hours before realising that Valerie Storie had survived. He panicked, dumped the gun on a bus and raced off to Liverpool to buy himself an alibi.

Hanratty responded, 'If I wanted to pretend I had been in Liverpool, I would have done it in a much better way than that. That is only on formality. I would have done something outstanding.'

Swanwick continued. Having realised that the three men in Liverpool could not be proved, because it was a lie, Hanratty had switched his alibi at the last minute to Rhyl, which was just another made-up story. Hanratty replied that the reason he decided to speak of the Rhyl story was because of all the 'disgusting evidence' that had been given in court by the prosecution and the real truth needed to be told. He was presumably referring to Bob Acott, Roy Langdale and William Nudds. If that was the case, his argument was flawed. Hanratty had briefed his counsel on 24 January about Rhyl, days before any of the witnesses had even stepped into the witness box.

Chapter Fifteen

Defence Witnesses

Hanratty had now given his version of the truth and Sherrard's job now was to introduce evidence that would support his claims.

Clearly, Hanratty's alleged trip to Liverpool on 22 August was a critical factor. The police had taken a statement from Olive Dinwoodie, the sweet shop assistant, who had said that the man she had seen in the photographs shown to her resembled Hanratty and the day on which it had happened was Monday, 21 August. She had been able to verify that by her granddaughter being present at the time and a lorry driver called Albert Harding visiting her in the evening when she relayed the conversation about the man asking for directions. She had been able to exclude the event happening on the Tuesday because she had been accompanied that day by the shop owner's brother, who had not been there when the man visited; nor had she seen Harding on the Tuesday. Therefore, she concluded, the only day it could have happened would have been the Monday and even then, the photograph merely resembled Hanratty. Dinwoodie was therefore not called as a prosecution witness, but Sherrard chose to make her give her evidence. The purpose of putting Dinwoodie before the jury was to cast doubt on her ability to recall the correct day.

She repeated what she had told the police, only moving the time of the visit from 3.30 p.m. to somewhere between 4.15 and 4.30 p.m., and she identified Hanratty in the dock as the man who resembled the photograph she had seen. Sherrard merely tried to show that she was probably making a mistake about her dates, principally because she was fixing them based on her granddaughter's presence, but Dinwoodie stood firm. She was not making any mistake. It seemed the attempt to cast doubt on the accuracy of her memory had failed.

Sherrard then introduced Robert Kempt into the witness box, a billiard hall manager from Lime Street. He told the jury that at some time between June and September of last year he was standing on the steps outside his billiard hall when a man, in his mid-twenties, around 5ft 6in tall, tried to sell him a watch. He had refused and told him not to go into his club to try to sell it. He was asked by Sherrard if he could identify the prisoner in the dock but he was unable to do so, saying he saw hundreds of people every day. Kempt was not the most helpful of witnesses but it did lend weight to Hanratty's claim that he had tried to sell a stolen watch, albeit only at some time during the summer.

The next witness was Terry Evans, the man with whom Hanratty had stayed when he first went to Rhyl in July and who, he now claimed, was the purpose of his trip in August. The police had first spoken to him before Christmas and had revisited him again recently, since the Rhyl alibi became known, to explore whether his house bore any resemblance to that being described by Hanratty.

He was a 28-year-old petty thief, well known in Rhyl, and Sherrard got him to explain how he had worked on the dodgems and how he had helped Hanratty out with a bed for the night on 25 July. The following day he had dropped him off at work but had not seen him since. He told the court that he had owned a taxi and while he knew Dixie's café in Sydenham Avenue, in August he had been working just around the corner at the Caravan Café. In cross-examination, he agreed that had anyone been looking for him in August, as Hanratty was claiming, it would have been easy to have found him. He was well known, distinctive by a tattoo of a star in the middle of his forehead, and the staff in Dixie's would probably have known he was only a few hundred yards away in the Caravan Café. Swanwick asked him about his convictions, which amounted to petty larceny and some driving offences, and asked him whether there was any reason why Hanratty would want to search him out as a person who would be interested in buying a £350 diamond ring. His reply was that there was no reason why Hanratty would think that. Asked to describe his house in Gwynfryn Avenue, he said he had a green plant in a stand and a coat rack in the hall, and you could just about hear the sound of trains shunting. His bath was white, though boxed in by a duck blue/green surround. His mother, who regularly went to the house was 50, about 5ft 3in and 'fatty'.

It was odd that the prosecution had not called Evans as a witness as he was able to confirm that he could easily have been found in Rhyl in August and it was unlikely that Hanratty would perceive him as a 'fence'; it cast doubt on the credibility of the alibi.

If there was ever anyone more important as a defence witness than Hanratty himself, it was Grace Jones, the landlady who had been traced only three days earlier by Gillbanks and who may have been able to identify the prisoner as the man who had stayed at her guest house in August. If she could do that to the satisfaction of the jury, it was inevitable he would be acquitted.

When she had arrived at court, she was seen by two local officers from Flintshire Constabulary, who quickly realised she was there to give evidence for the defence.[1] As a result, a call was made, and police officers visited her address. They spoke to her daughter Brenda, who handed over the hotel register, and they photographed the inside of the property.[2] It was all quickly despatched to Bedford.

Jones began by confirming she lived at the property with her husband, a 30-year-old daughter and 15-year-old son. She described her boarding house, including the fact, like Hanratty had said, that she had a green bath in the attic. Some of the other detail provided by Hanratty matched her property, though much did not.

She told the court that she had been shown the photograph of Hanratty that had been taken in court a couple of weeks ago, pointed to him and said, 'Well, I feel as if I have seen him at our house.'

It was between the dates of 19 and 26 August, she said.

When it was Swanwick's turn to re-examine her, he asked for an adjournment over lunch given the nature of the story that was now being presented to the court; he needed time to explore it. Gorman agreed and instructed Jones, as was the normal procedure with any witness, not to speak to anyone about the case.

When lunch was over, one of the jury members told the judge that some of them had seen Jones in conversation with Terry Evans, the witness immediately before her, and felt they ought to report it. Jones was ordered back into the witness box and explained that she had merely asked him about where to go for lunch. Evans was now recalled and when he was asked about it, he said rather more. He told Gorman that he had asked Jones about whether she had recognised Hanratty in court and she had replied, 'I think so.'[3]

This was a serious breach of court rules. Fundamental to British justice is that a witness should only give evidence that they know of themselves and should therefore not speak to any other witness who might influence them. Despite being warned by the judge, she had done so and was again recalled. This time she admitted discussing the appearance of Hanratty and Evans had asked her whether she knew him. Her reply had been, 'I am almost sure of him.'

A map of Rhyl was handed to her and she explained where her boarding house was in relation to other landmark locations. It was just off the High Street, close to the bus and railway station, near the Odeon cinema, close to a betting shop and opposite the Windsor Hotel. Kinmel Street was, she agreed, as easy as any place to find in Rhyl, reinforcing the point that if Hanratty had wanted to tell the police or his solicitor where the boarding house was, it would have been simple.

As soon as it had become known that Ingledene was to feature in the trial, the police had visited and seized any books that may have helped with tying down dates of visitors to the property. Jones had not brought any with her and Swanwick produced one for her to examine. There followed a series of exchanges between the two of them about whether this was the book that recorded details of guests or whether it was the one that visitors were invited to sign. She was unsure, she said, before saying that the visitor book from last year had been thrown away. The one produced by Swanwick did include details of guests but the pages were falling out as they were not fastened and they had become mixed up and out of date order.

One thing that seemed to be established was that, importantly, for that particular week there had been one vacant room in the property, which was a single room and that was the one, she said, that Hanratty must have stayed in. She added that it must have been a Tuesday, though when asked how she knew that, she could not give an explanation. The point she made was that there was a vacant room, number 4, though this room was at the front of the property, whereas Hanratty claimed he had stayed in a rear bedroom.

The police had examined the boarding house records, poor though they were, and had traced three of the residents who had stayed there that week. One was Joseph Sayle, a union man who had been in Rhyl on business and had stayed at the property in room 4 from 21 to 24 August – he had the receipt to prove it. Hanratty could not have stayed in room 4. Another witness, Thomas Williams, who had stayed at the property more than once, said that he had been there all that week and saw no one of Hanratty's description. In fact, this combination of witnesses showed that there were only two rooms not used by guests, including the one with the green bath, and these needed to be available for Grace Jones and her family. Further, the former residents made it clear that breakfast time had been busy that week and it emerged that the dining room had five tables, all of which were occupied by the guests including a number of young children. Hanratty had said that the dining room he ate in had only two tables and he had seen no one. It seemed Hanratty could not have stayed in Ingledene that week.

Before court rose for the weekend, Swanwick questioned Jones once more on her identification of Hanratty – she said she couldn't honestly recognise him now because he had different-coloured hair. It was true that his hair colour was different from what it had been back in August and the comment seemed relatively unimportant.

When court resumed on the Monday, Terry Evans was asking to return to the witness box. He had been worried all weekend because he knew that he had not told the complete truth. He now told the jury that after he had had the conversation with Grace Jones in court the previous week, after she had said that 'she was almost sure' she recognised Hanratty, he had said, 'Well, I suppose the reason you might not have recognised him straight away was the colour of his hair.'

This explained her comments in the witness box before the weekend and demonstrated that what Jones had said about Hanratty's appearance was not her own account but had been the outcome of her conversation with Evans. When she was recalled on the Monday morning, Swanwick now produced a second book seized from her bed and breakfast establishment. This time, it showed that the boarding house had two extra bedrooms not disclosed by Jones for which she could give no reason. This new book contained details of all guests and she spent a great deal of time trying to decipher the handwriting. In short, she was unable to say which room was which, who had stayed in which one, whether they were singles, doubles, large or small. She seemed to have little knowledge of the property and repeatedly contradicted herself. With the spare room 4 now accounted for by Joseph Sayle, Swanwick demonstrated that on the weeks after the murder, there were numerous vacant rooms and any one of them could have been occupied by Hanratty, if indeed he had stayed there at all.

Jones, upon whom the defence were relying so heavily, had shown herself to be an unreliable witness who had been willing to speak to another witness and was wholly incompetent at managing the records at Ingledene. When the police had visited her boarding house during the trial to inspect her books, they had taken a statement from her daughter, who said that neither her nor her mother were sure at all about Hanratty being there.[4] This had become clear. Whereas her starting position had been that someone who looked like Hanratty had stayed in a single room on Tuesday, 22 August, her evidence at the end was that someone who may have been Hanratty may have stayed, at some time, in the summer of 1961.

Sherrard now started to conclude his defence case by introducing a number of witnesses who could either say something positive about Hanratty's character, deflect the attention away from him or simply challenge the integrity of some of the prosecution witnesses.

Mary Meaden had been the young woman who had been introduced to Hanratty by Louise Anderson and she told the court that in the very short time she had known him, a week or two, he had never behaved improperly or violently towards her. They had kissed only once.

Meike Dalal, the Swedish woman who had been attacked in East Sheen, gave evidence that her attacker had tried to sexually assault her and had claimed to be the A6 killer. In a subsequent identification parade she told the court that she had identified Peter Alphon, albeit this was not strictly true, and he had since been proved innocent of the allegation. Similarly, Audrey Willis told the court that she too had been assaulted by a gunman at her house in Old Knebworth the day after the A6 incident and gave a description of man with dark brown, smoothed-back hair. Neither of them identified Hanratty in the dock as the man responsible and the implication was clearly that these two unsolved crimes were committed by Peter Alphon. If he had committed these offences, surely, Sherrard suggested, it was not inconceivable that he had been the man responsible for the murder of Michael Gregsten and the attack upon Valerie Storie.

Two convicted prisoners were produced, David Emery and Nicolai Blythe, who stated that it had been Emery that had walked the exercise yard with Hanratty at Brixton prison as a matter of routine and Roy Langdale, the man to whom Hanratty had allegedly made his confession, was a liar.

And finally, Sherrard examined a witness, who had been found only the day before, relating to the abandoning of the stolen Morris in Ilford on that Wednesday morning. His name was Matthew Hogan, Paddy as he was known, and he told the jury that it had been he who James Trower had been collecting that morning when he said he heard a Morris crashing down through the gears. Hogan said that he too had seen the car, but it happened twenty minutes before Trower had even arrived that morning. In short, Hogan was saying that Trower was either mistaken or lying. However, when cross-examined, he said that the Morris he had seen was either cream or fawn in colour and not grey like Gregsten's. When Swanwick asked him why he had not come forward before now, he said he didn't want to get involved and decided to 'keep his mouth closed'. Questioned further, despite the fact that he knew the abandoned Morris was involved in the A6 murder, he had read about it in the newspapers and had even been with Trower when he was first spoken to by the police, he had said nothing. He had, he thought, seen the murder car, yet had told no one; importantly, not even the police or his friend, Trower. He did nothing to affect Trower's evidence and had clearly not seen the stolen Morris. Like Jones before him, had been shown to be an unreliable witness.

When Hogan left the witness box, the case for the defence closed. No more could be said. Nothing could be added. Apart from the summing up of their arguments, Swanwick and Sherrard had done their jobs and it would then be in the hands of the jury.

Chapter Sixteen

The Jury's Deliberation

With the evidence concluded, both sides summed up their cases to the jury. Sherrard spoke first and, as he told them, it was a difficult task since not only did he have to get all the important points across insofar as Hanratty was concerned but he had to anticipate what the prosecution would say after him.

His opening message was that this crime was committed by a local maniac probably sleeping rough in a field. The description of the gunman could fit any one of a number of people and in any event the killer's supposed profile did not match Hanratty; certainly, he could not be described as a sex maniac. He specifically referred to Hanratty's blood group of 'O' secretor and reminded the jury that more than 30 per cent of the population had that group and it added no weight whatsoever to the prosecution case.

Identification was the major factor and this was something that was so weak, so precarious, that the jury ought to ignore everything to do with it. Given Valerie's dreadful circumstances and the momentary glimpse she had had of her attacker, plus her earlier wrong identification, it made her wholly unreliable. So too, he continued, should the jury dismiss the witnesses who saw the Morris being driven that Wednesday morning. They were simply wrong.

Liverpool had featured highly throughout the trial and Hanratty's account hinged around the evidence of Olive Dinwoodie. Sherrard argued that the prosecution had done nothing to rebut anything Hanratty had said he had done on 22 August when he had travelled there by train. Dinwoodie had said that Hanratty had been in Liverpool the day before when there was ample evidence to show that he had been in London that day. She was clearly wrong and on the basis that she had said that the conversation she had with the man must have been either the Monday or the Tuesday, it must have been the latter; even the billiard hall manager tended to support his story, he suggested.

In relation to Rhyl, Sherrard told the jury that a false alibi is not in itself an indication of guilt. They needed to assess Hanratty's reasons for choosing this path. Even so, and despite her terrible ordeal in the witness box, the 'miracle witness', Grace Jones, had merely said what she remembered. It amounted to little, given her terrible memory, but there she was, a woman fitting the description given by Hanratty, in a boarding house, again matching the description in a town where Hanratty was known to have visited the month before. No one could say which room was occupied at which time and there existed the possibility therefore that Hanratty was simply speaking the truth. Her evidence could not and should not be ignored.

Then there was the whole question of Peter Alphon. He could not be ignored either and given the evidence of the two unfortunate women who were attacked in their homes – could the jury be sure that he might well be responsible for the A6 crime, which was similar in so many ways? Specifically referring to the criteria by which Acott had eliminated him, he said the police investigation of Alphon was rather less than satisfactory.

Sherrard questioned a prosecution case that relied on identification from highly unreliable witnesses such as Nudds and Langdale. This was such an important point since Nudds had implicated Hanratty in the possession of the gun at the Vienna hotel and Langdale's evidence amounted to what was almost a complete confession. They were scheming career criminals who would say anything to get attention and their evidence must be ignored.

Drawing to the end of his address to the jury, Sherrard devoted much time to his criticism of Bob Acott. He had broken the rules, had presented selective evidence and behaved unprofessionally throughout. He systematically attacked him over the contents of the interviews, his conduct surrounding the identification parades and his investigations into Hanratty's pleadings of innocence, notably the inability to find break-ins admitted by him. His evidence gathering in both Rhyl and Liverpool had been selective, relying only on what suited him. He was the central plank of the prosecution case and serious questions had to be asked about his integrity and credibility. The whole case was based on either unreliable or circumstantial evidence, and given that, it was the duty of the jury to acquit the defendant.

In summarising the prosecution case, Swanwick needed to present all the key evidence as well as dealing with those matters raised by defence counsel and, specifically, the alibi.

He started by dealing with what he called the four red herrings. Firstly, this crime was not committed by a local maniac sleeping rough in a field somewhere; the gunman had no local knowledge, as demonstrated by his continual questioning about road layouts and directions, and it was clear that he knew the London area well. Secondly, there was absolutely no evidence that Peter Alphon was involved and he had been eliminated from the investigation almost as soon as his name first appeared. Thirdly and fourthly, the attacks on Dalal and Willis in their homes were committed by someone of a completely different description and there was no connection between them and the attacks on Gregsten and Storie. The red herrings dismissed, he then turned to the evidence.

Picking up on the blood group of Hanratty, it was true that a third of the population had the same group and that alone showed very little other than he could not be eliminated. But then consider, he said, of that 30 per cent, how many of them were of the right height, the right age, had blue eyes and brown hair, spoke with a cockney accent, used the word 'kip', were careful about their appearance, were boastful, a bad driver, had spoken about getting a gun, had a near-matching criminal record, had stayed in a hotel room where cartridges from the murder weapon were found and knew both the Harrow area and the way to Bedford? On top of that, three people, from three different locations had identified the defendant on identification parades.

He dealt with the attack upon Acott's character and credibility. Hanratty had shown himself to be a liar on many occasions and all his allegations about Acott fabricating the contents of the telephone calls and interview were unfounded. He certainly did not break the rules as was suggested and there was much evidence that he was trying to be as fair to Hanratty as possible. He had pointed out to him that he had been given numerous opportunities to prove his innocence but had not taken them. At one point, it should be remembered, Sherrard even had to apologise for making a false suggestion when examining Acott in the witness box. It was a matter for the jury whether they believed the officer or the defendant.

He acknowledged the dangers of relying on the likes of Nudds and Langdale but insofar as the Vienna hotel was concerned the documents showed that Alphon had not occupied room 24 and the only person who had been in it between the night before the murder and the day the gun was found was Hanratty. And how odd was it that Nudds had spoken to Hanratty about the number 36 bus just a matter of weeks after Hanratty had spoken to his friend Dixie France about the convenience of hiding stolen property under the seats of buses? As for Langdale, the jury could dismiss the notion that he was motivated by money to give false evidence. Yes, he received payment from a newspaper but that was in January, just before the trial, whereas he had made his statement to the police the previous November. His motivation was speaking the truth about a murderer.

He then turned to the first of the two most important elements. He would deal with the alibis later but for now he needed to deal with the thorny issue of identification evidence. Acknowledging Valerie's fleeting glimpse of her attacker's face, though she had heard his voice for five hours, and that she had picked out a wrong man on an earlier parade, he reminded the jury that she had taken eleven minutes to pick out the prisoner, not twenty minutes as Sherrard had erroneously claimed. In fact, she had made up her mind after just five minutes that she knew who her attacker was but she had decided she wanted to hear them speak first, which they did, twice. Take out the logistics of having to wheel her in a bed up and down a line of men on a number of occasions, and her identification had been relatively swift, and positive.

As for Skillett and Trower, they were unequivocal in their identification and Trower's evidence had not been shaken with the sudden production of Paddy Hogan claiming he had got it wrong. Identification evidence being as it was, less than ideal, these three witnesses had been as good and reliable as any.

Swanwick spoke briefly about the notion of an alibi. A true alibi is one that demonstrates unequivocally by independent evidence, be it human, by documents or by something else, that the accused person could not possibly have committed the crime. Ideally, it is provided in good time so that it may be investigated thoroughly and proven beyond all doubt. The hallmark of a false one is one that is provided at the last moment with little or no time to investigate its veracity. The ideal false alibi is based on real events, with real people and real places but at another time; the events did happen but not when the accused says they did. This case, he said, had all the classic hallmarks of a false alibi. It was correct that the defence need not say anything, but on this occasion they had and despite Hanratty's claim that the prosecution and defence had the same amount of time to investigate it, this was not the case; the defence had a head start of thirteen days.

Swanwick suggested that once Hanratty had realised that Valerie Store was still alive he knew he needed a false alibi to save him from the hangman's noose. He had gone to Liverpool on 24 August, which would have been the first day the newspapers were reporting the incident, and again on 7 October, to create one.

One of the most important points to note, which Swanwick took time to emphasise, was that Hanratty knew that the story about the three men in Liverpool was not true. They had never existed. Yet, he now claimed he was in Rhyl. The jury would need to consider why, if the new alibi was true, did he not mention it straight away and, more importantly, why did he not try to find people who could prove it for him? Additionally, if the Rhyl story was true, why bother manufacturing a false one in the first place?

Swanwick reminded the jury that Hanratty had told the France family that he was going to Liverpool on the Monday, but he did not go. The reason for that was because, he now suggested, he acquired the gun that night, just as he had described it to Langdale, and had gone to the Vienna hotel to play with his new acquisition, hence the discarded cartridges. After having committed the murder, now looking for an alibi, he had gone to Liverpool and was suggesting that he had tried to sell a stolen watch to a man outside a billiard hall. There were two problems with this – Kempt said he recalled the incident, but not the day it happened and Hanratty, despite giving the perfect description of the inscribed Omega watch, had claimed it had been stolen in a burglary, of which there was no trace.

As for the sweet shop incident, even if it did happen on the Tuesday, which it did not, his train did not arrive in Liverpool until 4.45 p.m. and by the time he had washed, eaten and travelled there he could not have been in Dinwoodie's shop until well after she said the incident took place. This was probably another piece of information he had gleaned and again used it for himself. One issue in particular that suggested he had bought or borrowed this information was that his account of who he spoke to and what was said varied significantly from what Dinwoodie said. It was as if the message had got lost in translation and he asked the jury to imagine they were playing the parlour game where one person whispered something in somebody's ear, they then repeated it to the person next to them, and so on. What eventually came out the other end was different to that which had been put in at the beginning. This is what probably happened to Hanratty. He had been told of the incident but the conversation and the actors in the scene had become altered. There was no evidence, Swanwick told the jury, that Hanratty was in Liverpool on the Tuesday and at best there was someone who looked like him who had been in the shop or he was simply telling a true story that had happened on another day.

Focusing next on Rhyl, he made the obvious point that despite Hanratty having a remarkable eye for detail, remembering how he had broken into a house and exactly what he had stolen and the man with the cufflinks and the biro on the train, he was very vague about the location of the boarding house, despite it being so very easy to find. The discredited Grace Jones had admitted that herself, and yet he had told no one. It had not been possible for him to have stayed at Ingledene on 22 and 23 August because there was no room and he made no mention of how busy it had been there that week. Jones herself was unreliable and dishonest, and her bookkeeping, which the defence had not tried to introduce, did nothing to support the alibi – if anything, it disproved it. Despite not recognising the other residents, Sayle and a Mr Such, who had stayed there for three and four nights respectively, she had managed to remember Hanratty, who had stayed there, allegedly, for only two.

Swanwick finished his address with the following words:

> Where does all this lead? To where does the evidence point? In my submission, it leads and points inevitably and inexorably to one conclusion and one conclusion only; the guilt of the accused.

Mr Justice Gorman's summing up lasted ten hours spread over three days, during which he emphasised to the jury the need to look at the case coolly and objectively and with no hint of emotion. He described Valerie as giving her 'agonised evidence' but said, 'Let us forget the sorry picture, the tragic picture of a woman whose life is blasted.'

Before retiring, the jury members asked if they could have a copy of the court transcript, which would have amounted to nearly 1,300 pages of evidence, but their request was refused. It was 11.22 a.m. on Saturday, 17 February when they eventually went to their jury room, twenty-one days after the proceedings had begun and which, after over 100 witnesses, had become the longest criminal trial in UK history.

The atmosphere in the courthouse was tense with more than eighty police, counsel and newspaper reporters pacing the entrance hall on what was described as 'a snow of cigarette ends mounting under their feet'.[1] The Hanratty family were gathered together awaiting the outcome of their son's fate, while outside hundreds of people were loitering and would remain there until the verdict was delivered. Hanratty himself sat in his cell below the court, while Janet Gregsten waited on the end of a telephone.

Just over six hours later, the message leaked out that the jury were returning but the tension disappeared when it was realised they wanted to ask the judge a question. They wanted more guidance on what amounted to reasonable doubt and the value of circumstantial evidence. Gorman pointed out that he had never used the phrase 'reasonable doubt' as it often led to confusion. They must be satisfied so that they were *sure* of the defendant's guilt before they could convict, he told them. As for circumstantial evidence, it was evidence that pointed inevitably to one conclusion and they must consider it all to see if they are satisfied it does lead to that conclusion, in this case the defendant's guilt.

They were sent back to the jury room but an hour and a half later they were back with another question. The judge read it out. 'Is it possible for us to have some tea, please?'

Hanratty was returned to his cell once more.

By 9.10 p.m., though, they had reached a decision. When the foreman was asked for the jury's verdict, he replied, 'Guilty', and it was a verdict upon which all eleven were agreed.

After a guilty verdict is returned on a charge for which the court has only one sentence available, there is no further part for prosecution or defence counsel to play. There is no place for arguments about the judge considering a reduced sentence nor any purpose in putting forward any mitigating factors that may affect the sentence. There was only one more formality to carry out.

As was customary, Hanratty was asked by the judge whether there was anything he wanted to say regarding why sentence of death should not be passed. White-faced and choking, he found it difficult to talk. He snapped his fingers, and after a long pause, said, 'I am not innocent.'

Some observers would comment that they half-expected to hear some sort of belated confession but it seemed his nerves had got the better of him. He continued: 'I am innocent my Lord, and I will appeal. That is all I have to say at this stage.'

Mr Justice Gorman donned his black cloth and said, 'James Hanratty, the sentence of the court is that you suffer death in the manner authorised by law, and may God have mercy on your soul.'

It was over in an instant. On hearing the verdict, Hanratty's mother collapsed and fourteen minutes later the convicted prisoner was being driven to the condemned man's cell at Bedford prison.

In a hospital 40 miles away, the television was broadcasting the evening news bulletin in Valerie's ward. She stared at its screen; no one else seemed much interested. Most patients were reading or resting; some were already asleep. In the silence she listened to every word the newscaster had to say. In what had been the longest criminal trial in British history, she said, Hanratty had been found guilty and would be hanged. In Valerie's own words, she recalled, 'I listened intently, briefly closed my eyes and said quietly to myself, "Thank God it's all over."'[2]

★★★

James Hanratty did appeal against his conviction and on 12 March 1962 he appeared at the Court of Criminal Appeal in London with his parents and brother, Michael, sitting in the public seats. Michael Sherrard addressed the three judges, claiming that, among other things, the trial judge had not given sufficient detail in his summing up to the jury. Lord Parker did not agree:

> No one who had read the summing up could believe for an instant that there was the slightest unfairness, partiality or failure to go into details which showed, as one would expect from this judge, a very conscientious task and a job well done.

In a thirty-minute ruling, read out the following day, Lord Parker dismissed the appeal and was satisfied that there was an abundance of evidence upon which the jury must have been satisfied and there had been no errors made by Mr Justice Gorman.

The defence team, though, were not ready to give up. They were in possession of more statements that had been obtained from people in Rhyl but whom they had chosen not to produce as witnesses either at the trial or the appeal hearing.[3] Simply, their evidence did not help Hanratty in any way. But, with the appeal now lost, they sent the details to the Home Secretary, Rab Butler, in the hope that there was sufficient doubt that could justify a reprieve and commute the sentence to one of life imprisonment. Butler read the documents but concluded that he had been unable to find sufficient grounds to justify him recommending Her Majesty to interfere with the due course of law. Sentence of death should be carried out, he concluded.

There was probably never a more sensitive time for people to be hanged in Britain. Its abolition was being actively sought, and debates in Parliament, since the hanging of Timothy Evans twelve years earlier, had often discussed replacing it with life imprisonment. But it was not only rational debate that occupied people's minds; letters started to flood in to the police: 'You can't hang Hanratty. He didn't do it. I did,' one anonymous writer claimed.

Another said: 'Dont hange the man. She is to blame the girl who got shot she is now good and you Will be sorry. James Han Ratty is not a MURDER Just don't hange him or the will Be nother Murder.'

Another, to a newspaper, also claimed responsibility: 'I killed Gregson on the A6. Now I have killed again on the A9. You will see that this letter is posted in Leeds. By the time you get it I will be miles away. HANRATTY, the man convicted, is innocent. I will not see an innocent man killed hung. I know what it is like my brother was hung and he was innocent. I KILLED GREGSON HANRATTY IS INNOCENT.'

On 4 April, James Hanratty became the last person to be hanged inside the walls of Bedford prison.[4] A crowd of around 250 people had gathered outside, including a small group of Cambridge undergraduates waving anti-hanging posters, but at eight o'clock that morning, the man convicted of the A6 murder was executed.

PART 4 — THE AFTERMATH

Chapter Seventeen

Betrayal and Silence

Four days later, on 8 April 1962, Valerie returned home. She had looked forward to this moment, but it had suddenly arrived and she was nervous. For the past seven months everything had been done for her by the 'wonderful hospital', but no longer would she have dedicated, professional staff to help her through the hours of therapy she had endured trying to balance and 'sit up like a baby'. No longer would there be someone there to encourage her to play table tennis or archery, to go swimming or pull weights, activities that had helped to build up her strength. There is no record of what immediate medical support she received, either at home or as an outpatient, but it would be unlikely to match that at Stoke Mandeville. Efforts had even been made to encourage her to walk and she had managed, at one point, to pull herself along on a frame for up to 10 yards. It was some measure of encouragement that by the time she was eventually released from hospital, she was able to dress herself completely, could get out of bed, albeit with some difficulty, and was able to get in and out of a chair.[1] Physiotherapy had concentrated on her upper body strength as it was that which would allow her to have some level of mobility. All that support was now gone but getting out of hospital was something she had been dreaming of since the beginning of the year.

One of her biggest pleasures was being reunited with her pet cat, Whisky, who doted upon her and she now posed in front of newspaper cameras clutching the animal in her arms. Her mother had already taken the decision to give up work in a local shop in Cippenham Lane to look after her daughter. 'It is my duty,' she said, 'to be with Valerie until she gets used to things and some alterations are made to the house,' though Valerie was adamant, perhaps a little naively, that starting life at home again would not impact adversely upon her parents. 'Mum, you're not staying at home for me. I am not an invalid. I can look after myself,' she said.

The day 4 April had, for her, been grim.[2] A man had been executed and she was a contributor to that. 'But I've no regrets and I wouldn't have had things any different,' she said to reporters. And now, more than seven months after she had set foot outside the house on that fateful evening, she was home. Yet even though she was enjoying the simple things like a cup of tea in her living room, she was focused on what, to her, was important.

'I want to go back to work as soon as possible. I want to go rally driving again.'[3] She knew that she would no longer be as good as some of the other competitors but she was a good navigator and the prospect thrilled her – quite an incredible stance given the events of the previous year. She was in a positive frame of mind and did not dwell on the fact that she could no longer walk:

> To worry about things that you can't do, to my mind is negative. You accept where you are and you go on from there. You live today for tomorrow. Tomorrow is another day and that is what you have to aim for.[4]

Despite saying on the day of her return home that her ambition was to be independent of her wheelchair, years later, she would say that, 'I knew I would never walk again. I accepted that. The important thing to me was not that I couldn't walk, but would I ever drive again?'[5]

She also knew that by being able to drive she could return to work and earn money. Neither of her parents could drive. Her father had previously owned a motorcycle before he married but he had never owned a car and Valerie was adamant that the time would come when she would be able to take her parents out for the day. She was absolutely clear in her own mind.

'My plans now are to live a normal life. I am not an invalid and I want to be treated like a normal person.'[6]

Her father returned to work at Camp cycle dealers, a couple of miles away in Farnham Road, and Valerie adapted to her new living arrangements: the converted downstairs bedroom and the new bathroom with its system of bars and pulleys that would enable her to move around more easily. Her parents had built it out of their life savings. The doorways throughout the downstairs were widened to allow her to pass from room to room but other than the fact that she could no longer go upstairs, life in the immediate aftermath was beginning to settle down.

To an extent, she had been shielded from press interest while she had been in hospital. The only exception to this was when she had been allowed out in

February to attend a friend's wedding and newspaper reporters had turned up uninvited. But now she had returned home, she once more became the focus of attention. In reality, she was a private person and never sought publicity, but she appreciated that she had become a public figure although, deep down, she believed that anything appearing in the newspapers was a 'seven-day wonder' and people had very short memories.[7]

But generally, in the summer of 1962, she had nothing against the newspapers and so when approached by the *Today* magazine to write a series of articles about her ordeal, from her perspective, she saw no reason to turn down the opportunity. They were offering £300, which she would give to her parents in return for the money they had spent on adapting their home. She met with the reporter, told her story, and the articles, written in her name, appeared over three consecutive weeks in June. The result was described by her as 'a betrayal'.[8]

The article headlines were dramatic. 'Once I had a secret love – then came Deadman's Hill', read the first, followed by, 'I play cat and mouse with the man who killed Mike' and lastly, 'I wanted Hanratty to die'. She was horrified at the portrayal of events: 'They embroidered the truth and put words into my mouth which most definitely weren't there.'[9] The only good thing to come out of the exercise,' she joked, 'were some rather good photographs.'

Damage had been done. She had been through an incredible seven-month journey in hospital, had given evidence at the trial and watched as Hanratty's execution had been announced on the television. Now it was time to rebuild her life and by allowing the world to hear a true account from the woman who was there, raped and shot at the side of the road, it was meant to be cathartic. But an unhealthy relationship with the British press had been triggered.

This experience was countered by a piece of good news, though. The month before, arrangements were being discussed between Valerie and her boss at the laboratory for her to return to work on a part-time basis.[10] Since she had started working there in 1955 her duties had included the analysis of car accidents by attending accident sites where she measured friction marks using a portable skid-resistance tester. This would no longer be possible but arrangements had been made for her to return to work in the laboratory, where she could continue with analyses and other types of experiments.

Knowing that she was restricted to a wheelchair, the laboratory had made small modifications to help her move around the building and in May she received a letter advising her that it had been cleared by her doctor that she could return to work. She had taken on some minor administrative work while she had been in hospital, but she could now return to the place she loved, the place where she had met Michael. Two days later she was back in the office, initially part-time, but after the installation of a number of ramps and a disabled toilet she was able to return to her pre–August 1961 hours.

Life back at the laboratory seemed to carry on where it had left off. There were about 100 people working there and it was, as Valerie described it, one big, large, happy family.[11] She found people friendly and was treated as just another member of staff. But it may have masked an underlying atmosphere. Two weeks after the shooting, the police had turned up at the research laboratory and interviewed everyone in an attempt to not only understand the relationship between Valerie and Michael but to establish whether or not the motive behind the attack rested within the laboratory walls.

Most of those spoken to were aware of the relationship between the two of them and had known that Michael was married. No one had a bad word to say about them personally but many had frowned upon the courting. Michael's boss considered him to be an extremely hard worker, though highly strung and definitely of the nervous type. He had confronted him over his relationship with Valerie and pointedly told him that no good would come of it and his career might even be affected. The scientist had responded by saying that he would try to break off the liaison but despite his best efforts he had been unable.[12] Others found him to be very helpful, though often reserved, but one member of staff knew of his attraction to the opposite sex and inferred that he had been posted to Langley from another branch due to him having another illicit affair.[13]

It is unclear whether Valerie knew about Michael's boss challenging him, specifically remarking later that she was unaware whether he had been spoken to by any of his friends and emphasising that she had not been 'warned off' as newspapers would later suggest.[14] Her return seems to have been a period of celebration rather than any hushed up embarrassment surrounding the widely known affair and how it all ended in tragedy. She knew that everyone was aware of the situation but felt that they simply accepted it.

Her return, though, was a complex dynamic. She had brushed it all off, the killer had been hanged and she wanted to resume life as normal. She had no obvious pangs of guilt that, had it not been for the illicit relationship, Michael may very well still be alive. Her relationship had not only been out in the open but Janet, whom she had met on a couple of occasions, was completely aware of it.[15] Others may have seen it differently, of course, given her perceived immoral behaviour, but if they did, Valerie was wholly unaware. She had been made welcome, the building had been adapted and she was given work commensurate with her physical and mental abilities. Life was ready to move on and, for a while, a routine was established. She settled into her office-bound role acting as liaison officer between the laboratory and the police and co-ordinated the attendance at road accident scenes.

When in hospital, she had made it known that once discharged she would be needing some sort of motor vehicle to get around. She had heard that the government would provide her with a Mini, but the lady from the Ministry of Health who had come to see her quickly disabused her of that notion. 'You'll have to have an ordinary invalid carriage,' was the official decision.[16] And that was what arrived on her driveway in August.

'It was a bit of a culture shock,' she said. 'I had passed my first driving test in 1958 and to go back down to three wheels, I would need to take another.'

She passed and for the first time since August the previous year, she was able to take to the road again. It allowed her to get out of the house, to gain some level of independence and to fulfil her ambition of being able to help her parents. On Saturdays, she would go shopping with her mother, although the one-seater invalid carriage had no room for a passenger.

'She would follow me along on her bicycle and, in fact, sometimes she would go quicker than I would.'[17] Occasionally, 'On a downhill stretch with a good following wind it would just about get to 29 miles per hour.'[18]

She christened it her 'flying machine'. It drove her nutty, she quipped, but at least she was back in the driving seat and another level of normality was starting to return.

Over a year had now passed since her 'accident', as she referred to it, and while it undoubtedly would have occasionally occupied her thoughts, she was very much determined to put the matter behind her. There had been some correspondence in *The Times* newspaper about the strength of the evidence at the trial, though more about the convicted murderer's medical history, which, it was being argued, should have been put before the jury. There were also some arguments about the safety of the conviction, and with the country moving towards the abolition of the death penalty, others were arguing that even if Hanratty were guilty, his mental background may well have precluded him from being hanged. Sidney Silverman, the Member of Parliament who was advocating the abolition of capital punishment, wrote that 'not even the most passionate advocate of the death penalty has ever been in favour of executing people who were mentally sick or whose guilt was doubtful'.[19]

The first book about the case was published in 1963. *The A6 Murder: Regina v James Hanratty – The Semblance of Truth* by Louis Blom-Cooper, himself a barrister, argued that the English criminal system was flawed. Using the Hanratty trial as a case study, he argued many things but concerned himself with evidence that had not been put before the jury, specifically that Hanratty had been diagnosed in 1952 as a 'mental defective' and that the detail of the relationship between Michael Gregsten and Valerie Storie should have been made known. It had not. He did not argue for Hanratty's innocence, simply that the accusatorial system employed in the English courts was unfair. However, assertions of Hanratty's innocence began to appear.

In July, the newspapers revealed that another man had now confessed to the murder and that a 10,000-word document that outlined the detail had been submitted to the Home Secretary. It was discussed in the House of Commons when Fenner Brockway, Valerie's local MP, argued that the report contained such damning evidence that only a public enquiry would suffice. He cited a Mr X as the man confessing to the crime, and had the jury known about this, a different verdict may well have been reached. Henry Brooke, the Home Secretary, studied the dossier in detail and discussed it with senior officers at Scotland Yard as well as his political advisers. The confession, he concluded, was wrong in many material instances and indeed this was the third such confession by different people since Hanratty had been convicted. There was nothing in the report that justified a public enquiry and the matter was closed. But a 'Hanratty is innocent' movement had begun.

On 8 August 1963, Valerie took possession of a car. A real one. She would be able to get rid of her 'flying machine' and instead be back in charge of four wheels instead of three. With some irony, she had chosen a Morris 1000 traveller, an estate version of the car in which she had suffered her ordeal two years earlier. She had chosen it because she wanted more flexibility. The 'flying machine' had been good up to a point. She had been able to carry the shopping home while her mother cycled on ahead, but she desperately missed being able to take her parents out for the day. She had to take yet another driving test, her third, as it was a car that had been specially adapted for a 'disabled person' to drive without the use of legs, and she passed.

She had been restricted in her choice, since whatever car she bought needed to have doors that opened fully, almost 90 degrees, to allow her to pull alongside in her wheelchair and slide across into the driver's seat. A Mini would still have been her preferred choice but as she pointed out, 'Whereas I could no doubt have fallen gracefully into a Mini, I couldn't get back out again.' Not only could she get in and out but this car was an estate, allowing her to carry her wheelchair around with her. Her driveway at home was very narrow but obligingly the next-door neighbours had removed the adjoining fence, which gave her room to park it on the drive. The world now opened up. She had achieved her ambition to be able to take her parents out for day trips and made the most of the opportunity. They went out for meals or anywhere her parents chose, and in December, she drove them to central London to see the Christmas lights.

The year 1964 was perhaps the quietest and happiest time of Valerie's life after her 'accident'. She described it as, 'a very peaceful, perfect home life'.[20] She had settled into work, had become as independent as she could have hoped and she was able to look after her parents. There was no financial compensation in the early 1960s for anyone who had suffered from a criminal injury and though, in time, she would become a little bitter about this, she had accepted it. The tranquillity, however, was about to be disturbed.

When, in the summer of 1963, the House of Commons had dropped the 'Hanratty is innocent' debate, a businessman, Jean Justice, had picked it up. Justice had befriended the mysterious Mr X, the man who had allegedly confessed to the murder of Gregsten, and was ready to publicly name him. In October 1964, he published a book, *Murder v Murder: The British Legal System and the A6 Murder Case*. No British publisher would support it as it was potentially libellous, but he had found an outlet in Paris. The name of the 'real' A6 murderer was none other than Peter Alphon, the man earlier arrested by the police in September 1961 and who had not only denied any involvement but had been eliminated from the investigation.

Justice detailed how Alphon had since made a series of confessions[21] and he had no doubt at all that this man was the real killer. He alleged that not only were Valerie and Michael forced by the murderer to have sexual intercourse in the car but Valerie, to hide the truth, had been 'conditioned' by the police to tell the story she did. Justice's book made little impact other than exposing Alphon as the man who, after the hanging of Hanratty, now admitted to the crimes. What affect it had on Valerie is not known, but little reference is made to it in her notes and so it may be assumed that she carried on regardless, probably half-expecting that from time to time people would write about the murder.[22]

What would have affected her more was the death of her father in December at the age of 59. Valerie thought that he had coped better with her 'accident' than had her mother but it is impossible to imagine the effect it must have had upon him when, just over three years earlier, his only daughter had been abducted, raped and shot in such hideous circumstances. On top of that he had needed to deal with the added complication of Valerie being involved with a married man, although there is no record of how he reacted to this disclosure. He had suffered a coronary thrombosis seven years earlier and he seemed to

have overcome that, but now it was just Valerie and her mother, and the paralysed woman in the wheelchair became the family breadwinner.[23]

But life needed to keep moving on and Valerie, as she promised she would,
returned to the rallying scene and attended a number of the treasure hunts
that she used to attend with Michael. Her outings, however, seem to have been
short-lived, though she continued to attend the monthly meetings of the West
Middlesex Group of the Civil Service Motoring Association and eventually
was asked to edit their monthly magazine, *The Sump*. She was keeping herself
busy and remained close to her mother, continuing with the regular day trips
in her car.

Meanwhile, Parliament was busy in 1965 debating the possible abolition
of the death penalty for certain categories of murder. When in April, clauses
of the Bill were being explored in the House, the Hanratty case was repeatedly cited, often inaccurately. There were no calls for the conviction to be
overturned at this time, but the name came back into the public consciousness. When the Bill was taken to the House of Lords, Fenner Brockway,
now Lord Brockway, was quick to name Hanratty as a reason why the death
penalty should be abolished. 'There was grave doubt,' he said to the House,
'that James Hanratty was guilty of that murder.'[24] In addition, another peer,
Lord Russell of Liverpool, published a book, *Deadman's Hill: Was Hanratty
Guilty?*, which echoed the same sentiment that Hanratty was innocent and
he scripted a series of weaknesses in the prosecution case that, he argued,
proved his point.

The potential miscarriage of justice arguments were powerful and in
November the death sentence was officially suspended in Britain. The names
Hanratty and Timothy Evans, unsafely convicted for the murder of his
daughter in 1949 at the infamous Rillington Place address in west London,
would become closely associated with the abolition of capital punishment.
As a consequence of the change in the law and an application made to the
Home Secretary by his family, in February the following year, Hanratty's
body was moved from Bedford prison and reburied in consecrated ground at
Carpender's Park cemetery, Watford.

The following year, Valerie's name would become a regular feature in the
House of Lords. In August, Lord Russell of Liverpool, his book published
and widely read, took to the floor to demand an independent commission to
investigate Alphon's admission and to determine whether there had been a
miscarriage of justice. Valerie's name was mentioned repeatedly.

By the autumn, it was clear that the saga was not going to go away. Even
Valerie's own Member of Parliament, Joan Lestor, like Fenner Brockway

before, was insisting that Hanratty was innocent and had met with the Home Secretary to make her point. She had written to Valerie asking to visit her but she had got short shrift. On one of the rare occasions that Valerie responded to letters, she told her MP, 'Nothing can be gained by your coming to see me since you firmly but very mistakenly believe that Hanratty was innocent. There is absolutely no doubt of his guilt.'[25]

The BBC approached Valerie and asked if she would be prepared to take part in the reputable *Panorama* programme, which she saw as an opportunity to counter the recent imbalanced reporting. She seemed to have attached little weight to the experience she had four years earlier when she was misrepresented in the *Today* magazine and how upset this had made her, and agreed to be interviewed. Filming ahead of the programme's broadcast, Valerie told the interviewer, 'Why have these people taken it on themselves to try to whitewash Hanratty? I was there, these people weren't. Hanratty was guilty. I know. I was there.'

When the programme was screened in November 1966, however, it was significantly biased. An emphasis was placed on Valerie making the earlier erroneous identification, none of the prosecution case was commented upon and selective witnesses were criticised, taking their accounts completely out of context. Peter Alphon's confession was central, supported by witnesses from Rhyl remembering things they could not recall at the time of the trial and, understandably, James Hanratty senior claimed his son was not guilty. 'He told me himself he was innocent and I am convinced he was innocent,' he said.

The programme was widely criticised in the press: the *Sunday Telegraph* of 13 November described the BBC's use of sensationalist journalism as 'intolerable', while Robert Pitman in the *Daily Express* wrote: 'Our state TV service has decided to denigrate the police and add further agony to the shattered life of Miss Storie.'

As for Valerie, it was the final straw. Three times she had agreed to speak to the media and on the last two occasions she had been let down. As she later scribbled down on her note pad:

I had become totally disillusioned with the false representation of the world of the Press. No one seemed capable of spelling my name correctly or getting my age right so the chances of any part of the reporting being factual was remote.[26]

She felt she was perceived as an immoral woman who had sent an innocent man to the gallows and it was time for all that to end. 'I think that was the one situation which made me think then, well, I've had enough of this. I'm bowing out of public life if that's what public life is all about.'[27]

And so she did. It would be another thirty-five years before she again spoke to the media. She began her long silence.

Chapter Eighteen

The Gathering Storm

At the same time that Valerie decided to observe silence, a new Criminal Justice Bill was going through its reading stages in Parliament under the stewardship of the Home Secretary, Roy Jenkins, who only a few months before had granted Timothy Evans a posthumous pardon from his wrongful conviction in 1950. Part of the new Bill was seeking to change the law over last-minute alibis by introducing a requirement that advance notice should be provided to the prosecution in plenty of time for them to be investigated, a clear reference to the Hanratty case. Another part was seeking to change the law so that no longer would juries be required to return unanimous verdicts, but if necessary, a majority one. Sidney Silverman, the Labour MP who had successfully piloted the abolition of the death penalty through Parliament, opposed it on the grounds that all jurors needed to be sure to convict, not just simply a majority. He cited the jury in the Hanratty case, whose deliberation for ten hours was ample evidence, he claimed, that they must have had extreme doubts about their decision.

Michael Foot, a labour backbencher at the time, joined forces with his colleague and Valerie's MP, Joan Lestor, in asking for an enquiry into the Hanratty case due to the concerns that had been aired and the belief that new witnesses had been identified in Rhyl who had not been available for the trial. At the same time, another labour MP, Tom Driberg, asked for an enquiry on the grounds that, according to his information, Rhyl fairground worker Terry Evans had been told not to tell the whole truth at the trial; newspaper reports were reporting similar messages. While Jenkins dismissed Driberg's information, it became impossible not to bow to pressure and in January 1967 Detective Chief Superintendent Douglas Nimmo from the Manchester City Police was appointed to investigate the specific claim that Hanratty was in Rhyl on 22 and 23 August 1961.[1]

In addition to a number of articles from the *Daily Telegraph* and *Sunday Times* and a piece appearing in the magazine *Private Eye*, Nimmo was provided with correspondence that had passed between the Home Secretary, Joan Lestor MP and Lord Russell of Liverpool all claiming that there were a number of witnesses in Rhyl who could prove Hanratty's innocence. Russell had made it quite clear that he would have preferred an independent enquiry rather than one led by the police.[2] Perhaps the most significant information of all that was given to Nimmo was the transcript of the *Panorama* programme itself, which claimed that Hanratty was more than likely in Rhyl and there were new witnesses who could prove it. This was his starting point and Nimmo interviewed everyone involved in the programme.

Each of the people who were spoken to now said that words had been put in their mouths by the BBC reporter and his objective had been to prove Hanratty innocent. Terry Evans had effectively been employed to find new witnesses, and one had indeed been found. His name was Charles White Jones and on screen he claimed he had spoken to Hanratty on the night of the murder. Not only had he been the person who had directed him to Grace Jones' boarding house, but he had also told him that he was looking for a man called Terry who worked at a fairground. It was remarkable that he could suddenly recall this, five years after the events, but had not come forward at the time. Now interviewed by Nimmo, Jones admitted he had been set up by Evans to say the things he did and nothing he had said had been true, though he was grateful for the £10 he had been paid by the Corporation. Nimmo described him as 'pathetic, illiterate, vague and confused'. Nicknamed in Rhyl as Charlie Cockles, Jones claimed that the BBC reporter, John Morgan, had only wanted to prove Hanratty's innocence and thought perhaps he was 'putting things in my head'.[3]

Two years later, Lord Donovan would say in the House of Lords:

> It is shameful and a public disservice that a national institution like the BBC should seek, on the shallow basis of a shallow investigation of the facts, to lead the public to believe that an innocent man has been convicted and executed. It is not merely shameful, but downright dishonest, when the principal witness (Charles White Jones) for this implied assertion goes back on his evidence to remain dumb about his recantation.[4]

The irresponsible reporting exposed, Nimmo then focused on the overriding claim that new witnesses had been found, other, of course, than Charlie Cockles. Two people whose names were frequently cited were Margaret

Walker and Ivy Vincent, who claimed they had seen Hanratty on the night of the murder in Rhyl. However, both Walker and Vincent had been interviewed not only by the police but also by the defence team during the trial. Neither had been able to positively identify Hanratty, nor could they pinpoint the date. It was independently shown, in fact, that Vincent's recollection was wholly inaccurate. The point, though, was that both these witnesses were available to the defence at the time of the trial and they chose not to use them. Having lost the appeal, both Walker's and Vincent's statements were sent to the Home Secretary by Kleinman and their evidence was taken into account when considering the reprieve. Their names were not new but they had lingered and now Nimmo closed down this suggestion.

During the course of the enquiry, twenty people were spoken to as alleged potential witnesses; three had already given evidence at the trial, eight had had their details passed to the defence at the time and eight others were unable to add any further information.[5] Only one person had not been interviewed.

Chris Larman had made two statements on 16 and 21 February 1962 saying that he had seen a man in Rhyl, who he recognised by the published photograph as being Hanratty, on the night in question. Unfortunately, Larman had now moved to Australia and was not seen by Nimmo, but his details had been known to the defence and had they thought it helpful to have pursued him, doubtlessly they would have done so. Even Kleinman, reported in the *Sunday Times* in December 1966, said that if Gillbanks had found anything of interest, he would have acted upon it either at the time of the trial or in time for the reprieve.

The Nimmo report was submitted to the Home Office in March 1967 concluding that no further information had been unearthed and that the Rhyl alibi was false. However, Lord Russell of Liverpool and the Hanratty family decided that they would visit Rhyl; they would do their own investigation.

Armed with photographs of James Hanratty's funeral, which of course had no evidential value, and which was clearly, though understandably, an emotive gesture, they spoke to Grace Jones' daughter, Brenda Harris, and once again to Margaret Walker and Ivy Vincent, who now once more claimed they were sure that Hanratty was in Rhyl on the night. This remarkable turnaround was reported back to the Home Office and Nimmo was required to interview them again, this time in the presence of solicitors acting for the Hanratty family. This resulted in Vincent saying much the same as she had said before – that she could not really remember, but Walker now thought it must have been Hanratty she had seen as the photograph of him she had been shown was so much like his father. In other words, she was identifying the photograph she had seen, not the man she claimed to have seen in Rhyl. As for Brenda Harris, who was available to the defence at the time of the trial, she now claimed that Hanratty had been in the attic and not in the room her mother had claimed, something that had been explored in great depth at the trial and dismissed by the jury.

The Nimmo investigation had once more heightened the attention being paid to the A6 murder and it would have been of some relief to Valerie that the report had concluded that there was nothing to support the Rhyl alibi and perhaps, she hoped, this would now be the last time it would be mentioned.

It was not to be.

On 12 May, a press conference was called in the Hotel du Louvre in Paris and Peter Alphon announced to the world that he was the A6 murderer. It brought the country's press to attention.

He had been befriended by Jean Justice, the barrister who had published his book three years earlier and which contained his so-called confession. Shortly after the trial had finished, Alphon had turned up at the Hanratty family home, admitted to making the confession and even got his cheque book out offering to pay them compensation. Understandably, this had led to a great deal of ill feeling between them, resulting in Alphon at one point getting involved in a scuffle with the family outside a tube station in London. He was charged, though later acquitted at court, but threatening phone calls to the family followed. When Lord Russell later published his book, Alphon's reaction was to make similar threatening phone calls to him as well, for which he was fined and bound over to keep the peace. At the same time as the BBC was creating the Panorama programme in 1966, journalist Paul Foot wrote an article in *Queen* magazine naming Alphon as the murderer.[6]

Foot was someone who was strongly siding with the Hanratty family and had even attended his burial when his body had been moved to Watford the previous year.

Alphon now told the gathered journalists that he felt he had been so persecuted that he wanted to drag British justice through the mud. He admitted carrying out the A6 killing and said that he had killed Gregsten and 'half-killed our friend Miss Storie'. The police, he said, were now trying to hush up the fact that they hanged an innocent man. At one point, according to later newspaper reports, he 'rambled on' about Russians, Nazis, Bertrand Russell and miniskirts, which, he mused, showed a moral decadence in Britain. He was, as one observer put it, 'drunk and highly excited almost to the point of hysteria'.[7] Although, according to the *People* newspaper, Alphon was quick to retract his confession, Paul Foot quickly telephoned him and carried out his own interview, which then appeared in the *Sunday Times*.

In it, Alphon claimed that he had been approached by a 'central figure', a right-wing fascist who had strong views about immorality among married people. He had his sights on Gregsten and Storie and asked Alphon to stop the affair. He boasted that he could do the job and he had received £5,000 in payment after he had carried out the murder. It had been Dixie France, he said, who had acquired the gun, who had been a mutual friend of him, Hanratty and the 'central figure'. The field had been pointed out to him where the couple met regularly and after he had been to the dog stadium at Slough that night,[8] he had gone to the field, found them and had decided he needed to rape the girl. But they had become cocky and he considered that they needed to be killed, although he also claimed that he had shot Gregsten in self-defence. Afterwards, he had given the gun to France, who had hidden it on the bus and planted the cartridges in the hotel room at the Vienna. When France then went into the witness box to give evidence against 'his friend', he had rung him up time and time again and told him that if Hanratty died, so too would he.

Of particular interest was the reference at the end to his threats towards Dixie France if Hanratty was to hang. Two days after Hanratty lost his appeal, France had committed suicide by gassing himself. He had been an ill man before the trial but his involvement in the case eventually took its toll. He had been a crucial witness for the prosecution, as had his wife and daughter, but with his own criminal background, it would have been an unnatural thing to do to support the police in a prosecution. Many writers since have theorised as to why he took his own life but now here was Alphon implying that it had been his pressure on him that forced him to commit suicide.

He filled in a lot of the blanks, but essentially this appeared to be a story fabricated from using established facts and introducing some fantasy. Everything he said could have been gleaned from the trial, which he had attended frequently, or from the newspapers.

One journalist at the press conference asked of him, 'Now, there seems to be three different opinions of you. People think you're either a liar, a killer or that you're mentally disturbed and unbalanced. Which are you?'

Alphon replied, 'Maybe it's all three.'

Journalists present were sceptical, and few felt that Alphon's confession was other than attention-seeking fantasy.

However, those few felt that the fight was worth continuing. Certainly, from 1967 onwards, there was a small, yet vocal group, including the distraught Hanratty family, who continued to campaign to prove Hanratty's innocence. Jean Justice and his barrister friend Jeremy Fox had been pushing the Alphon issue for a number of years but with Paul Foot, a respected journalist with concerns about not only the Rhyl alibi but the entire police investigation, a nucleus of agitation was formed; it became known as the A6 Committee.

More newspaper articles now followed and further demands for an independent public enquiry were made in the House of Lords. In November 1968, Lord Brockway fuelled the sentiment that the police could no longer be trusted and an enquiry, conducted by a body other than them, was the only way forward. There were, though, some dissenting voices. In response to Brockway's demands, Lord Leatherland said:

> Does not my noble friend think, that some consideration ought to be given to the feelings of the girl who suffered, and is still suffering, in connection with this case, and that the more this question is ventilated along the lines upon which it has been ventilated today, probably the more suffering it will cause to that girl.

Brockway responded:

> I have the deepest of sympathy for the paralysis of her body which has occurred from this case, and that it is not out of any lack of sympathy for her that I put these questions.

The A6 Committee was now gathering momentum. A letter was sent by the Hanratty family to the Prime Minister asking for a public enquiry and Joan Lestor wrote once more to Valerie inviting her to join. Valerie later wrote:

> In times of trouble one could always go to one's MP and ask for, and possibly receive help and understanding. However, my MP joined the rebel cause, became embroiled in a committee set up to prove a miscarriage of justice and had the temerity to write to me asking me to join it.[9]

She never replied to the letter.

On 10 December 1969, Beatle John Lennon announced he was joining the committee to support them in their cause and announced he would fund a film about the campaign.[10] Lennon and Valerie never met but she said in 2001:

> I felt it was very ironic that he himself died by the bullet and it flashed through my mind that when the news came through that John Lennon had

been shot and killed, I felt, well now John Lennon, you know what it feels like to be shot.[11]

A hint of bitterness was beginning to emerge.

On 23 March 1970, the A6 Committee held a public meeting in Bedford ostensibly to raise awareness of their concerns. Not only did they invite the eleven jurors from the trial – though there is no evidence that any attended – but that day, they despatched a telegram to Valerie at her place of work. It read:

> You are invited to the Corn Exchange in Bedford to refute any allegations that may be made against you at our public meeting tonight 7.30pm. A6 Murder Committee.

Quite apart from its intimidatory wording, it was delivered to Valerie at the laboratory at 4.30 p.m. that afternoon, which 'added insult to injury'. Had she been minded to attend, which she most certainly was not, it gave a woman in a wheelchair three hours to travel the 60-mile trip. So incensed was she, that she instructed solicitors to write to Jean Justice, to express her feelings.

> We take a most serious view of the terms in which the telegram was couched containing as they do threats against Miss Storie. When the Hanratty trial took place, Miss Storie gave her evidence and was subjected to cross examination thereon. We think it is monstrous that she should now be subjected to 'allegations' directed against her by yourself and your committee and we must warn you that we shall, on Miss Storie's behalf, vigorously protect her interests.[12]

The Corn Exchange meeting seemed more to be a platform for aiming criticism at individuals rather than a political lobby group concerned about the country's criminal justice system.[13] Placards were placed around the building declaring Bob Acott had 'rigged the case', the State had murdered Hanratty and Peter Alphon was the real murderer. There were a number of speakers and Foot publicly declared that Janet Gregsten had been behind the plan to scare the couple and that Hanratty had subsequently been framed. Mary Hanratty spoke about the police corruption concerning Kerr's missing notes and James Hanratty senior criticised Sherrard for not properly defending his son. It may have been a coincidence, but two days after the meeting, the Hanratty family received a letter from the Prime Minister's office telling them that no further action was to be taken; officially, the matter was closed.

In December that year, the former Home Secretary, Rab Butler, who had authorised Hanratty's execution, received a writ alleging negligence in office in that he had wrongfully decided against a reprieve in the light of the additional evidence from the Rhyl witnesses. It was dismissed by the courts the following year but the campaign continued.

The A6 Committee was built around the Hanratty family and Jean Justice and Jeremy Fox, the latter of whom at least had some knowledge of how the criminal justice system worked.[14] But its main protagonist was Paul Foot, the journalist who had already made his mark in the case with an article in *Private Eye* in 1966.

There is little doubt that Foot held a genuine concern for the Hanratty family and a much wider distrust of the establishment, in this particular case, the police, the courts and the Home Office. He had spent much of his time visiting witnesses around the country, extracting different versions of events that conflicted with the evidence that had been gathered during the police investigation. He would have been frustrated by the lack of progress with the committee's efforts to obtain a public enquiry and so, with all the information he had gathered over the last four years, he wrote a book, one that would resonate for decades and have a profound impact on the reading public.

Who Killed Hanratty? was published in 1971[15] and it sought fundamentally to undermine the entire police investigation and criminal justice system. Foot wrote meticulously to create a narrative intended to convince the reader that Hanratty had been wrongly convicted.

The key features were there. The Kerr incident in the layby was a police cover-up designed to arrest an innocent person, the prosecution witnesses were all either wrong or not to be believed and the entire investigation into the Liverpool alibi was flawed and corrupt. There were, though, two key themes on which he concentrated his attention: Alphon and Rhyl.

Alphon was the real killer and he outlined a theory based on what the eccentric Londoner had told him. In fairness, Foot had managed to get access to Alphon's bank accounts and established that after the killing he had received more than £7,000, which for an unemployed wanderer did need some explaining.[16] As for Rhyl, Foot named people whom he claimed to be new witnesses who could prove Hanratty's innocence.[17] In reality, two of these had been spoken to by the defence in 1962 and one had come forward seven years later to say that a man she saw in the seaside town 'could have been James Hanratty'. A fourth person was the elusive Chris Larman, who had moved to Australia but whom Foot had managed to track down in 1968. Larman, though, had already been seen by the defence and they had decided that his evidence, if anything, could do more harm than good and they chose not to use him. None of the new names took the case any further forward.

Hanratty was a man of low intelligence and a burglar, Foot argued, with an appalling disciplinary record in prison.[18] There were no traits of violence within him and, as he himself admitted in one of his last letters from prison to his family, 'Though I am a bit of a crook, I wouldn't hurt a mouse.' It was a quantum leap for someone like him to suddenly become a rapist and murderer. However, Foot did not explore this idea in any great detail but rather left it that this was someone who quite clearly could not possibly have carried out the attack.

Foot's book was to be far reaching; it most certainly influenced the course of political events and he made a number of valid criticisms of the police, notably their poor investigation concerning the Stanmore burglaries, Hanratty not being invited to sign his interview notes and some unanswered questions around the Hanratty/Storie identification parade. Insightfully, he frequently brought to the surface the issue of the disclosure of material in the possession of the prosecution that had not been passed to the defence, a topic that would pervade the following decades. It is wrong to examine the law of the 1960s through modern-day eyes but Foot made the valid point that had the defence been made aware of everything in the possession of the prosecution, their defence may have been adapted accordingly. That said, there is nothing disclosed in Foot's book that proved Hanratty's alibi, although his argument was that had a jury been aware of every single detail it may have painted a more doubtful picture. In this regard, Foot was critical both of the prosecution and the defence.

While Foot wrote what appeared to be a forensic analysis in trying to establish that the police investigation had been anything but transparent, he was a journalist and, quite properly, did not have access to information that witnesses had provided to the police, relying to a large degree on newspaper reports. As one example, Acott's visit to Ireland had been the subject of considerable journalistic attention at the time with much speculation as to the purpose of the trip. Foot described it as 'one of the least distinguished periods of an undistinguished enquiry' and said that 'Acott shamefacedly returned without his quarry'. In fact, the detective had travelled to Ireland to investigate the postcard 'Ryan' had sent to the address in Wood Lane, as a result of which he was able to conclusively show that 'Ryan' was really Hanratty. Because he and his journalist colleagues had not been aware of this, Foot reached the conclusion it was an example of police incompetence.

He also readily accepted the word of witnesses who presented themselves to the A6 Committee, and by doing so fed a story that gained huge publicity and reinforced the Hanratty family's insistence that their son was innocent. However, it was an accomplished piece of work that achieved its purpose.

It had its detractors though. For instance, Parliamentary Under Secretary Dick Taverne QC pointed out that Foot had failed to mention the significant sighting of Hanratty in Liverpool on 9 October and it was this event that may have formed the basis of his alibi.[19] He made the point that it did not matter what weight anyone would wish to attach to that piece of evidence but if Foot was going to publish, at least let it be balanced.

Interestingly, Professor Keith Simpson, the pathologist who had examined Valerie's injuries in the days after the attacks, and had subsequently followed the case with interest, said:

> No one engaged in the case, as I was, and entirely disinterested in the innocence or guilt of the accused, could fail to be impressed by the weight of the [prosecution] evidence. I myself do not doubt that the Crown case has in no way been seriously dented by the books and articles written about the case.[20]

Valerie though, struggling at home and trying to rebuild her life, was beginning to feel the pressure by all that had been written. In fairness, Foot had written to her, twice it seems, in the preceding years, inviting her to comment but she did not reply. She would later write that the book was 'regarded highly', but continued:

> A recognised left-wing, anti-establishment author took the facts, ignored most of them and expounded his idea of the sequence of events of the night of 22/23 August 1961 and the subsequent trial and came up with a winner.

She went on:

> If we pause for just a moment, only one person really knew the truth – that was me, because horror upon horror, although I was there, fiction in this instance was far better than fact, so anything I might have said was not to be taken into consideration. Take any book, article, which purports Hanratty to be innocent and Valerie Storie is dismissed in a variation of the few words 'she was shot and paralysed for the rest of her life.' No more, no less – 'for the rest of her life.'

It justified her decision to remain silent, she felt, despite numerous requests from the national newspapers now asking for an interview. One even suggested to her that, 'The implications of the new study and the ones which preceded it are, I would have thought, grave enough for you to make some kind of rebuttal.'[21]

She thought otherwise and consigned the letter to her filing cabinet.

As much as she had been disgruntled by Foot's analysis, she pressed on with her life. Despite what was being portrayed in the newspapers, more practical issues were confronting her. In 1973, her Morris Minor Traveller came to the end of its life and she replaced it with a Marina estate, a car she fell in love with and would keep in her garage until long after she would eventually lose the ability to drive altogether. Work had increasingly become more interesting and she began a period in her life when she was once more settled and engaged in some 'highly intensive research' with her team at the laboratory. As she wrote later, 'I like to think I played an important and integral part in this piece of research.'[22] It was during this period that Valerie met Adrian Hobbs, a man who would become a lifelong friend and in time would unearth the *Storie Papers*.

Her job was to collate all of the accident reports and act as liaison officer between the laboratory and the police in a project aimed at better understanding the causes of road accidents. It was a crucial piece of work that in time would lead to improved knowledge of the relative roles of the road user, the road environment and the vehicle in accident causation. She would take the initial call from the police and get in radio contact with the investigating team, who would then visit the scene and carry out their investigation. She organised interviews with the drivers of the vehicles involved, compiled the accident files and prepared the data for entry onto the computer. The role brought her into contact with Ken Wells, a Scenes of Crime Officer for the local force, who was given the task of liaising with Valerie at the laboratory.

'She was a lovely lady,' he said, 'always smiling, always pleasant and always very particular about her appearance.'

She may have been destined to a life in a wheelchair, he thought, but she was very determined that she should be treated as if nothing had happened. She was always complimentary about his accident night photography and they used to just sit and have a chat over a cup of tea or coffee, though they never spoke about what had happened to her. He knew her background, of course, but always felt it inappropriate to ask; she never mentioned it, so neither did he. She was simply getting on with her job and loving it.[23]

But while she was enjoying every minute of her work, the political narrative was running in parallel. There had been a few more debates in the House of Commons about the case where calls for a public enquiry persisted but Roy Jenkins, as Home Secretary, resisted them. However, in 1974, that was to change. The arguments for reviewing the entire case were powerful and had become a recurring theme. In June, the Home Office conceded the point and decided that an enquiry would be carried out. It would not be a public forum where witnesses could attend and give evidence, but it would nevertheless be a formal enquiry carried out by a Queen's Counsel. He would examine not only everything that had been cited before but also any other documents or pieces of information that anyone wished to have taken into consideration. Lewis Hawser QC was appointed to carry out the task.

The volume of material submitted for his assessment was vast. The Hanratty family, through their appointed solicitor Geoffrey Bindman, was allowed a personal audience and he pleaded that all of Paul Foot's well-reasoned arguments should be considered. The evidence of every person named in the original investigation and the Nimmo report as well as Foot's book was revisited alongside more documents that had been provided by the defence and the police.[24]

In April the following year, Hawser published his findings. His remit had been not only to consider the evidence insofar as it related to the jury's verdict but also to decide whether, in view of the new material, it could cast any doubt upon that verdict. He found nothing, he reported, to suggest that the evidence did anything other than fully justify the jury's decision.[25] He specifically pointed out that all the evidence showed that Hanratty did not stay in Rhyl on 22/23 August, although it did not preclude the possibility that he had stayed there on some other occasion.[26] His final paragraph read:

> My conclusion is that at the end of the day the case against Mr Hanratty remains overwhelming and that the additional material set into the framework of the case as a whole does not cast any real doubt upon the jury's verdict.

It seemed to draw a line under the affair and despite *Private Eye* magazine (for which Paul Foot was a columnist), under a title of 'Hung, Drawn and Hawsered', criticising the outcome, perhaps, the matter was finally at an end.

The conclusion of the Hawser report would have been welcomed by Valerie; and she needed some good news. Two months earlier her mother had died and her last years had not been happy ones. Each time the Hanratty story hit the front pages, reporters would knock on the door at Anthony Way asking for an interview. On every occasion Valerie refused to speak to them. They were persistent though and would peer through the windows, shout through the letter box or 'any damn thing they liked to do in order to try to get a story'.[27] Her mother had been a very gentle person and she found the intrusion into their personal lives deeply upsetting. Since her father had died eleven years earlier Valerie had felt the need to protect her mother from all the press interest but her patience had worn thin as their antics became increasingly invasive, though somehow she had managed to control any public outburst of emotion.

Privately though, with the constant pressure of the Hanratty campaign while she was confined to her wheelchair, she harboured angry thoughts:

> I've always said I don't blame the Hanratty family for their campaign and trying to prove their son was innocent but it was all the others that joined it. I don't know how the campaign began. There was somewhere in somebody's mind, a seed of doubt. It attracted those people that I call left-wing trendies, anti-establishment, anti-monarchy, anti-hanging, anti-anything that is good and traditional in this country.

Since coming out of hospital thirteen years ago, she had needed her mother to help her into bed every day and turn her during the night. As time went on, and certainly in the months leading up to her death, Marjorie would often comment on how concerned she was that when she eventually died her daughter would have to go into some sort of home and she knew how her temperament would not allow that. This worrying had made her ill, a factor that probably accelerated her death at the age of 68.

But now she was gone, things had to change. It is clear that at some point Valerie would benefit greatly from a daily care service who would visit and help. She was also fortunate to have the help of Adrian Hobbs,[28] the engineering friend at the laboratory, who installed grab handles suspended from the ceiling that she used to get herself in and out of bed. He installed a similar system in her lavatory and very cleverly designed a mechanism through which Valerie could slide from her wheelchair into her car and then use a system of pulleys to move and store it in her garage, enabling her to close her car door; when away from home, she used another wheelchair stored in the back of her car. The grab handles, pulleys and ropes were a lifesaver and brought comfort to Valerie.

The paralysis, though, had given her a strange sensation and she later remarked, 'If I shut my eyes I have no idea where I am in space. I am just a head and shoulders. I don't know where the rest of my body is.'[29]

Over the two years following her mother's death, she learned to cope with the everyday household chores such as cleaning and gardening. Being in a wheelchair and living alone made everything many times harder than it would normally have been but she mastered the use of a carpet sweeper. She had tried using a vacuum cleaner but she kept on getting tangled up in the wire and repeatedly she would accidentally pull the plug out of its socket. She arranged for someone to put her garden plants in tubs and in the summer she could water them by wheeling herself among them. Washing she did by hand and it would be many years before her house was eventually fitted with a washing machine.

She liked cooking and had taken it up since her mother had died. In fact, it had been a stark reminder that when she arrived home from work, she realised there was no longer any food for her waiting on the table and she had to either get on with it or starve. She felt it had been intuition, that just before her mother passed, they rearranged the kitchen so that she could get access to the oven door. Before that, she had been unable to reach in and her mother had to do everything.

Some years later, trying to make the best use of the upstairs of the house, which she was unable to use herself, she had taken in a lodger and from time to time he would wheel her to the shops. On one occasion in Oxford, while negotiating a pavement, she somehow slid out, due probably to her refusal to use a lap belt to hold her in. No damage was thought to have been done but after a week or so she realised that when she lifted her leg to get into bed, she could hear a crunching sound. Having had enough of hospitals, she asked a medical colleague at work to examine it, who quickly diagnosed a broken leg and arranged for her to be admitted. The lower leg was broken in four places and it had been her paralysis that had prevented her from feeling any pain. She persuaded the doctors to put a plaster on as high as her knee and then simply went to her car and drove home. She was not one for any fuss.

She recuperated at home and it was during this period she began to realise that this was where she preferred to be. Initially, she needed to carry on working, not least for the money, but by 1983, she had had just about as much as she could take. Although not entirely unrewarding, life at the laboratory had been challenging for the past few years. She had been promoted twice, wrote articles for the British Medical Association and carried out research on behalf of the Blennerhassett Committee to establish acceptable levels of alcohol in drivers and how that contributed to the cause of road accidents.[30] But it had become less enjoyable and her daily regime was becoming difficult. Every morning she got up at quarter to six in order to leave home by eight and then had to travel 16 miles to the laboratory, which had by now moved to Crowthorne. After work she made the return trip, arriving home at six in the evening, and the weekends were taken up with cleaning, washing and gardening. She was now 45 years old and she wanted to spend what was left of her life doing the things that *she* wanted to do. After all, she had been led to believe that the life expectancy of a paraplegic was only fourteen years, and that milestone had been and gone eight years ago. As she reflected later, 'I was past my sell-by date,' and decided to call it a day.[31]

With the daily grind of getting to and from work over and no more frequent callers from the newspapers, she, once more, began to rebuild her life. Almost immediately, she heard an appeal on the radio asking for volunteers to record articles for the blind. She got in touch and soon she was part of a network of people involved in 'talking newspapers', which were broadcast all over the world.

The following January she joined the Cookham Women's Institute, something she felt she needed to do for her mother; Marjorie had always wanted to join but had never got round to it. Her first visit was during an afternoon that was packed with about fifty or sixty people, who instantly saw that the newcomer was in a wheelchair. They did not know what she would be capable of or even who she was; she certainly did not advertise her past. For her, the first few months seemed to drag a little and she questioned whether she was doing the right thing, but eventually she found herself enjoying her time with a group of people who she later realised were the Institute's committee; she had found a new group of friends. In time, she would divulge the circumstances of her being incapacitated – her accident – but it never became a major talking point.

During her time there, she was appointed the Institute's Press Secretary, which, given her history with the media, was somewhat ironic. She later recalled:

> It just enhanced my view of the media, because I would send in a report once a month but what came out in the paper bore no resemblance to what I wrote at all, which just goes to show that you never believe anything that you read in the newspapers; I proved that many a time.[32]

Her point was demonstrated when an article written by a renowned author appeared, ironically in the *Police Review*, arguing that there remained a 'strong suspicion' that there had been a miscarriage of justice at the Hanratty trial.[33] Treating it with the contempt she felt it deserved, Valerie read it through, highlighting in a bright pink felt-tipped pen every time a name was misspelled.

Instead of Storie, Gregsten and Acott they appeared as Storey, Gregster and Alcott. She wrote at the top of the page, 'What a pity they cannot spell in the first instance.'[34] Her point was not so much that this was laziness but if the researcher did not even know how to spell the protagonists' names, what reliability could be placed on the rest of the article?

To add to this, the following year, Paul Foot had a second edition of his book published that contained a postscript criticising the Hawser report. It is right to say that Foot identified what he considered to be some dubious judgements on some of the detail expounded by the QC, but overall, he merely re-rehearsed some of his earlier thoughts.

The WI, though, was not Valerie's only passion. She taught herself calligraphy, producing some rather ornate letters with an obvious ability to keep a steady hand; one of her friends later said that she was really rather good at it. She loved reading historical works of the Tudor and Stuart periods and joined local history groups. But her overriding passion was researching family history, which would become a lasting, lifetime hobby for her. Through a chance conversation, she discovered that one of her new friends knew someone who knew her parents and grandparents. She tracked them down and found the man who once had been at school with her father. It somehow reconnected her with her parents and memories of happier times. In her notes, she makes reference to a later occasion when she 'had a dramatic meeting with cousins in Harwell',[35] though quite what this entailed is unclear.

She was now happy and knew her decision to give up work had been the right one; her life was again fulfilling. She had the occasional letter from people claiming to know the identity of the real killer but by and large the fuss had died down.[36]

And in 1990, a lift was finally installed in her house. She had for a while been making enquiries about the prospect of having one fitted but she never really thought it feasible. For the first time in twenty-nine years, she saw the upstairs of her house. The lift was like Doctor Who's Tardis, she said, fitted so that she could wheel herself into it and it would 'disappear through a hole in the ceiling'. She had one of the old bedrooms converted to a study:

I always longed to have a study and after twenty-nine years of living down-stairs, suddenly one day I was able to go upstairs and it was a very, very weird experience. And then came the first time that I was upstairs and could look out of my window. The houses all around me looked so tiny and I thought I was sitting on top of the world, somehow.[37]

It seemed a small point for someone to be so excited about looking out of a bedroom window but the last time she had done that was on the evening of 22 August 1961, and Michael Gregsten had been downstairs waiting to drive her to the Old Station Inn. She was going out on a date with her boyfriend and they were going to discuss their future. That had been almost thirty years ago.

But the campaign to prove Hanratty's innocence, and thus discredit Valerie and blame her for his execution in 1962, continued.

Chapter Nineteen

The Campaign Continues

In 1991 another book was published that attacked the English court system and argued once more that James Hanratty was innocent. Ludovic Kennedy was a well-known journalist, broadcaster and author and his book, *Truth to Tell*, was a collection of his writings across a wide range of subjects. He concentrated, though, on miscarriages of justice, most notably Rillington Place, the Guildford Four and the Birmingham Six, but Hanratty featured as well, not only as a man wrongly convicted but principally because the case demonstrated the English adversarial legal system was not fit for purpose; Kennedy favoured the European inquisitorial system in much the same way as Louis Blom Cooper had argued in 1963.

Then in April 1992, Channel 4 screened *Mystery of Deadman's Hill*, a documentary that was little more than a revisit of all the issues that had been debated many times before in the courts, Parliament, radio, television and newspapers. But its presentation format was at least as prejudiced, if not more so, than the *Panorama* programme that had been screened twenty-six years earlier.

In fairness, its producer, Bob Woffinden, had written to Valerie on a couple of occasions stating his intention to make the film and his letter to her in December 1991 revealed the approach the programme would be taking. He wrote:

Our research into the case is now virtually complete. I'm afraid that our conclusions are broadly the same as those reached in previous investigations. We believe that the crimes were committed by Alphon; that Hanratty had nothing to do with the whole affair; and that Detective Chief Superintendent Acott was sadly misdirected … I believe there is real evil at the heart of this case. It all seems to have been frighteningly calculated, not just with regard to the crime itself, but in the way that another man was put in the frame afterwards … We have met Peter Alphon but briefly. He is still adhering to his basic confession of having committed the crimes and still regaling those in his company with his admiration for Adolf Hitler. He is an odious man, still living freely in London, as he has done all along. The other person involved with the crime is equally unpleasant.

This last sentence implied that he knew the identity of the person who had supposedly hired Alphon to carry out the murder, and candidly revealed his personal opinions:

The case is merely an example of the kind of judicial ineptitude that seems to have been so commonplace in recent years. Curiously, for a nation that invented Sherlock Holmes et al., we seem to have little idea of how to conduct actual investigations. This was another case bedevilled by startling investigative flaws.[1]

In short, Woffinden told Valerie that the wrong man had been convicted, Alphon was the hired killer and that the miscarriage had been a result of police ineptitude and corruption. Valerie ignored him, and in time, would come to greatly dislike the man.

The programme itself once again showed old footage of James Hanratty senior, who had now been dead for fourteen years, claiming his son to be innocent. Hanratty's last letters from prison were read out in detail and the message was that the young man had been framed. Acott had no idea about who the real killer was, the programme alleged, and the people who had made their eyewitness identifications were all wrong, particularly Valerie Storie, who had not been seen or heard from since 1966.

The programme's most powerful assertion was that there was some forensic evidence that had been withheld by the prosecution, which, with the advent of DNA technology, could demonstrate Hanratty's innocence. It also argued that the affair between Storie and Gregsten had been withheld from the public gaze and behind this lay the answer to why the attack had taken place.

Valerie asked Adrian Hobbs to watch the programme with her. She was concerned that she might get upset by it, but she laughed at its inaccuracies rather than show any concern about its central message; she had heard it all before.[2] She did feel sufficiently exercised, however, to write to her solicitor, who was monitoring media coverage on her behalf, and said that, 'If I was the Director of Channel 4, I would want to know why Mr Woffinden spent eighteen months producing a re-hash of old and very old footage and accomplished nothing.'

But with the programme's transmission and despite all she had done to move her life on and to be discreet about her past, once again her 'illicit relationship with her married lover' was broadcast across the UK television screens and the suggestion was that it was now only a matter of time before the truth was revealed. No doubt, she thought, all those new friends she had made and the new hobbies she had developed would be tainted by this pointless and biased reporting.

However, despite the potential for people viewing her differently, everything indicates that life carried on as before. Attitudes towards her seemed not to change. She had already been appointed president of Cookham WI and continued in that role until 1994. She joined the Old Paludians for Slough Grammar School, an 'old girls' group intended to bring together former pupils, and by 1993 she had been appointed their secretary. She regularly attended events hosted by the group and she avidly read all their newsletters. A former head of the school later said, 'She was an intelligent woman and we appreciated all she did.'[3]

By 1994, though, her health had started to deteriorate and her physical inability to move easily in bed had resulted in bed sores. She now needed help, and despite putting it off for as long as possible, she was admitted to Wexham Park hospital, where she once more returned to an environment that she had grown to hate. For the next six months, she spent the majority of her time in bed on her front, barely able to move, and found it incredibly difficult to eat. She became desperately unhappy and when Adrian Hobbs visited her he saw she was now putting on weight.

There was a lighter moment, though, during this prolonged period of unhappiness. Despite her deteriorating health and her generally depressed mental state, she had managed to maintain a level of mischievousness and in a matter that was actually quite serious.

A year earlier she had received a letter from Jeremy Fox, the friend of Jean Justice who had scripted the first book campaigning for Hanratty's innocence to be recognised as far back as 1964. His letter explained that he had spent the last thirty years exploring not who had committed the murder, but why she and Michael had been subjected to their five-hour ordeal. In other words, the book held the key to identifying the real killer. He had been in contact with Janet Gregsten, her son Anthony and Peter Alphon, and he wanted to know her views about the idea that someone had been sent to the cornfield to separate them for good. There was nothing new in this story, which had been born when Alphon made his half-hearted confession in Paris back in 1967 and been followed up by a number of people in their quest for a salacious story. Fox backed up his first question, though, with another about wanting to know the real reason why Janet had visited her in hospital in the first place. In fact, he pointed out, Alphon himself would soon be writing to the Home Secretary telling them that the police were told the names of the people sent to kill them and the matter had been brushed over.[4]

She would later say: 'All this nonsense of people being sent to separate us, hitmen, it's total rubbish, absolute total rubbish.'[5]

But, perhaps reflecting the contempt in which she held Fox, instead of simply not replying, noticing that the letter had been addressed to an incorrect house in Anthony Way, she opened it, read it, re-sealed it and returned it, endorsed, 'not known at this address'.

That had been a year ago, but now while in hospital he again wrote, three more times in fact, each one addressed to the same incorrect house. They were taken to her in hospital and again she opened them, read them, re-sealed the envelopes and sent them back.

His letter of 19 January built on his earlier ideas. He now claimed that Janet Gregsten, who sadly had died from a heart attack that week, had said shortly before her death that the man who had sent the gunman to carry out the attack had been none other than her brother-in-law, William Ewer. Allegedly, she had complained to him about her husband's affair with Valerie and had persuaded him to do something about it.

His final letter, in March, in which he complained about his letters not arriving safely, had a strange final paragraph. It read:

Peter [Alphon] and I firmly believe that she [Janet] was guilty – whoever it was she sent; certainly her guilt would be entirely consistent with your identification and the subsequent conviction of James Hanratty.[6]

Valerie sent it back marked 'unread'.

It was, perhaps, an incident that gave her a measure of light relief given her own wretched position in hospital. But the reality was that by now she had lost what little strength she had in her arms and her prospects were looking poor. It was for Valerie, the lowest part of her life since the shooting. Eventually, though, she was discharged and returned to Anthony Way.

'I came out of hospital really quite different than when I went in. I hadn't even got the strength to cut a slice of bread when I got home,' she said.

But there was worse to come. She could no longer get in and out of her car. Her driving days were over and 'it was a bitter pill to swallow'. The thought of being confined within the four walls of her house frightened her. It was not something she would be able to tolerate but help was at hand. The Slough dial-a-ride scheme, Out and About, later to become known as the Slough Community Transport Service, collected people from home if they were suffering with mobility difficulties. She began to use the service and, as seemed to happen with any group she joined, it was not long before she was invited to become part of its management team as the secretary and company director. Her scientific background gave her a greater understanding of the needs of transport and disabled people, and having been a user of the service for a while she pushed for changes and improvements to the vehicles. She also addressed the local council on how the town centre's facilities could be enhanced to make it a better experience for people in her position. So grateful was the Transport Service that later, when it acquired a new bus, they named it 'Valerie'.[7]

She pushed on with her family research through the Berkshire Family History Society, finding cousins she had never met before and, with her enthusiasm buoyed, even bought a computer in 1996, something she thought she would never do. She found it invaluable for her research and an effective way of getting hold of people. She would buy picture postcards of towns that were connected to her family, particular those in Scotland, a heritage of which she was very proud; on Burns night, friends would bring her round a haggis.

She and a friend, Pauline Hodges, whom she had met at the society in 1998, used to go off for days out, hiring the 'Out and About' minibus to visit villages where her ancestors originated such as Newbury, Cumnor, Aldworth and even Highclere castle.

'She was so organised,' Pauline said of her. 'She would get the Ordnance Survey maps, find a country pub for lunch and visit the churches where her relatives had been baptised and married and the graveyards where they were buried – not always easy for a wheelchair user.'

Determination and persistence had always been among Valerie's attributes; feisty, some would call her. The night of 22 August 1961 had been proof of that. She had mentally battled against her attacker for five hours, challenging him and doing what she could to frustrate his intentions. Had circumstances been only slightly different – a decision taken to run from the car or shout out to someone – things may have ended differently. For the past twenty years she had coped at home since her mother's death and had focused on getting on with her life and over the years these traits had not weakened. As one newspaper account would later say, 'this was a lady who never let herself be defeated by terrible adversity'.[8]

Pauline Hodges echoed those feelings. 'She didn't suffer fools gladly,' she said. 'She was a very determined lady, wouldn't accept anything on face value, had an excellent memory and was always questioning authority'; perhaps a result of what she had had to put up with for the past forty years.

At home she had no central heating in the house, only storage heaters and an old gas fire, and once when an engineer came to inspect them, he condemned the gas fire and put up a notice with a large red cross instructing her not to use it any more. As soon as he had gone, Valerie ripped off the notice and carried on as before. But her fascination with her own family history almost became her raison d'être, and she could have been excused for not paying attention to the slow build-up of newspaper articles once again being written and arguing for Hanratty's conviction to be overturned.

In 1996, the *Sunday Mirror* reported that Scotland Yard's Detective Superintendent Roger Matthews had been ordered to once again review the case and had allegedly told reporters that he felt Hanratty was innocent and that Gregsten had been killed as a result of a pre-meditated killing. The results of his seven-month reinvestigation had been passed to the Home Office and in January 1997, the *Independent* splashed the headline: WRONGLY HANGED: HANRATTY IS FOUND INNOCENT.

The reporters were now banging on Valerie's door again. They got the same response: silence. However, her local paper, *Slough Express*, picked up on the developments and claimed that, 'It seems, according to today's *Independent* newspaper that Hanratty's case is to go before the Court of Appeal where his conviction is expected to be quashed.'[9]

Another local reporter sent a letter and simply told her that she ought to make a statement once and for all. Another from *The Times* asked her to talk to them about the earlier theory that the murder had been committed by a hitman hired by the late Janet Gregsten and/or her brother-in-law, William Ewer, something that Jeremy Fox had written to her about three years earlier.[10] Again, she chose not to reply and maintained her silence.

But with this latest reporting, it was clear that the sentiment in the country was one of growing concern. Despite the fact that the circumstances had been examined repeatedly by the judiciary, journalists had succeeded in agitating public anxiety over the issue of wrongful convictions and were calling for yet another review.

Newspaper reports were one thing, but for Valerie to receive an offensive letter through the front door of her own home was another. A man from Lincoln wrote:

> I accuse you of sending an innocent man to his death. The fact is Miss Storie that you also identified another totally innocent man of the crime. The truth must be faced. You do not know who the murderer is. I hope fervently that you live long enough to hear James Hanratty declared innocent by the Court of Appeal. The man who should have been hanged now lives in Chalk Farm and his name is Peter Louis Alphon. You and Basil Acott, together, caused the death of an innocent man. You both lied under oath.[11]

By now, though, the Home Secretary, Michael Howard, had indeed received a further report from Scotland Yard and he made the decision to refer the matter to the newly formed Criminal Cases Review Commission (CCRC), a body established to examine potential miscarriages of justice with the power to refer the matter back to the Court of Appeal if they felt there was a real possibility that the conviction could be overturned.

It duly reported back in 1999 that it was of the view that there had been a number of material irregularities at the original trial that made the prospect of the conviction being overturned likely. Their principal finding was that there had been material in the possession of the prosecution that had not been passed to the defence and had it done so, the jury may well have returned a different verdict. The Commission based its findings on the law of 1998 rather than that which was in force in 1961, but said it had adopted a common sense approach and felt that a fair application of the 1961 rules would have allowed much more disclosure of withheld evidence.[12] They cited a number of examples but specifically raised the issue of sightings of the Morris Minor that might have damaged the credibility of the Ilford witnesses, the mileage recorded on the milometer of the car that showed that it had travelled a much further distance than was suggested and grave doubts about the procedures employed at the identification parades.

However, the Commission also touched upon the fact that the latest DNA techniques had been employed on some of the exhibits at the trial that showed marks found on Valerie's knickers and the handkerchief in which the revolver had been found on the bus came from the same person. Samples had been taken from Hanratty's brother, Michael and his mother, Mary, which showed that there were strong similarities between them and the profiled marks on the exhibits. The Commission wanted the body of the convicted man to be exhumed to recover samples of DNA as that would be the only conclusive way in which it could be determined if the marks could have originated from James Hanratty himself, but the family had objected to such a course of action. The family had no faith, the report said, in the validity of the scientific techniques and there could be no guarantee that the exhibits had not, at some time, become contaminated.

The earlier television programme screened in 1992[13] had made the point that evidence had been withheld at the time of the trial and the CCRC seemed now to be supporting that position. However, the programme had also suggested that modern DNA evidence could be the way forward, but suddenly the family did not want this pursued. The report concluded, however, that even if the DNA indicated that it was Hanratty who was the killer, the vast amount of irregularities that had occurred during the prosecution would outweigh it and they felt that the Court of Appeal would not uphold the conviction.

During this rather protracted period of Matthews submitting his report to the Home Office and the Commission referring the matter to the Court of Appeal more than two years later, television producer Bob Woffinden, who had made the programme *Mystery of Deadman's Hill*, published yet another book, *Hanratty: The Final Verdict*.

Woffinden began with the premise that the investigation had been inept and corrupt, and while the prosecution had based its case on disreputable witnesses such as Nudds and Langdale, the defence had relied on honest, decent people such as Grace Jones and Olive Dinwoodie. Woffinden introduced such views expressed by others about the perceived reason why Valerie and Michael were in the cornfield that night but the mores of the day had suppressed such idle gossip in the newspapers. The fact that the Morris was parked a mere 6ft into the cornfield, completely in view of any passing traffic or pedestrians, made such a prospect unlikely. Furthermore, Valerie had happily admitted to Bob Acott very early on in the investigation that they had been to the cornfield before for sexual purposes, so there was hardly any need to cover it up on this occasion. Valerie was furious about the suggestion and wrote in capital letters across her notepad 'REFUTE INSINUATION'.[14]

Woffinden, like others before him, named Alphon as the real killer of Michael Gregsten. Alphon had, of course, admitted the crime, retracted it and readmitted it again over the years, but when he was in confession mode he said that he had been asked to carry out the attack by an anonymous figure who wanted to teach the couple a lesson because of their immoral behaviour.

Inferences were drawn from that confession, and people had become more confident in suggesting that it had been Janet Gregsten who had set up the whole incident. She had tried in vain, so the theory continued, to get her husband to leave Valerie but had failed. There was only one thing left for it and that was to threaten and scare them off. Janet had, years earlier, repeatedly denied such suggestions and Valerie had dismissed it as rubbish.

But Woffinden ignored what Alphon had claimed and came up with a completely different theory: it was not that Gregsten and Storie needed separating but it was that Gregsten needed to be off the scene altogether because someone else wanted to occupy his place. Janet had an admirer. So, the question was, who was this man who wanted Gregsten out of the way and was prepared to take such drastic steps? By implication, it was William Ewer, brother-in-law to Janet and who fairly soon after the tragic events of 1961 had moved in with her and the children. This idea had been hinted at many times before, not least by Jeremy Fox when he had written to Valerie in 1995. Woffinden now said that Ewer had not been overly keen on Michael anyway, a view that is, in fact, supported by the statement Ewer had made to the police in the early part of the police investigation, and was quick to extend the hand of sympathy to the beleaguered widow.[15]

It was true that there was something different about Ewer, not simply because he had gone to bed with his recently widowed sister-in-law, but his name had crept to the surface immediately after the trial in quite bizarre circumstances and in a manner that may have tainted Valerie's attitude towards Janet.

According to a number of journalists, Ewer had approached them before the verdict had been reached and told them that in the week following the shooting Janet had been in his antique shop in Swiss Cottage when she had seen a man who she was sure was her husband's killer walking into Burtol Cleaners, the very place Hanratty had deposited his green suit for alterations and repairs. She based her opinion on the descriptions being circulated in the newspapers, but had certainly never heard of Hanratty and nor, at that time, had the police. She was so convinced that this was the man who had murdered her husband that she asked her brother-in-law to follow it up. Ewer went from shop to shop and eventually established that the man had gone into a florist to order some flowers for his mother, a Mrs Hanratty of Kingsbury. Ewer telephoned the police who, in time, with all the other numerous sightings of a man fitting the description flooding into the incident room, followed it up. Clearly, this did not lead to Hanratty being identified.

It was such an incredible story that the wife of the murdered man had, almost by intuition, found the killer, that doubts started to creep in about

Ewer's account. Janet would later deny all knowledge of such an incident and when spoken to some years after the event, Ewer himself diluted his story somewhat. His behaviour, though, fuelled Woffinden's ideas about his involvement, particularly as it had been him who had gone to the hospital with Janet to visit Valerie while she was recovering from her injuries in Guy's hospital.

Ewer remained with Janet until 1969 when she moved away with her children to Cornwall. There will always remain a hint of unseemliness about the relationship between Janet and Ewer but, accepting that Woffinden was carefully selecting which parts of Alphon's confession he wished to use in this conspiracy theory, it seems wholly unlikely that Ewer, a man who, according to Alphon, had wanted to split up an immoral couple, would then choose to move in with his sister-in-law so soon after her husband's death.

Woffinden considered Alphon to be a highly intelligent psychopath and also attributed the attacks (as had many others before him) upon Meike Dalal in Richmond and Audrey Willis in Knebworth to the list of crimes committed by him. However, when the CCRC eventually set out its report in 1999, it made it clear that there was absolutely no evidence that Alphon was involved in the A6 killing at all. In that regard, the Commission, the police and Hawser were all agreed.

But Woffinden's book, coupled with the referral of the matter to the Court of Appeal, now triggered the press to again splash the story.

'Woffinden is confident that the evidence he has uncovered will prove that Hanratty did not commit the crime,' reported the *Observer*.[16]

The *Daily Express*[17] reported under the headline of 'Evidence grows for Hanratty' that 'a wheelchair-bound recluse kept her long silence yesterday in the face of dramatic new developments in the campaign to clear the name of the man hanged 37 years ago for murdering her lover'. Alongside its opening paragraph rested a photograph of Valerie in her wheelchair. The editors were clearly readying its readership for the dramatic denouement that they felt was not now very far away.

The *Daily Express* was probably keen to talk to her after some casual comments she had made five years earlier, when she said that, 'If people want to stand up in court trying to prove the moon is made of green cheese and has little men in it, let them,' a clear dig at the pro-Hanratty campaigners.[18] Quite how this comment had got to reporters' ears while she was maintaining her silence is not clear, but she would later acknowledge saying it.

It was the *Mail on Sunday*[19] that was awarded Valerie's most cutting endorsement, which she scribbled across her copy of the article: 'The best fantasy yet!' Under the title, 'The lonely twilight world of the woman who sent Hanratty to hang', the readers were told that Valerie Storie was alone in her suburban sitting room when she heard the news (the referral to the Court of Appeal). It was the blow, the article said, that Valerie had long feared but half-expected. New DNA evidence and suppressed evidence were to provide the key to unlock the door to overturning the conviction. Worse than that, she would have to face the possibility that she had identified the wrong person and sent an innocent man to the gallows. And if that was the case, it continued, somewhere the man who had killed her lover and crippled her was living free.

With the allegedly lonely, crippled, mistaken woman vividly described, the newspaper went on to describe her house as a 'small home in Cippenham, Berkshire, an uninspiring suburb of Slough. She was unlike any others who lived in her street.' It was important to point out that 'thick net curtains shroud the windows, blocking out the sunlight. There is no knocker or bell on the front door but an entry phone to turn away unwanted visitors.'

The article continued by claiming that neighbours had stuck together to protect her from prying eyes and shopkeepers would not talk about her or her life. 'Yet,' it said, 'careful piecing together of this reclusive figure reveals the demons that drive a woman who will always have a place in British criminal history.'

It went on, citing inaccuracy after inaccuracy, about which Valerie later jokingly said, 'Oh my God. Save me from the media. I can't cope with it.'[20]

To an extent, Valerie may have expected a certain degree of unwarranted attention beyond reporting the facts, and her attitude was once more one of disdain rather than anger. But her equanimity was stretched when now-retired Detective Superintendent Roger Matthews, who had authored the report that had landed on the desk at the CCRC, wrote an article in the *Daily Mail*[21] entitled 'They hanged the wrong man'. In it he claimed that there had been a gross miscarriage of justice, though he omitted to explain how he arrived at that conclusion. But with a former senior detective and the newspapers reiterating claims of Hanratty's innocence, it is no surprise that some unsavoury by-products began to appear.

Playwright Michael Burnham was astounded that a man could be convicted on what he considered such flimsy evidence and decided he wanted to write a play about the whole affair. Simply called *Hanging Hanratty,* the play was performed at a number of different theatres in London and elsewhere.

The renewed publicity triggered more public reaction. One correspondent wrote to the *Daily Mail:*[22]

A senior investigating detective in the Hanratty case told me after the hanging that police planted the gun on the 36A bus to link it to the Vienna hotel where Hanratty had stayed. There may be many former policemen, scientific officers and others who know the truth but fear to speak out on this and other crimes.

In spite of this and other similar claims, Valerie remained silent.

Chapter Twenty

The Final Judgement

Despite the wishes of the family, on 17 October 2000, the Court of Appeal ordered the exhumation of James Hanratty's body; it was something they wished to consider at the same time as they assessed the seventeen points of appeal submitted by Michael Mansfield QC, who was now acting for the family.

His grounds largely echoed those identified by the Commission and it would be the role of the court to determine whether Hanratty's conviction was safe, and not, paradoxically, whether he was guilty; that had been a matter for a jury thirty-eight years ago. Mansfield argued that, procedurally, it was wrong for the Crown to try to introduce any new DNA evidence, but he was overruled.

Despite the Hanratty family's thirty-nine-year-long campaign to ensure that everything possible should be done to prove their relative's innocence, they now objected to the exhumation on another ground: it would disturb the body of his aunt, who was buried with him in the same grave.[1]

The court, though, had made its decision. Hanratty's body was exhumed and a bone sample was taken from the remains, which showed conclusively that Valerie's knickers and the handkerchief in which the murder weapon had been found contained James Hanratty's DNA.[2] It was a significant development. It allowed the appeal process to move forward and the court could now consider this new evidence alongside the more fundamental proposition put forward by the defence that the original prosecution had been so materially flawed that the conviction, regardless of the DNA evidence, should be set aside. A hearing was set for May 2002.

The news that Hanratty's DNA matched the staining on the police exhibits was startling and unexpected. The referral from the Commission to the Court of Appeal had raised hopes among Hanratty supporters that at last justice was to be done, but suddenly this all changed. The matter needed to be formally put before the court and strangely the conviction might still be overturned if it was thought the trial process had been flawed.

The scientific revelation brought the reporters to Valerie's front door once more, but for the first time in thirty-five years, she felt ready to talk. She had been vindicated and she wanted the world to know that Hanratty had not ruined her life, and allowed a photo to be taken of her in her living room. It was more likely than not that she was unaware that the appeal was more than just a mere formality and Hanratty's conviction could be quashed, but she could hold back no longer. It had been him who had raped her and she had been right all along.

In the *Mail on Sunday* the tone was much more upbeat about Valerie, the person. No longer was she the recluse who lived in uninspiring suburbia and remained hidden behind net curtains. She now lived in an airy Berkshire home and was a remarkable woman who had remained steadfastly silent, courageously getting on with her life despite her disabilities. Suddenly her appearance and her interests in life were the focus and not the fact that the crippled loner had been mistaken in her identification. In fact, the paper said, 'she appears to be just another pensioner quietly enjoying her retirement' reading romantic novels and carrying on with charity work.[3]

Television companies again wanted her attention and she could see the groundswell starting as confidence increased in Hanratty's conviction being upheld. She had been silent for thirty-five years but she could see that the time had come to tell her side of the story.

Earlier she had put out a statement entitled, 'To co-operate or not', in which she set out not only her conditions but a summary of the trauma she had undergone.[4] She started:

> To make it perfectly clear to all concerned, I am not obliged to say any-
> thing to anyone, at any time. I am an innocent victim in this unseemly mess
> because: I was merely raped, shot, left for dead after a nightmare scenario at
> gunpoint and I was a living witness to a murder – Hanratty would have been
> found guilty with or without me.

She named the television companies which had 'hounded her' and com-mented on the numerous authors and feature writers 'of varying standards and proficiency' who had plagued her. Journalists had tried to contact her sometimes by post but more routinely by banging on her front door, looking through her windows and poking about in her front and back garden 'picking up sundry scraps of rubbish'. On one occasion, she had become so frustrated and upset that she was reduced to swearing and told one reporter to 'fuck off'; her mother would not have approved.

Notes pushed through her letter box spelt her name incorrectly and got dates wrong – once by ten years. One article had even said she had died in 1995 and that she had begun to believe that the wrong man had been convicted.[5]

She finished what was effectively a press statement, by saying that if anyone wanted to speak with her they would need to pay tens, if not hundreds, of thousands of pounds to her charity, Slough Community Transport and Shop Mobility, and signed off, 'Take it or leave it.'

Many wanted to take up her offer. Suddenly they wanted to portray her as the woman who had been proven right after all this time. She accepted two offers of donations to her Slough charity, including one from an independent production company who carried out a series of interviews with her and which became the subject of a television programme by Channel 4 the following year.

One particular issue was the relationship between her and Michael. It had been largely hushed up during the trial and over the past few years various articles had been written that had focused on the 'lover' relationship. None of this had been put before the jury but the time now seemed right to raise the subject and she confirmed that she was now happy to speak about it. The relationship had been a full, intimate one since 1959 and there is little doubt she had been completely smitten with Michael. When asked, she did not deny she was in love but neither did she admit it. This should be compared to words she uttered as she lay in the layby forty years earlier when she was asked whether the dead man lying next to her was her husband. She had said no, but they were 'in love'.[6] Perhaps the passage of so many years had made her more circumspect when it came to talking about the relationship and she was comfortable about building in distance between them. When Michael had secured new, rented accommodation in Maidenhead the night before the attack he had told the landlord that his fiancée was waiting outside in the car, possibly because it was true that they had agreed to marry but, equally possible, a white lie as a means to influence the landlord to allow them to live together, or at least allow her to visit and stay over. Throughout the journey between the cornfield and the A6 Valerie routinely called him 'darling' and there is little doubt that deep affection was there, although such life-threatening situations would be susceptible to a last-gasp outburst of emotion. Yet, with the passage of time her attitude seems to have hardened.

When now asked specifically whether marriage had ever been discussed, her reply was quite emphatic. 'No. There was never a question. It was never discussed.' She added more clarity.

> I've never really said this before but the relationship we had, really had run its course. I don't think we would have been together, inasmuch as we were together, if this hadn't have happened. I think by the time a further six months had gone past, then the relationship we had would have been over. I'm quite sure that our friendship, our romance if you like, had run its course and this has always been to me a very ironic thing that this happened and so much pain has been caused to so many people. Another few months and it wouldn't have happened.

There were a number of instances when Valerie's recollection of events of forty years earlier were inaccurate: days of the week, timings and so on, which is only to be expected. But recalling such human emotions as love and affection is less likely to vary. It is more likely that at the time she felt strong affection towards Michael, may even have privately felt she loved him, but with the benefit of time realised that it was more of an adventurous crush rather than true love. There is no evidence that Michael loved her but there is plenty to confirm that he was attracted to her, physically and mentally. When first spoken to in the hospital following the attack, she had mentioned more than once that marriage had been discussed, but forty years later this was now reversed. This disparity was never put to her since her earlier comments had never been made public and, in any event, would have had no bearing on why Hanratty carried out the attack. It is possible that she may have forgotten that she had mentioned in her very first statements that marriage had been discussed as it had never been spoken of since, not even at trial. It is equally possible that over the years she had somehow distanced herself from the trauma from which she undoubtedly suffered by blocking out certain memories, some form of dissociative amnesia, though this seems unlikely given that she was able to recall most of the detail of what happened that night. Her parents certainly said that they had no knowledge of an intimate relationship between the two of them, even though she had brought him home from work that night.

It will always be a moot point as to whether Valerie genuinely believed that Michael was intending to marry her or deep down she knew that it was a pipe dream that would never be realised.

Yet, while her recollections about marriage had changed, her sense of guilt seems to have increased. When she returned to work in 1962, she sensed that everyone had simply accepted that she and Michael had been in a relationship that would have been seen as immoral by some observers. But as the years had gone by, she began to reflect on the fact that, whichever way she looked at it, she had been involved with a married man and that had only complicated matters. True, Michael was equally as liable and he and his wife had been ready to split, but the passage of time had made her feel that, perhaps, she ought to take some of the blame.[7] As she would later say, 'I paid the price for what I did.'[8]

During the rest of the interview, she opened her soul and told all; her innermost thoughts, her outlook on life and, of course, the events of the night of 22 August 1961. But most of what she said, including her revelation about her relationship with Michael, remained on the cutting room floor and she decided that it was time to write a book. If no one would tell her personal story, she would.

Newspapers did write articles, of course, and people were beginning to gain some greater insight into her side of the story but not everyone was convinced on the morality of the case.

One anonymous writer wrote to the *Daily Mail*, which passed the letter on to Valerie:

> I've read your account of events and I am totally appalled at your running down of Mrs Janet Gregsten. She is not here to say that she knew of her husband's affair with you and your saying she was neurotic and had threatened suicide (not surprising as he was carrying on with you). I well remember the reports when it happened and she did not know. Don't justify yourself. You were not in a field to discuss motoring – give readers some intelligence. It was a place to get on your back with someone else's husband, some poor children's father. If you hadn't been a common adulteress, two people would be alive today. Don't make your side right. You were an available whore who God has given justice to. You care not for his wife or the family.

The writer explained how his daughter had gone through a similar experience with her husband leaving her and having an affair:

> You could not have got a kinder, nicer person, trusting and loving and he abandoned her for a tramp like you. Whores like you do deserve to be shot and I am bloody glad you are suffering. So you damn well should.

In contrast, Valerie received a large number of letters of support, but none has survived, and they would perhaps have been able to provide a counterbalance to the question of 1960s attitudes towards infidelity. Morality aside, though, the important question now was whether the man who had destroyed their lives was, officially, James Hanratty. Valerie had taken a brave step in speaking before the Court of Appeal made its final judgement, but that would be the next step.

When the court resumed in April the following year, Mansfield accepted that if the court was satisfied that the DNA was indeed that of Hanratty he would undoubtedly be the murderer. But he argued that given that the exhibits – Valerie's knickers and the handkerchief in which the murder weapon had been concealed – dated back forty years, there was a very real risk that the marks could have been contaminated when being handled in the laboratory. Specifically referring to the semen found on the knickers, he pointed out to the court that similar stains had also been found on Hanratty's Hepworth trousers, which had also been subject to forensic examination. Due to the poorer standards of packaging and the handling of exhibits of the day, it was likely, he argued, that these had come into contact with a surface in the laboratory upon which Valerie's knickers had been placed and therefore any staining could have been passed, unwittingly, from one to the other. It was a perfectly valid argument.

Evidence from one of the scientists[9] involved in the original investigation told the court that while this could not be wholly eliminated, the likelihood was low, and even back in 1961, victims' and offenders' clothing were never in the laboratory on the same day. The judges explored in detail the chronology and the handling of each of the exhibits and they concluded that the risk of contamination was so remote that it could be safely dismissed. Furthermore, the handkerchief contained only mucus and only one DNA profile – Hanratty's. If this had contaminated by another profile left by someone else, then the argument would be that that other person's DNA had now fully disappeared leaving only Hanratty's. In the words of the appeal judges, the notion that such a thing might have happened was 'fanciful'.[10]

With the new scientific evidence now accepted by the court, it had to determine whether any of the seventeen arguments put forward by Mansfield demonstrated that the non-disclosure of material to the defence would have afforded them the ability to present a stronger and more informed case. And if that was the position, it then had to decide what the effect of such non-disclosure would have had and whether it amounted to something so serious that it had prevented Hanratty from having a fair trial.[11]

On 10 May, the court passed its judgement.[12]

The coincidences in the case, they pointed out, were remarkable. For it not to have been Hanratty responsible for the murder it meant firstly that three witnesses had been wrong in their identification. Moreover, Hanratty had the same speech characteristic as the killer, he had stayed the night before the murder in the room where the cartridges had been found, the gun was found in a location that he regarded as being a good hiding place, and his DNA had now been identified in compromising positions. The number of coincidences, they said, meant that they were not coincidences but overwhelming proof of the safety of the conviction from an evidential perspective. 'The DNA evidence made what was a strong case, even stronger.'[13] Insofar as any procedural irregularities were concerned, they were satisfied that they fell far short of what was required to lead to the conclusion that the trial should be regarded as flawed and the conviction unsafe, and consequently the court ruled that the appeal should be dismissed.

The two aspects of the case that had led to the most prolonged and heated public and legal debate were resolved by the Appeal Court decision.

Firstly, the court now threw light on why the police had circulated the wrong eye colour of the attacker early in the investigation. When Valerie made her very first statement in hospital on the day she was found in the layby, she made no reference to the colour of her attacker's eyes. The officers who had interviewed her then briefed Sergeant Christopher Absalom in order for the description that they had obtained to be circulated. For some inexplicable reason he translated the word brown as the colour of the eyes rather than, as Valerie had said, the colour of his hair. There had been a communication breakdown in the transference of information. This careless but innocent action triggered the catalogue of debate that exercised the minds of journalists, police officers, politicians, judges and barristers for decades. It was a simple error, but one that underlines Valerie's truthfulness, accuracy and integrity. She mentioned blue eyes to the police officer who had constructed her Identikit on 26 August and confirmed it again in her statement two days later. There should never have been any doubt about the colour of the attacker's eyes.

Secondly, the Alphon confessions had been conclusively shown to be false.

'By way of postscript,' the Lord Chief Justice said, 'we should record that it has been agreed by Mr Sweeney (prosecuting counsel) and Mr Mansfield that on the evidence now available [DNA], Peter Alphon could not have been the murderer.'[14]

From the day of the murder of Michael Gregsten and the rape and attempted murder of Valerie Storie it had taken just over seven months to arrest, try, convict and hang James Hanratty. It had taken another forty years for Valerie to be vindicated.

Chapter Twenty-One

The Final Years

Valerie was now 63 years old, four years older than her father had been when he had died in 1964. Her mother had been dead for twenty-seven years and since then, other than some home-care support, she had effectively fended for herself. She had originally been thrust into the public limelight as a young 22-year-old at a time when rape victims could be freely named in newspapers. The law had changed in the meantime[1] to provide anonymity for victims but that was the image people had in their mind's eye whenever they heard her name mentioned. But she had now suddenly become older, a white-haired woman in a wheelchair, and finally some measure of sympathy was flowing her way. The critics had fallen silent and she must have become aware of a book that had been published that, for the first time, argued for Hanratty's guilt.

Leonard Miller's *Shadow of Deadman's Hill* was not simply a retelling of events topped up with the latest DNA developments. He had originally believed in Hanratty's innocence[2] based on what he had read – like millions of others – but having closely analysed both Foot's and Woffinden's books, he saw that their narratives contained false assumptions and skewed observations. Careful editing, he said, was a tactic employed to paint Alphon in a far more sinister light than he actually was and when analysing Liverpool train times, Woffinden simply changed the data to make his theory fit. Whereas Foot had relied on newspaper accounts, Miller pointed out that 'simple [newspaper] statements end up horribly garbled, names get mis-spelled and remarks get mis-heard or otherwise distorted. Newspaper journalists, local or national, seem chronically incapable of transmitting any information with 100% accuracy.'[3] There was no evidence whatsoever, he said, to support any of the conspiracy theories, which seemed to have grown from nothing.[4] As for Woffinden's programme

The Mystery of Deadman's Hill, Miller said, 'it tells whopper after whopper' and is a 'triumph of misrepresentations'.[5]

Miller had captured much of what Valerie would have reasoned. Quite what she made of the book is not known since she made no notes about it, but a copy lay among her personal belongings. It did not go anywhere near telling her own story but if she had read it, she would have approved.

The following year, Ludovic Kennedy, who had been arguing Hanratty's innocence for many years, published another book, *Thirty Six Murders & Two Immoral Earnings*, in which he once again outlined a series of miscarriages of justice; strikingly, the James Hanratty case was omitted.

After the Court of Appeal issued its final judgement, Valerie made a lengthy press statement, the final paragraph of which read:

> I have never had a problem with the truth. My evidence has never changed, neither have I ever had any doubts. I repeat that James Hanratty was guilty of the crime for which he was hanged. James Hanratty killed Michael Gregsten. I know that because I was there. Please God, the judgement by the Lord Chief Justice sees not merely the end of yet one more chapter but the end of this book that has been part of my life for so many years. I would ask you now to respect my wish to be left in peace.[6]

But this carefully crafted script masked her stronger feelings, which she had scribbled down on paper while drafting her final say and doubtlessly were her early thoughts on what she would detail in her own book.

> Hanratty committed a crime and was found guilty and was hanged. I therefore have no fear of him. If anyone doesn't want to be punished then they, surely, don't commit the crime. If he hadn't been hanged, with life sentences meted out today, then he would be long out of prison. I would be terrified of every unusual sound or knock at the door. I could not ever relax.

Of the media, she wrote:

> The media have made my life very difficult. They have been intrusive and invading my privacy. They believe they have a right to know everything about you and find it difficult when you say, 'on your bike.' No one has ever listened to me before – media wise – so there was little point in raising my blood pressure. Now is the right time to speak, but make the most of it, I won't be doing it after today – hopefully.

About the books and articles that had been written:

> As the campaign went on it was getting, to my mind, more and more outra-
> geous. The printed words, the various films made, perpetuated this folklore
> almost until the average person in the street was only aware of these books
> and had no concept of the truth.

Of the police:

> I would like to pay tribute to the professionalism, dedication and absolute
> integrity of the original officers investigating this case: Harold Whiffen of
> the Bedfordshire Police and his team and then Bob Acott, Ken Oxford and
> their team from the Met. Bob, Ken and I remained in contact, watching
> with increasing horror, at the unfolding events over the years. We kept our
> counsel in the unshakeable belief that one day, somehow, the truth would
> be recognised.

Of the Hanratty family:

> They have had over forty years believing he was innocent and I have had
> more than forty years of knowing he wasn't. I don't bear the Hanratty family
> any ill will. I think the saddest thing to come out of these last few months
> is not the fact that they will have to accept that he did kill but that the very
> last words he wrote to his family, that he was innocent, was a lie. That must
> be very difficult for them.

But she had no axe to grind with the man who had destroyed her life:

> I am not bitter. You can't live like that. You destroy yourself, let alone every-
> one else. Hanratty is not a real person to me. I have always believed in capital
> punishment and he committed a crime for which that was the punishment.[7]

Any venom she had was reserved for authors such as Paul Foot and Bob
Woffinden, who had campaigned for years to prove Hanratty's innocence and
perhaps more worryingly for the guilt of a man, Peter Alphon, for whom it was
now proven beyond all doubt that he could not have committed the crimes.

'It has been said that even if Hanratty came back and said, "I was guilty,"
they still would not accept it,' Valerie said. 'They have built their case on this
myth and like a cancer it has grown to become pure folklore. What I do find

distasteful is that the family's belief in their son's innocence has been boosted so much by campaigners who have given them false hope.'

And finally, as if it was some afterthought, some measure of her despair and hope, she wrote on her notepad, 'You dream, and very rarely, you are not in a wheelchair.'

But she also had anxieties. It had only been in recent years that she had stopped waking up at two o'clock in the morning on 22 August each year, the exact date and time Michael had been shot. She now felt uncomfortable simply sitting in a car and hated it if anyone came to her house and tapped on her window, a reminder of the events in the cornfield. Neither could she any more go into a butcher's shop, the smell of blood bringing back memories of the odour inside the Morris Minor after Michael had been shot. But at least the newspaper stories were different now. Given the evidence placed before the Appeal Court, they all finally reported that Hanratty was guilty, some even claiming Hanratty had confessed to a Catholic priest moments before his execution.

★★★

By the time the Appeal Court made its final ruling, former Detective Sergeant Ken Oxford had died. He and Valerie had kept in contact by letter and phone over the years and exchanged Christmas cards, although his writing was so illegible that she had trouble reading it. He had been a big support for her not only during the investigation and trial but also in later years when newspaper reports and television programmes brought the matter to the surface time and time again. He was again in the headlines two years later when he arrested Christine Keeler during the Profumo affair and later, in 1976, he was appointed Chief Constable of Merseyside before eventually retiring in 1989 so that he could 'catalogue his books and music collection'.[8] Unfortunately, he died at a time when the matter was with the CCRC and it was looking likely that the conviction would be overturned.

Bob Acott too had passed away, although only the year before.[9] In recent years, he had suffered two strokes that had 'ruined his eyesight, memory and balance', and had needed to deal with journalists who had continually libelled him in newspapers and which had forced him to sue, successfully, for damages. Although his passing was before the ultimate court ruling, he would probably have been aware of the scientific findings that pointed towards Hanratty's guilt. He had always been sure that he had got the right man, and in letters to Valerie he reinforced the point that he too had always maintained his silence.

Acott, and less so Oxford, had been criticised almost from when the news first broke in 1961. The confusion over the colour of the eyes was the starting point and this, and almost every other aspect of the investigation, had become a target for criticism ever since. Each time their names were mentioned, their deceit, in the eyes of the public, multiplied. In reality, there is nothing to suggest that they were anything other than honest, hard-working people who worked tirelessly to build a prosecution case. Perhaps the biggest single issue that occupied their minds was the alleged involvement of Peter Alphon.[10] Acott had explained in the witness box his rationale for pursuing him but its context was never really understood.

Alphon was never, as so many thought, 'the first suspect'. When Alphon's name emerged, a file was raised. When James Hanratty became a suspect, he too had a file raised. In terms of procedure, especially in a case as significant as this, the police do not simply get a lead, follow it and if that turns out to be someone who clearly is not responsible, file it and start on the next one. When names are passed to police incident rooms, as Alphon's was, they tend to flood in. Sometimes they are just descriptions of 'suspicious' people who were seen getting off a bus somewhere but who seemed to match the description of the killer, or the caller had a next-door neighbour once who used to sleep rough at night and always looked the type 'who would do that sort of thing'. The police themselves generate people of interest based on description and the modus operandi of criminals in their system, of which there are, and were then, many thousands. All these have to be analysed and a judgement made over which should take priority. But the point is, those priorities are dealt with simultaneously by a large number of officers. When Alphon's name, or Durrant as he was first known, was first telephoned in on 27 August, he was just one of hundreds of names that had been fed into Acott's system. It is true that he seemed of interest due to his evasiveness, but he was just another name.

Where Acott exposed his vulnerability, and what in hindsight was perhaps a regrettable step, was to go to the press and say that he wanted to speak to him in connection with the murder. Of course, everyone was going to think he was a suspect; that was the only logical conclusion. It is a largely undefinable area to determine when someone moves from 'a person of interest' to 'a suspect', but there was little doubt that he needed to be traced, interviewed and either implicated or eliminated because of his connection with the Vienna hotel. That was what Acott did but it was an error to name him publicly. For Alphon's part, he did nothing more than take full advantage of the situation. Hitherto, he had been an unemployed man who wandered the streets of London allowing his mother to fund his nomadic lifestyle. Suddenly, there were newspapers and television companies, and as time went on, a barrister and businessman who became fascinated with him and he was, for once in his life, centre stage.

But it was Acott's overall integrity that was challenged by the campaigners. He was, they said, corrupt. To an extent this was based on what Hanratty was telling his legal advisors. It is fair to say that Acott could have done a better job over the handling of the interviews with Hanratty, the arrangements for the identification parades and the disclosing of information to the defence. Part of that fell to prosecuting counsel to discharge their responsibilities under the law but the principal responsibility rested with the police. But as the Court of Appeal eventually ruled, all of this fell far short of saying that justice had not been done. Acott was not corrupt. He was a police officer doing his best – occasionally he could have done better.

Following the court ruling, Valerie received an unexpected letter. It was from Anthony Gregsten, the youngest son of Michael, who had not been 2 years old when his father had been murdered. It was a kind, compassionate and thoughtful letter that told Valerie that throughout all the years of torment she had endured, and among all the suggestions that she had been responsible for the ruination of a family, Anthony told her that 'her courage had not gone unnoticed'. Even more encouraging was that he had never had a problem with Valerie's relationship with his father, and his mother had never had a bad word to say about her; she had remained open-minded and kind-hearted right up to her death in 1995.

Much of the letter concerned his personal thoughts about his relationship with his older brother, Simon, who had recently reported his own version of events in the newspapers[11] but which Anthony knew was quite wrong and inaccurate. It also contained more information about his mother's and their relationship with Bill Ewer, but that should remain private.

However, he was hugely critical of both Paul Foot and Bob Woffinden and how they had treated his mother and how, over the years, they developed the theory that Janet had in some way been responsible, or at least had been the catalyst, for the murder. She had needed to deal with people looking at her in a 'knowing' way and when, as a young boy, he had first read Foot's book and learned of the accusations, the effect on his mother had been huge. She needed to reassure him that the suggestion was untrue and, in time, he came to realise that, but it had been extremely painful. Foot eventually had back-tracked on the theory, but much damage had been done and Anthony was in no doubt that his and Woffinden's treatment of her had accelerated her death at the premature age of 64. He had received not one word of apology from either of them and had been most upset when seeing their smiling faces at the Court of Appeal hearing.

Anthony had dissected their books and compared them to the television programme *The Mystery of Deadman's Hill*, which Woffinden had produced, and pointed out the inconsistencies. Anthony's comments are contained in a private document but he pointed out that if you asked anybody what they knew of the A6 murder, the only name they would respond with would be Hanratty; the victims' names are rarely remembered. Anthony and his family had suffered badly at the hands of the campaigners and Hanratty had shattered their lives, but enclosed in the letter was a photograph of his father's final resting place at Golders Green crematorium; it was a poignant and thoughtful gesture.

Valerie would have reflected on this letter and welcomed the message that Janet had not thought ill of her. She herself had expressed regret over the leaked, private conversation she had had with Janet in Guy's hospital in 1961, but other than that she recognised Janet for what she was; a kind and loving mother to her two sons.

There is one thing, should Anthony or any of the Gregsten family today read this account, about which they should reassure themselves. In an article in *Best* magazine in 2002,[12] Anthony was quoted as saying that his mother, who had never really got over the identification of her husband as he lay on the side of the A6, had been unable to identify him properly because his face had been 'blown off'. This is not true and Janet was able, greatly upsetting as it must have been, to recognise him. If it is an abiding memory that Michael was left in such a sorry state, it can be dismissed once and for all.

Despite everything that has been written about the Gregsten family, it is clear that both Michael and Janet were loving parents. Their marriage, like so many others, suffered from its problems, but this was a normal family whose lives were simply ripped apart.

Valerie was touched by what she had read and responded immediately. It was a reply that demonstrated her sadness about how people's lives had been affected; not just hers, but others: the Gregstens, the Acotts, the Oxfords.

Valerie was once asked whether she ever thought about what her life would have been like had she not been in that cornfield in Dorney Reach. She was characteristically blunt:

No. What's the point? You can't ever go through life saying, what if? The two words that I have never, ever, ever, ever uttered in my whole life is, why me? Those two words are so destructive. You can't say, why me? Why did it happen to me? You would end up mad if you do and you just have to get on with life. Don't sit down and wail about it. You get up, get out and do something, that's been my philosophy and I can honestly say, with my hand on my heart, that I have never broken that vow.[13]

But with the incessant banging on her door and windows by reporters now over, and despite her speaking more openly to the media, she remained disappointed that the world still did not know the real Valerie Storie. She had remained silent since the *Panorama* programme in 1966 all the way through to 2001, when news of the DNA began to emerge; thirty-five years of pent-up frustration. People needed to know why she decided to remain silent and how she had maintained a strength of character that had allowed her to rebuild her life. She gathered together the list of books and articles that had been written, sorted the hundreds of newspaper articles that had been printed, jotted down a list of the key events and sketched out the ideas for her book.[14]

She was emphatic about not only portraying the real Valerie, the person behind the wheelchair, but wanted to pay tribute to her parents, who had been 'distressed beyond belief'[15] by the press intrusion that had, she felt, contributed to her father's death. When the events of August 1961 came along, their world had been shattered and for a family that had been so unassuming and private, it was an undeserved, devastating blow.

Under a heading of 'Myths, Legends and Downright Lies', she wrote:

How did a crime in 1961, which so horrified the nation by its senseless cruelty, degenerate into folklore within forty years – folklore which bore little semblance of truth.

Thousands of words have been written expounding ever more bizarre theories, some of which would be laughable even in a genuine work of fiction let alone a supposed factual happening.

No one – certainly not me – can blame the Hanratty parents for disbelieving the case against their son. What mother anywhere in the world would ever accept the fact that her son was a murderer? The other side of the coin, however, is that every murderer has a mother.

So the family protest his innocence and start a campaign. Someone takes up the cudgel and voices a doubt – after all, how can this petty crook, imprisoned a number of times during his twenty five years, be someone who kills in cold blood?

It could have all ended at this point but something far more sinister takes over. Those with a cause, an axe to grind begin to take an interest. Here is a possibility of an outlet for their beliefs; anti-establishment, anti-police and anti-capital punishment. This fits the bill so easily.

These persuasive men of letters, sow the seeds of fiction, find a theory and somewhere there will be a phrase or action which, when taken entirely out of context or totally mis-quoted, fits this theory.

Now the link is found, the whole story grows, flows like a malevolent cancer, eating away at reality, poisoning any semblance of truth to fit the cause.

She had a number of chapter headings written down and had begun to write the detail of what had happened to her, but suddenly it stopped. Perhaps she lost enthusiasm or maybe she just simply got tired. The years had taken their toll on her. Even as late as the 1990s, when the story was reaching its denouement, the occurrence of reporters banging on her door, shouting through her letter box, her neighbours being chased down the road to get an inside story, had worn her out. It had even got to the stage that when leaving her house, she had taken to wearing a towel over her head to protect herself from the photographers. Her life had become miserable and for now, in all probability, she decided that the book would need to take a back seat.

In a rather ironic twist, she turned her hand instead to researching local history and in 2005 she gave a presentation about a murder committed in 1853 at Burnham Abbey; perhaps she felt qualified to talk about it or simply she was finding an easier way to talk about such things.

She obviously did a good job, though.

'Hanratty victim turns super sleuth to solve a murder', her local newspaper reported.[16]

She was described as a white-haired woman who enthralled her audience demonstrating a dry sense of humour and having a no-nonsense attitude, but when asked about her own experience she quickly stopped the conversation in its tracks, insisting that it had no bearing on her current life. She reinforced her position. She had kept silent for thirty-five years, had spoken only once when the verdict was confirmed, and then returned to her own world.

In the years that followed, Valerie would visit attractions such as Brighton Pavilion, Hampton Court and Buckingham Palace, places that made her feel happy, but her health was once more starting to deteriorate. She was making more frequent trips to Stoke Mandeville hospital for operations and treatment as her body started to slow down due to her years of immobility. One of the nurses at the hospital, Tracey Geddis, who came to admire Valerie for her strength of character and wit, once went to see her in the intensive care unit after one of her operations, only to find that she had already been sent back to her ward. In an expression of affection, she described her as a 'hardy old bird' who seemed to just brush off such traumatic events. Valerie, she said, was stubborn, tenacious, had a twinkle in her eye and was a wise person who had compassion hidden behind a hard exterior. So proud of her was she, that she once had a photograph taken of the pair of them and proudly displayed it on her office wall.[17]

At home though, Valerie always felt cold and her day carers had to put cushions underneath her to try to keep her warm. Everything was becoming an effort. She wanted to continue with her book but she realised now that it was beyond her capabilities. She made her decision. The world, after all, would not now hear her side of the story, her years of torment and how, despite being plunged on occasions into the depths of despair, she had held out and fought through the battle that had been brought so abruptly and catastrophically to her front door in 1961.

By 2015, she was seriously ill and one of her legs became infected, due probably to a lack of blood circulation after years of immobility, and needed to be amputated just below the knee, a very sad chapter in a lifetime battle over her health. The following year, on 26 March, at the age of 77, she passed away in the same house in which she had been born. Well over 100 people attended her funeral and many commented that Valerie was a kind, yet strong woman who they would miss very much. Her chosen hymn, 'Flower of Scotland', rang out,[18] almost as a last message to her parents; they were in her thoughts to the end.

Other than her press interviews in 2001, she had maintained a dignity of silence for nearly fifty years and would have left this world satisfied that she had.

Epilogue

So, What Really Happened?

There are two perennial questions at the heart of the Hanratty case. Why would a mild-mannered, urbanised petty thief suddenly turn into a rapist and murderer? Why would he be in an isolated cornfield, armed with a gun, in the first place?

There remain, of course, many gaps in our knowledge of what happened and we will never know some of the more probative detail such as Hanratty's precise movements before and after the attack and exactly when, where and how he acquired the murder weapon. The following is an analysis that can be accepted in whole or in part, or simply rejected; it is more than likely that there are different views and what follows is an opinion.

What then, is known about James Hanratty?

A point made by many commentators was that he was a 'mental defective', a phrase that appeared in his medical history as early as 1952, when he was found unconscious in Brighton and diagnosed as feigning amnesia. This phrase, unacceptable today, has its roots in Victorian legislation. It was used, and frequently misused, by clinicians and other professionals in their writings but disappeared from the medical lexicon as the century progressed. It is likely that the doctor who examined Hanratty was referring to his intellectual capabilities rather than any personality trait, and in any event, he may not have been qualified to attach such a categorisation given the limited amount of time he had to examine the patient.

Hanratty's mental state, however, was never an issue at trial, and even though, in the disputed police interview, he suggested that Acott had given him the opportunity to declare diminished responsibility, his counsel never relied on that as part of their defence. Hanratty's argument was simply that he was not in the cornfield and therefore could not have committed the crime.

A related issue arose in the days before Hanratty's execution: that the country should not be hanging people who were suffering from some type of mental disorder, but that was all rather a belated and desperate attempt to prevent him from being executed. He was examined prior to his trial in terms of his fitness to plead, which he was, but that fell far short of any structured assessment. Thus, his mental state was largely ignored at the time and has only been addressed in the various books that have appeared in the years since his death.

That said, an article appeared in *The New Statesman* in 1962[1] entitled 'The Criminal Psychopath', authored by psychiatrist Anthony Storr, in which he asked, 'If proper diagnostic facilities were available, could such a man [as Hanratty] be halted in his career of crime at an earlier stage so that tragedies such as the A6 murder might be prevented?'

This followed reports that Hanratty had been described as a 'potential psychopath' by a doctor at Wormwood Scrubs and the Medical Officer at Durham prison had indeed diagnosed psychopathy.[2]

Psychopathy has been traditionally used to describe a personality disorder that involves persistent antisocial behaviour, reduced empathy and remorse, and extreme egotistical traits. The term has often been used interchangeably with 'sociopathy', although some authors suggest psychopathy has a biological origin with sociopathy being a result of predisposing social factors. However, the term 'psychopathy' is not, and was not, included in the first edition of the *Diagnostic and Statistical Manual of Mental Disorders* published by the American Psychiatric Association in 1951 and current at the time of Hanratty's trial.

The current manual, DSM-5, defines ten types of personality disorder[3] that are determined through a series of personality assessments carried out by mental health professionals involving psychometric tests and semi-structured interviews. Of course, none of this is possible in the Hanratty case, as the diagnostic tool of the time appears somewhat flawed based on contemporary research and there is insufficient information to compare against current criteria. However, by applying current thinking to what is thought to be known about Hanratty, some measure of his personality may, perhaps, be determined.

Hanratty had a high opinion of himself that manifested itself in traits of cockiness and arrogance. There are numerous examples of this, even extending to his prowess in being a professional criminal who made sure he left no fingerprints at his crime scenes; it was, he said, 'his business'. In custody, while awaiting his appearance at court, he told one of his police gaolers that he had stolen well over £3,000 worth of jewellery and furs while he had been on the run, but had only managed to get £750 for his haul.[4] When first arrested, he even acknowledged, albeit the precise detail of the conversation was disputed, that he had wanted to arm himself with a gun so that he could become a 'stick-up man'.[5]

He mixed with the grand, stayed in expensive hotels and could have sex whenever he wanted, he claimed. The first was a lie, the second only an infrequent luxury he could afford and the third is open to question. It was a deceitfulness that reflected a desire to embellish the facts indicating a grandiose image of self-worth and a sense of egotism. In short, he had a compulsion to unnecessarily and habitually lie and it appeared as though he wanted very much to mix with the top criminals while in reality being no more than a housebreaker.

He had a cunning edge to him, often masked by his inability to fully cover his tracks, but he employed tactics to try to ensure his criminal behaviour remained undetected, such as assuming a fictitious name and dying his hair different colours. Quite how he considered those measures would be successful in his housebreaking career is not entirely clear but it demonstrated a veneer of guile that he believed would give him some measure of protection.

Feelings of remorse and guilt seemed absent as he routinely crashed cars, whether they were hired or stolen, and abandoned his window cleaning business, which had been set up by his father, without a hint of guilt about dumping his ladders in someone else's garden. Walking away from his job on the dodgems in Rhyl, which had been given to him only the night before by someone who had been prepared to offer him a chance to earn some money was, for him, acceptable. These may appear on the surface to be small points, maybe just a simple case of irresponsibility, but it indicates a man who had no empathy and had no awareness of the effect of his behaviour upon others.

His family had taken him back under their roof after his release from prison but he had simply walked out, not wanting to take advantage of the fresh start being offered. Since leaving school he had run away on numerous occasions, committing crime and gambling, and had left his mother distraught. Interestingly though, five days before the attack in the cornfield, he sent his mother some flowers together with a message reading, 'Don't worry, Mum. All my love, your son, Jim,' presumably trying to reassure her over his continued absence.[6] Once he knew he was wanted for the murder, he continued to send bunches of flowers and after he was convicted, in the days leading up to his execution, he sent numerous letters to his family expressing loving feelings towards them.[7] However, before that, there appears little to show that he had any meaningful concerns about his family who, by their accounts, were constantly worried about him.

Breaking into people's homes was not a problem for him: stealing was easier than working, and it seemed that if he wanted something, he would take it. While in prison he purposely committed disciplinary offences, nineteen in all, and made four escape attempts, demonstrating not only poor levels of behavioural control but at the same time, ensuring a maximum sentence.[8] Accepting that, as a general rule, nobody chooses to be in prison, Hanratty appears to have had little desire to go out into the outside world and get a job, and all the time he was getting fed, watered and surrounded by fellow inmates from whom he could learn, he seemed content.

His criminal behaviour in the months leading up to the attacks in Dorney indicates that he appears to have enjoyed the risk and the impulsiveness of stealing other people's cars, driving around the country and committing break-in after break-in. None of it seemed planned but rather a means to get money to survive as well as providing a host of activities about which he could boast to his friends. His motivation to move up the criminal ladder may have been because he was simply bored with the mediocrity of burglary, although probably inspired by tales from his fellow criminals.

His dealings with the France family and Louise Anderson before the murder reflects a willingness to use some measure of subterfuge, and to that extent, a degree of planning to achieve his own ends. With Anderson, he simply charmed his way into her life as a means to securing somewhere he could stay for the night as well as establishing a new outlet for his stolen property, but with the Frances, the closer he got to the day of the abduction and murder, the more he equivocated about when he was going to Liverpool. He could have had no idea that he would soon encounter a couple in a car, but his behaviour indicates that he knew that when the time came for him to venture out with a gun, he would need a cover story.

His sexual experiences are, unsurprisingly, difficult to determine. By his own admission, and to an extent this was corroborated, he courted a number of girlfriends, although whether any of them progressed to a full sexual relationship is impossible to determine with any certainty, despite his claims. He also admitted to using a Soho prostitute on occasions, although there is no evidence of this. He proposed marriage on at least two occasions to women after only dating them a few days but whether that was a means to secure a sexual relationship or simply a sign of immaturity or impulsiveness is debatable.

Regardless of the sexual relationships he achieved, there is nothing to show that he developed any form of intimacy with anyone. Other than his immediate family, there is no evidence that anyone was close to him or regarded him as someone they could spend time with, perhaps indicating that closeness was not something he desired or of which he was even capable. Abandoning his family, arguably, fits with this behaviour but it was certainly the case that he routinely failed to remember people's names.

These characteristic traits of irresponsibility, impulsivity and risk-taking coupled with a lack of any sense of empathy for others may well be regarded today as someone suffering from antisocial personality disorder. Of course, the extent to which this may have applied to Hanratty cannot be conclusively determined since, as already noted, there is no means by which any structured assessment may be carried out, but at least this is a possibility. If this analysis is close, given the health warnings around a lack of meaningful data, then this is the type of person who walked out of prison in March 1961, having been incarcerated for the previous three years, and headed back to London to pursue his criminal career.

Upon release, he needed to get money and stealing was all he knew. His first port of call, literally on the day he was released from prison, was to a receiver of stolen property to whom he expressed his wish to 'promote' himself in the criminal world from housebreaker to armed robber.[9]

In time, he would secure his weapon but for now he returned to the routine of breaking into houses in Ruislip and Northwood, where he carelessly left his fingerprints. He did not restrict himself to the south of England, though, and in late July he and a friend of his stole a car, he claimed, and ended up in Shrewsbury, followed by 'a bit of a police chase'. The pair had split up and Hanratty made his way through the Welsh countryside, partly on foot, partly by hitch-hiking, and ended up in Rhyl on 25 July, where he picked up temporary work on the fairground. The following morning he simply failed to turn up for work. As a parting gesture, he made off with a pair of shoes belonging to the man who had put him up for the night.

Having once more shunned his parents' home in Kingsbury and reacquainted himself with Dixie France and his daughter Carol, who helpfully dyed his hair for him, he adopted a nomadic lifestyle sleeping where he could, shifting between their flat, various hotels and, as the weeks went by, his new-found friend and antique dealer, Louise Anderson.

Housebreaking then became a bit of a hit-and-miss affair, sometimes lucrative, other times, less so. The desire, and quite possibly the need, to arm himself may have been driven by the dire financial position in which he found himself, and midway through August he took steps to find a gun. This, of course, is probably the most significant gap in our knowledge: when and from whom did he acquire the .38 calibre Enfield?

Acquire it he did, and for a while, he may well have secreted it in the Frances' cupboard without their knowledge; after all, he would need somewhere safe to keep it as he moved between people's houses. On Sunday, 21 August he dropped by the France household, declaring his intention to travel to Liverpool the following day to visit his aunt, and asked Charlotte to launder his clothes for him. He was wearing his new Hepworth suit, which he had bought only three days earlier. The following day, the Monday, he returned for his clothes, remaining there until seven o'clock in the evening. When he eventually left, he in all probability had the revolver with him.

Despite saying that he was going to Liverpool, he stayed in London and was seen later that evening in the Rehearsal Club in Soho. Around eleven o'clock, he checked into the Vienna hotel, though now using the name J. Ryan. What he did inside room 24 is another gap that cannot be filled but at some stage, at least two spent cartridges fell onto the chair beside his bed in the darkened alcove. On the face of it, it seems that Hanratty believed that he had instilled in people's minds that he was now in Liverpool, he had assumed a false name, provided the hotel with a fictitious address and had experimented with his newly acquired weapon.

The following morning, after breakfast, he gathered his belongings and headed off to Louise Anderson's shop, just over a mile away; he most likely had some stolen property to sell. With his transaction complete, and armed with his gun and a pair of gloves, he set off to explore.

By his own admission, he suspected by now that he was wanted for house-breakings in Ruislip and Northwood, and despite the fact that he had changed the colour of his hair and had assumed the false identity of Jimmy Ryan, he probably considered that his normal territory of leafy Middlesex was too risky.

When he was not stealing cars, his usual modes of transport were trains and buses and now, given his concerns about Middlesex, it would have been sensible to do his day's 'business' somewhere else and he headed for Paddington railway station, a five-minute walk.

Less than an hour away from Paddington were Slough and Maidenhead stations; Taplow, where Valerie and Michael would later go for a drink, nestled in between the two. Exactly where he disembarked is not known, but from each of the stations there was a local bus service. More likely than not it was Maidenhead, from which there was a regular bus service to Dorney, via Taplow, one bus stop in the village being 400 yards along from the cornfield used by Valerie Storie and Michael Gregsten.

Given that, by his own admission, Hanratty was at Paddington station that morning and, years later it would be proven that his DNA was on Valerie's knickers, the most likely sequence of events is that Hanratty toured the Maidenhead and Dorney areas that day, on foot and/or by bus, scouting for houses to break into. At this point, it can be seen that all the ideas about being armed with a gun and carrying out a 'stick-up' were coming to a head.

By half past seven that evening, it is probable that he was already in the Taplow and Dorney area just as Michael and Valerie were leaving Anthony Way to drive to the Old Station Inn. They only stayed there for an hour before setting off for their cornfield. By the time they arrived around nine o'clock, Hanratty would have been walking through the village, possibly looking for a suitable house or simply heading back towards Taplow to catch the train back to Paddington. Either way, he was, if you can believe his fellow criminal in Brixton prison, walking across a field when he came across the Morris Minor, a possible means to get home, of course, but he noticed that there were two people inside. Not a house, but an opportunity had at last presented itself.

Just how events then unfolded were determined by the type of person that Hanratty was. He drove the agenda and he imposed himself on Valerie and Michael in a way that seemed reasonable to him and at a level of criminality to which he aspired. At the point when he tapped on the driver's window, his idea would have amounted to nothing more than pointing his gun at his victims and demanding their valuables. That was only one step beyond simple stealing and it would be a great coup. He would get into the back seat to make sure he would not be seen by any passing motorist or pedestrian, steal whatever they had, and his mission would be accomplished. He would be able to boast for hours about his conquest, no doubt exaggerating the facts, but the reality would be, he had become a 'stick-up man' and no longer would have any need for the dreary business of housebreaking.

But the occasion overtook him. His impulsiveness, and the suddenness of stumbling across the car, placed him in a position of finding himself parading his newly found criminality over an absolutely terrified couple. They were responding to everything he said. It was, for him, a dream come true, and he had no concern for the couple's predicament. They had property to be stolen and he was going to take it, and as the minutes ticked past, it would have occurred to him that much could be made of this unravelling adventure. It was his sense of thrill and his complete lack of empathy for the frightened couple that allowed him to enjoy his 'cowboy' moment as he demanded the ignition key and rattled the bullets in his pocket. He added to the occasion by telling them a mix of half-truths and blatant lies about his prison life in an effort to let them know that they were dealing with a seasoned criminal and someone to be reckoned with.

He had to steal something; he needed money. Quite when his thoughts switched from stealing to something else cannot be known but very quickly it seems, another idea was forming in his head as he waved his gun in the direction of the frightened young woman in the passenger seat. For now, he demanded their cash and watches, something with which they immediately complied. He added a bit more terror by telling them that if anyone should come near, he would shoot them.

There is nothing to suggest that Hanratty had ever planned to shoot the couple. The position he found himself in was his perfect dream, an immature fantasy coupled with a longing for the big time, but murder was never on his mind despite the fact that he was armed with a loaded revolver. It would be a combination of circumstances and the accumulation of hours of unparalleled excitement that would create the environment for that to happen.

His thinking, of course, can never be known but as he spoke to the couple in the front, ordering them to be quiet while he thought, he most likely fantasised about a sexual liaison with the woman, in much the same way as he had done with many other women. She was young enough, like his other girlfriends, and she was now in front of him under threat of being shot; fantasy had turned into reality.

Each time the couple asked him what he wanted he told them to keep quiet and it is evident that he was thinking as he went along. His sexual fantasy aside, he would have mused over how he could get more excitement from the moment and then get himself back to London. It would have been easy to simply make them get out of the car and then drive off, though it is a small but important point that he had probably never driven a Morris Minor before and was possibly unsure about how to drive it – it was not the sort of car he normally stole. The flaw in that plan, though, was that the dream would be over too quickly and he would have lost the opportunity to carry out his lustful thoughts. He clearly thought about making the man get out so he could drive off with the woman but that was too risky. She would probably try to escape or attack him in panic and the man, now in the field, would suddenly become a witness to his adventures. He needed more time to think.

Evidently, the idea came to him. He would lock the man in the boot and that would leave him free to do whatever he wanted with the woman. But that would not have been easy for him to achieve. Once the man suspected that he had eyes for his girlfriend, the dynamics could change and the course of events could go horribly wrong. He therefore invented a new story. He was hungry, he told them, and needed something to eat. They offered to drive him somewhere so that he could get something but that was not really his plan. He ordered the man out of the car and reverted to his original idea.

He would have been conscious that even though it was dark, while he was standing out in the field, there was a chance the couple would see his face. He needed to do something about that and used the handkerchief from his pocket to cover it up. He knew that he would not be needing it that night to wipe away any of his fingerprints, as he was wearing gloves.

But his plan did not work. The couple argued that the car had a leaking exhaust and if he forced the man into the boot there was a chance that he would slowly suffocate with the fumes. He did not want that. That is not what he did. Until now, he had never been a violent person but he loved the thrill of frightening this unfortunate couple. Bowing to their pressure, he told the man to get back into the car and made the decision to drive off.

As they headed along the now deserted roads, he had only an idea that if they headed in the direction of London, it would at least solve the problem of how to get back. The couple kept on asking him for directions, which confused him for he was not sure where he was. Very quickly they arrived at the junction of Marsh Lane and the A4 and the man driving the car paused, waiting for directions; Maidenhead was to the left, Slough and London to the right.

What he said next provides a hint of a clue as to where he had travelled that day. He told them that he had had enough of Maidenhead and that he knew the Bear Hotel there. It is another gap in the story, but given what he said, it is likely that he had eaten there earlier in the day.[10] Now, not wanting to return there, he directed them to head towards London, Northolt in fact. This was his home territory and if he wanted to, at least he could slip away quietly from there.

But he was still thinking. The couple kept on asking him what he wanted and he probably wrestled with the idea of being dropped off somewhere or stealing the car. But he still had not fulfilled his dream and the idea of groping the woman was still there. For now, though, he would simply hold them captive and gave them directions to head towards London.

He allowed them to stop to buy some cigarettes. He did not smoke but the man in the front did and he probably thought that if he let him buy some, there was less of a chance that they would try to do something silly like trying to escape.

As they neared his home territory, though, all the indications are that he purposely directed them away from London. Stealing, by this time, was clearly no longer his motive and he checked to see whether there was sufficient fuel in the car for a longer journey. There was not and he ordered them to put 2 gallons into the tank. All the evidence suggests that, with the car now full, Hanratty just needed to find a lonely spot where he could somehow free himself of the man, grope the woman and then escape. They would not be able to recognise him as he had a handkerchief across his face and he had been careful by ordering them to always face the front. They could have no idea who he was.

He told them to keep driving north, with no real idea about where he was, though he knew he was heading roughly in the Bedford direction. He knew the area as he had a receiver there he used on occasions. At one point, when a car overtook them and the front-seat passenger waved at them, he knew something was wrong and he ordered the man to stop. He checked the back of the car and could see that no lights were out, but something had happened. He began to think that the couple, who had been talking quietly to each other as they had listened to his directions, had done something to attract attention.

The point where Hanratty realised that the couple had been whispering to each other and that somehow they had attracted attention to themselves may have been the moment that he adopted a more aggressive attitude towards them. Until then, they had been compliant, but that had now changed.

He had been with them now for almost five hours and he had made a few pounds out of it as well as feeling pleased with himself that he had carried out what, for so long, he had been dreaming about. But now here he was, miles from anywhere, and he wanted to finish off the evening with what he considered to be the ultimate prize.

Somehow, he needed to find a lonely spot. He instructed the driver to turn down little side roads but none of them appeared isolated enough. They drove on further and just after the village of Clophill, he saw an entrance. He ordered the man to drive in, turn the car around to face London – he wanted a quick getaway – and turn the engine and lights off.

Now the adrenalin would have been coursing through his veins, but still he was thinking about what to do next. He made the man get out of the car, opened the boot and found some rope. He forced him back into the driver's seat and made him remove his tie, which he then used to bind the woman's wrists together before securing the other end to the door handle. He now needed something else to secure the man and told him to pass back the duffel bag that he could see in the front passenger footwell. But the man moved too quickly and, thinking that he was about to be attacked himself, he pulled the trigger, twice.

Until then, Hanratty had graduated incrementally above his normal level of criminality. He was a car thief and a housebreaker but for the past twelve hours he had been wandering around with a loaded revolver in his pocket. That was a step up from what he had ever done before, but it was something he had managed to achieve and he doubtlessly would have felt emboldened by his own behaviour. Having been provided with the scenario of a compliant pair of victims, for it to be suddenly challenged with a perceived threat, explains why the trigger was pulled. Despite the constant waving about of the gun, there had been no specific threat to shoot Michael and it had happened in a split second. His knee-jerk reaction indicates that he probably thought that he was about to be overcome and the pulling of the trigger may well have been nothing more than a panicked response. It still amounted to murder since it seems he had purposely pointed the gun at Michael's head and shot twice, but it assists in trying to understand his actions.[11]

However, his focus remained on the woman. She started to scream but he was emotionally detached from her fear. He could not empathise with others and had no remorse for what he had just done, and with the man now dead he could no longer stand in his way. He now had complete control of the situation and forced the woman to kiss him before ordering her into the back of the car. Stupidly, he told her, she tried to grab his gun and in all probability she had been annoying him all evening. She had tried to prevent the man handing over the ignition key in the first place and he was sure she had been up to something when that car had overtaken them and had tried to speak with them. Frustrated with her stubbornness, he forced her back into the seat, ordered her to remove her knickers and glasses, told her to pull off one of his gloves and then raped her. Immediately afterwards he ridiculed her for being sexually inexperienced and she put her under-garments back on. It had been quick, but he had got what he wanted.

Hanratty would now have been concerned that there was a witness to his crimes that night. He had taken precautions to cover his face but he would have been worried, nevertheless. At one point he had told her his name was 'Jim', and he would need to deal with that in the same way as he had previously with the fingerprints he had left at burglaries. He needed to get rid of the evidence.

But his immediate concern was that he needed to get away and, not wanting any blood on him for he knew how things like that could get him caught, he forced the woman to drag the man's body from the car.

Now he needed to drive off and he told the woman to show him how the gears worked. She showed him and she went back to sit beside the body of her dead boyfriend. He was ready to go but a last-minute thought probably entered his head. All this could be for nothing. He may have entered the top echelons of the criminal league, but there was someone who could make his world suddenly come crumbling down.

He stood a few feet away from the woman now looking up at him and hesitated. He spun her a yarn about needing to knock her out, but he knew deep down what had to be done if he was to survive this ordeal himself. His life had always been about getting what he wanted, with no sense of understanding about how his behaviour impacted on anybody else. This trait rose to the surface. Not only did he shoot her, but he emptied all his remaining rounds into her body, reloaded and shot again. A quick kick to make sure she was dead, and he drove off in the direction of London.

What Hanratty had done over the past few hours had been the result of a gradual process, not an execution of some grand, well-thought-through plan. His bravado and ego had taken over and as his victims increasingly acquiesced to his demands, his confidence had grown. It was his immaturity and lack of any sense of responsibility that had culminated in the shooting of Michael and the raping of Valerie.

It is rather unhelpful to examine his behaviour from a perspective of trying to understand why, as he has been described, a petty thief would suddenly and inexplicably turn into a rapist and a murderer. He was not a petty thief; he was a professional housebreaker who had become more institutionalised over time as he spent year after year in prison. There was nothing petty about him, and his criminality was his occupation; even he referred to it as his 'business'. This professional criminal's character traits of arrogance, lack of empathy and total disregard for anyone else's feelings removed any barrier to him having sex with someone in circumstances when he was in a position of power, something he had been working himself up to over the last twenty-four hours, if not much longer. It is no less understandable for a professional criminal with his personality traits to turn his hand to rape and murder than it is say, for a plumber, a banker, a sportsman, a car dealer or a software engineer to do the same. Prisons up and down the country house many people convicted of serious crimes who held down responsible jobs, many of whom had no previous convictions before they committed their crime. Peter Sutcliffe, the Yorkshire Ripper, had only two convictions, one for going equipped to steal and another for theft of tyres, before he went on to murder thirteen women and try to kill seven others.[12] John Haigh, the acid bath murderer who dissolved six victims in sulphuric acid, had convictions only for fraud.[13]

With Hanratty now having fulfilled his desires, his focus turned to escape and self-preservation. Where he drove exactly when he left the A6 layby that morning is not known. Four hours later, the car was found in Avondale Crescent in east London with minor damage and with a mileage reading that suggested it had travelled further than the shortest route between Bedford and Ilford. In the same way that he had no real plan when he had stumbled across Valerie and Michael in the cornfield, neither did he have one when he drove back along the A6.

The first thing he had to do was to abandon the car and it needed to be somewhere that would not be connected to his own business in west London and Middlesex. In fact, the opposite would be better, and he turned his sights on east London. He sped along the streets of Essex heading into London not really caring about who else was inconvenienced by his dangerous driving. He was unaware that several people saw him as he raced along Eastern Avenue and screeched to a halt in Avondale Crescent. Happy that he had abandoned the incriminating car, he could simply have caught the underground train at Redbridge station just a few yards away and within half an hour he would have been back within the safety of central London.

Where he stayed that night is not known. He had any number of places he could have slept and any number of left luggage lockers where he could hide the gun. But the following day he woke to the news that the woman he had shot had somehow survived. It was time to panic.

He needed to get rid of the revolver and the jacket he had been wearing in case there was any blood on it. Where he discarded it will never be known and it was never found, but disposing of the revolver would be easy. It could have been any bus, but he boarded the number 36A, which edged past Paddington railway station on its way to south London, and slid it underneath the back seat on the upper floor where previously he had hidden his unwanted jewellery. He would most probably have dumped the cheap watches there too if he still had them, but he had given them back to the woman.

With all the incriminating evidence safely dealt with, all he needed to do now was to establish an alibi and he would be in the clear. Liverpool was his best bet. He had been there before and he clearly believed he could rustle up some sort of fabricated story to show that he was miles away from Clophill at the time the bullets were being fired. He boarded the train at Euston and some hours later arrived in the city to explore his options. One thought that occurred to him was to despatch a message to his friend Dixie to imply that he had been in Liverpool for a few days and then all he needed to do was fill in the blanks.

There is little doubt that Hanratty spent that day moving around Liverpool trying to think of ways to cover his tracks. By his own admission, though there is nothing to corroborate it, he tried to bribe people into putting themselves forward as false alibis but his crime was too serious for others to perjure themselves.

There is no doubt that he frequented the Scotland Road area of the city and equally little doubt that at some time he had ventured into the tobacconists and sweet shops that littered the area. On one of his visits he may well have seen Olive Dinwoodie serving behind the counter with her granddaughter but it was not on Tuesday, 22 August. Neither had it been the day before, or if it had, it meant that Hanratty had travelled to Liverpool and back in a day and been in the Vienna hotel by 11.30 p.m. He would have had the time, but it seems rather an arduous day for someone who was happy to sleep wherever he found himself any particular night.

Lewis Hawser QC, who carried out the review in 1967, thought that Hanratty had in fact visited the shop on the Monday but Bob Acott, in the witness box, appeared not to agree with him. His thoughts, though, went with him to his grave. It is, though, wholly unlikely for Hanratty to have been in Liverpool on the Monday if all the London witnesses are to be believed.

Dinwoodie was only one piece of the jigsaw, of course. It is possible that Hanratty tried to sell a stolen watch to Robert Kempt as he stood outside his billiard club. It is almost certain that at some time he deposited his suitcase with William Usher at the left luggage office at Lime Street station, but neither occurred on Tuesday, 22 August.

While he was in Liverpool, the news broke that the gun had been found on a London bus, but he probably thought that the weapon could not be connected to him and so returned to London and stayed on the Friday night in a hotel. The next day he went to see the France family. His confidence would have had an even bigger boost when he saw that the police were looking for a killer with brown eyes. He flew to Ireland, which is where he left his clues that Jimmy Ryan was really James Hanratty, and when he returned, he proudly turned up at a number of people's houses with his newly acquired Sunbeam. For now, he 'self-demoted' himself back to housebreaker and conveniently stole a jacket to replace the one he had disposed of, which possibly bore traces of Michael Gregsten's blood.

When the description of the killer's eyes suddenly turned to staring and blue he would have become nervous, but when Peter Alphon was arrested he would have thought that he had avoided the noose. Confident that was the case, he drove across to see one of his girlfriends, Gladys Deacon, and took her for a drive to Bedford to visit one of his receivers. Doubtless, he passed near the layby on the A6, with most likely a gratifying sensation rushing through him knowing that this was where he had been 'promoted' and, he thought, had left no clues.

But within forty-eight hours, Alphon had been released and eliminated from the investigation, followed quickly by the police knocking on his parents' door, only asking about burglaries, but it was unsettling. Worse still, Dixie France appeared not to be believing his story about his trip to Liverpool. France's suspicions were probably aroused when the gun had been found under the seat of a bus, somewhere Hanratty had boasted to him about hiding his stolen jewellery.

Eventually word got to him that he was wanted for the murder but it is likely that he genuinely believed that he could not be connected to it. There were no fingerprints on the gun and he had been disguised the whole time. But he needed to firm up on his alibi. He telephoned Bob Acott, taunting him that he was an innocent man and could prove it, and went back once more to Liverpool, stealing a Jaguar to get there, to shore up his defence. It could have been on this occasion that he spoke to Kempt and Usher. It may even have been then that he actually went into Dinwoodie's sweet shop, for it is known that at this time he sent a bunch of flowers to his mother from a shop in Scotland Road a matter of yards from where the sweet shop was located. This probably happened and, for the purpose of creating a false alibi, he simply shifted it across to the day of the murder.

There were many weaknesses with his Liverpool alibi but the most damning was the fabricated story of staying with three criminal associates who could vouch for him. It dawned on him that this tissue of lies was going to send him to the gallows and so, continuing with his propensity to tell lie after lie, the Rhyl alibi was born. That too, did not stand up to scrutiny. Like Liverpool, there is little doubt that he had, at some time, stayed in Rhyl, possibly in late July when he had turned up at the fairground. On that particular night he stayed at Terry Evans' house but there was every opportunity for him to have got to know the town, its cafés, its streets and either before or after 22/23 August he may even have stayed at one of the guesthouses. It may possibly have been Grace Jones' Ingledene, but if it was, despite many arguing that his description of it fitted perfectly, in truth, there were many inaccuracies.

His journey of adventure that began when he came out of prison in March 1961 with his head full of grandiose ideas had fallen flat on its face. One person was dead and another had been crippled for life. He was hanged, and left in his wake a trail of emotional devastation not only for the Gregstens and Valerie Storie but also for his own family, who were convinced that he was a man wrongly convicted.

He was not.

Bibliography

Blom Cooper, L., *The A6 Murder: Regina v James Hanratty. The Semblance of Truth* (Harmondsworth: Penguin, 1963).

Foot, P., *Who Killed Hanratty?* (London: Jonathan Cape, 1971).

Foot, P., *Who Killed Hanratty?* (St Albans: Granada Publishing, 1973).

Foot, P., *Who Killed Hanratty?* (London: Penguin, 1988).

Franklin, C., *Woman in the Case* (London: Robert Hale, 1967).

Justice, J., *Murder v Murder* (Paris: Olympia Press, 1964).

Kennedy, L., *Truth to Tell* (London: Bantam Press, 1991).

Kennedy, L., *Thirty Six Murders & Two Immoral Earnings* (London: Profile, 2002).

Miller, L., *Shadow of Deadman's Hill* (London: Zoilus Press, 2001).

Razen, A., *Hanratty: The Inconvenient Truth* (Amazon, 2014).

Russell, Lord, *Deadman's Hill* (Oxford: Tallis Press, 1965).

Simpson, K., *Forty Years of Murder* (London: George G. Harrap, 1978).

Woffinden, B., *Miscarriages of Justice* (London: Hodder and Stoughton, 1987).

Woffinden, B., *Hanratty: The Final Verdict* (London: Macmillan, 1997).

Notes

Chapter One
1 Statements of Marjorie and John Storie, 23 August 1961.
2 Medical records from Stoke Mandeville hospital.
3 Transcript of C4 interview, 2001 – tape 1, p.9.
4 Statement of Valerie Storie, 23 August 1961 and Report of Detective Superintendent Acott, 10 November 1961, pp.42–48.
5 Transcript of C4 interview, 2001 – tape 1, p.10.
6 Statement of witness EC, 24 August 1961.
7 Transcript of C4 interview, 2001 – tape 2, p.10.

Chapter Two
1 Transcript of interview with Detective Superintendent Acott, 24 August 1961, p.23.
2 Statement of Valerie Storie, 23 August 1961.
3 Given the man's self-proclaimed criminal record, CT and PD probably referred to corrective training and preventive detention, sentences meted out by the courts to recidivist criminals.
4 Statement of Valerie Storie, 28 August 1961.

Chapter Three
1 *London Illustrated News*, 7 October 1961.
2 Transcript of trial, p.76.
3 51p in today's decimalised currency.
4 *Daily Express*, 19 February 1962.
5 Transcript of trial, p.80.
6 Ibid, p.81.
7 Ibid, p. 82.
8 Statement of Valerie Storie, 23 August 1961.
9 Transcript of interview with Detective Superintendent Acott, 11 September 1961, p.35.
10 Ibid, p.49.
11 Transcript of trial, p.83.

Chapter Four
1 Transcript of interview with Detective Superintendent Acott, 11 September 1961, p.51.
2 Ibid, p.53.
3 The post mortem was performed by Professor Keith Simpson at Bedford hospital on 23 August 1961.
4 Transcript of interview with Detective Superintendent Acott, 11 September 1961, p.62.
5 Ibid, p.55.
6 *Daily Express*, 19 February 1962.
7 Statement of Valerie Storie, 23 August 1961, p.9.
8 Police list of items recovered from basket. The *Storie Papers*, folder 38.
9 Report of Detective Superintendent Acott, dated 10 November 1961, p.56 and statement of W.C., 24 August 1961.

Chapter Five
1 Statement of Sidney Burton, 23 August 1961.
2 A police inspector would later describe the item as pyjama trousers. It is known that inside the green and white duffel bag from which the killer had removed the item to cover the head there were three sheets, three green and white pillow cases, a pair of pyjamas, pale blue trousers, a top and some pants. It is an anomaly and one that may be explained by Kerr's state of shock.
3 Statement of John Kerr, 23 August 1961.
4 Transcript of trial, pp.126–128.
5 Report of Detective Superintendent Acott, 10 November 1961, p.57, and statement of Peter Wortley, undated.
6 Transcript of trial, p.133.
7 Dr John Parkes.
8 Statement of R.P., 23 August 1961.
9 Statement of Douglas Richard Rees, annotated 24 August 1961, p.8.
10 Hawser report, April 1975, paragraph 121.
11 Victor Terry was convicted of the murder of John Pull in Durrington, Sussex, on 10 November 1960 and was hanged at Wandsworth prison on 25 May 1961.
12 Capital murder also involved murder through furtherance of theft, resisting arrest or murder of a police or prison officer.
13 Transcript of C4 interview, 2001, pp.37–38.
14 Statement of Gwendolyn Mary Rutland, 23 August 1961, p.8.
15 Statement of Allan Madwar, 24 August 1961.
16 Statements of E.R. and Doris Athoe, 24 August 1961.
17 Transcript of trial, p.145.
18 Transcript of C4 interview, 2001 – tape 1, p.39.
19 Handwritten notes of Valerie Storie, folder 2.
20 Transcript, of C4 interview, 2001 – tape 1, p.39.
21 Statement of Edwin Cooke, 26 August 1961.
22 Transcript of trial, pp.372–400.
23 Ibid, pp.116–125.
24 Simpson, K., *Forty Years of Murder*, 1978, p.134.

25 The conductors were witnesses E.B. and P.P. who made statements on 25, 26 and 31 August and SM who made a statement on 26 August 1961.

26 Report of Detective Superintendent Acott, 10 November 1961, p.34.

27 This is distinct from photofit technology, which emerged in the 1970s and which replaced the use of hand-drawn images with photographs of facial features.

28 *Slough Express*, 1 September 1961.

29 As a result of the Beck case, the Court of Appeal was introduced in 1907.

Chapter Six

1 Police Constable John Copp, Harrow Road police station.

2 Miller, L., *Shadow of Deadman's Hill*, 2001, p.32.

3 The occupier was George Pratt.

4 Transcript of trial, p.303.

5 Ibid, p.242.

6 *Daily Mirror*, 21 September 1961.

7 Detective Sergeant Arthur Kilner.

8 *Daily Mirror*, 21 September 1961.

9 *Daily Mail*, 21 September 1961.

10 The hotel register showed that a Mr Bell did cancel his reservation that day and he had been allocated room 6.

11 Statement of Florence Glickberg, 22 September 1961.

12 Statement of Detective Sergeant Arthur Kilner, 18 September 1961 and statement of Peter Louis Alphon, 27 August 1961.

13 *Daily Telegraph*, 23 September 1961.

14 *Daily Mirror*, 23 September 1961.

15 Alphon said this in his interview with Detective Superintendent Acott, although it is not known whether he was actually paid any money.

16 Notes of interview between Detective Superintendent Acott and Peter Alphon on 23 September 1961.

17 Statement of Inspector Kenneth Nayer, 19 October 1961.

18 Statements of Harold Hirons, 30 August 1961.

19 A further witness, P.A., also attended the identification parade and selected Alphon but this was in relation to the purchase of a coat in a shop and carried no weight in respect of the murder investigation.

20 Statement of Inspector Kenneth Nayer, 25 September 1961.

21 Statement of Detective Sergeant Ken Oxford, 28 September 1961.

22 Transcript of trial, p.139.

23 Ibid, p.633.

Chapter Seven

1 Snell had convictions for shop-breaking, larceny and wandering abroad.

2 Notes of interview with Florence Snell by Detective Superintendent Acott, 25 September 1961.

3 Nudds had convictions for stealing, taking vehicles without consent, receiving, shop-breaking and assault.

4 Report of Detective Inspector Farrell, 27 September 1961.

5 In fact, Hanratty sent a number of postcards to his friends and family and even asked strangers to write cards for him. Source: Statement of C.R., 1 November 1961.

6   The driver of the other vehicle was Arthur Sindall, who was also driving a hire car.
7   Report of Detective Superintendent Acott, 10 November 1961, p.107.
8   Statements of Ann Pryce, 10 October 1961, Jean Rice, 11 October 1961 and transcript of trial, pp.406–407.
9   France had numerous convictions for larceny, stealing, unlawful possession of property, and frequenting and running gaming houses.
10 Statements of Charles France, 3 and 14 October 1961.
11 This was confirmed by her dentist, Renee Birkhahn. Sources: Statement dated 18 October 1961 and transcript of trial, p.220.
12 Transcript of trial, p.218.
13 Statement of Jean Rice, 11 October 1961. In 1961, there were no speed limits imposed on the new motorways.
14 There is no police record that confirms this incident, but in a statement made by Ann Pryce, she mentioned that when she last spoke to Hanratty in the Rehearsal Club, she had been unaware at the time that two police officers were inside the club. This may have led to some sort of chase.
15 Statement of Winston Gardner, 18 October 1961.
16 It was true. He stayed there on 3 and 8 September 1961. Source: Statements of P.B., 26 September 1961 and K.M., 27 October 1961.
17 Statement of Louise Anderson, 7 October 1961.
18 List of items seized from her shop, Bedfordshire Police archives.
19 Statements of Louise Anderson, 24 October and 7 November 1961.
20 Transcript of trial, p.491.
21 Donald Langton.
22 Report of Woman Police Sergeant Clapperton, 5 September 1961.
23 Report of Chief Inspector Reginald Ballinger, 24 October 1961.
24 Statements from a number of the Hanratty family.
25 Statement of Gladys Deacon, 10 October 1961.
26 Ibid, 11 October 1961.

Chapter Eight
1   The interview took place in the Deputy Chief Constable's office.
2   Transcript of trial, p.512.
3   Ibid, p.495.
4   Ibid, p.508.
5   Ibid, p.647.
6   Statement of Inspector Robert Salisbury, 17 October 1961.
7   Doctor Guttman and Sister Wilson. In all, twenty-six people were present. In addition to the volunteers, the suspect and his solicitor, the hospital staff and Ballinger, also present was a uniformed inspector, the Chief Constable of Bedfordshire, three detective superintendents, a detective inspector and two detective sergeants.
8   Statement of Valerie Storie, 18 October 1961.
9   Statement of Chief Inspector Reginald Ballinger, undated.
10 Report of Detective Superintendent Acott, 10 November 1961, p.119.
11 Report of identification parade by Chief Inspector Reginald Ballinger.

Chapter Nine
1 Detective Constable Pugh.
2 Transcript of trial, p.857.
3 Statement of Olive Dinwoodie, 17 October 1961.
4 Actual train times: Bedfordshire police archives.
5 Hawser Report, paragraph 185.
6 Miss Ashman.
7 Report of Chief Inspector Ballinger, 24 October 1961.
8 *Daily Telegraph*, 24 October 1961, p.15.
9 Nimmo Report, p.15.

Chapter Ten
1 In 1971, the assizes were renamed as crown courts.
2 The disclosure of unused material was, and remains to this day, a much-heated legal debate. The law was not consolidated until 1996 when the Criminal Procedures and Investigations Act made it mandatory for the prosecution to supply all information to the defence – save for some rare exceptions – which had the potential to undermine the prosecution case.
3 *Daily Telegraph*, 24 November 1961.
4 *Daily Telegraph*, 25 November 1961.
5 Handwritten note: The *Storie Papers*, folder 25.
6 Statement of Louise Anderson, 6 December 1961. This was not the first time Hanratty senior had tried to influence witnesses. On 1 November he telephoned Gladys Deacon accusing her of lying over the telephone conversation she had with his son on the day he was arrested. Source: Statement of Gladys Deacon, 1 November 1961.
7 Guy Owen.
8 Linda Walton.

Chapter Eleven
1 *The Guardian*, 3 July 2003.
2 Obituary, *The Times*, 2 November 2012.
3 It was standard practice at the time to prefer only one charge where a capital offence prevailed.
4 Transcript of trial, p.45.
5 Ibid, p.47 and 50.
6 This was a conversation between Hanratty and Sergeant Absalom when he was being held at Ampthill police station awaiting his first appearance at court.
7 Many years later it would emerge that Acott had suggested that each of the parade participants wear a skull cap to hide their hair, but for some reason the idea was dismissed. Source: Court of Appeal 2002, paragraph 145.
8 Report of Detective Superintendent Acott, 10 November 1961, p.35.

Chapter Twelve
1 12 February 1962. Woffinden, 1997, p.148.
2 *Daily Telegraph*, 31 January 1962.
3 Detective Chief Inspector F. Davies.
4 Transcript of trial, p.622.

Chapter Thirteen
1 Foot, P., *Who Killed Hanratty?*, 1971, p.234.
2 Transcript of trial, p.737.
3 Ibid, p.757.
4 Ibid.

Chapter Fourteen
1 Transcript of trial, p.780.
2 Nimmo Report, p.64.

Chapter Fifteen
1 It is not clear why the two officers from Wales were present but it may be expected that having someone with local knowledge of the area available would have been helpful to Graham Swanwick.
2 Nimmo Report, p.47.
3 Transcript of trial, p.896.
4 Nimmo report, p.24.

Chapter Sixteen
1 *Daily Telegraph*, 18 February 1962.
2 Handwritten notes of Valerie Storie, folder 2.
3 Margaret Walker and Ivy Vincent. Both had claimed they had seen someone similar to Hanratty in the summer of 1961 but their recollections were vague and unreliable.
4 The hangman was Harry Allen, Chief Executioner 1955–64.

Chapter Seventeen
1 Medical records from Stoke Mandeville hospital.
2 *Daily Express*, 9 April 1962, p.11.
3 Ibid.
4 Transcript of C4 interview, 2001 – tape 2, p.3.
5 Ibid.
6 *Daily Express*, 13 April 1962.
7 Transcript of C4 interview, 2001 – tape 2, p.3.
8 Handwritten notes of Valerie Storie, folder 2.
9 Ibid.
10 Barbara Sabey.
11 Transcript of C4 interview, 2001 – tape 2, p.19.
12 Statement of witness VJ, 7 September 1961.
13 Statement of witness EM, 7 September 1961. There were a number of witnesses who confirmed that Michael had been transferred to Langley due to him having an affair with a work colleague.
14 Transcript of C4 interview, 2001 – tape 1, p.11.
15 Transcript of C4 interview, 2001 – tape 2, p.9.
16 Ibid, p.23.
17 Ibid, p.20.
18 Transcript of C4 interview, 2001 – tape 1, p.6.

19 Letter to *The Times*, 5 July 1962.

20 Transcript of C4 interview, 2001 – tape 2, p.26.

21 The first one was a series of drawings that, when held at a certain angle, showed the word 'murderer'.

22 An updated version of the book, Crime de la Route A6, was published in France in 1968.

23 Medical records from Stoke Mandeville hospital.

24 Hansard, 19 April 1965, column 576.

25 Letter from Valerie Storie to Joan Lestor, 14 November 1966, folder 27.

26 Handwritten notes of Valerie Storie, folder 2.

27 Transcript of C4 interview, 2001 – tape 2, p.34.

Chapter Eighteen

1 He was assisted by Detective Chief Inspector Charles Horan.

2 Woffinden, B., *Hanratty: The Final Verdict*, 1997, p.341.

3 Nimmo Report, paragraph 163.

4 Hansard, 21 May 1969.

5 Grace Jones, Terry Evans and Arthur Webber gave evidence at the trial. Brenda Harris (daughter of Grace Jones), Ernest Gordon, Joyce Roose, Lynda Fagan and Doreen Thomas (Dixie's café staff), Margaret Walker, Ivy Vincent and Robert Fish (who later withdrew his sighting) were all people whose details were provided to the defence during the trial. Albert Croft (barber in Rhyl), Charles White Jones, William Jones (husband of Grace Jones), Gwyn Jones (son of Grace Jones), Brian Sandford, Pearl Hughes and Kenneth Portlock (people propped up by Evans for the Panorama programme) and Frederick Davies (saw Hanratty in Rhyl in October 1961) were unable to add any information.

6 Foot, P., *Who Killed Hanratty?*, 1971, p.266.

7 Report of Assistant Chief Constable, Bedford, 13 May 1967.

8 He claimed he had seen a dog called Mentals Only Hope run in a race and afterwards he had left for Dorney.

9 Handwritten notes of Valerie Storie, folder 2.

10 The film never made a public appearance until 1972.

11 Transcript of C4 interview, 2001 – tape 2, p.33.

12 Letter dated 6 April 1970 from Messrs William Charles Crocker solicitors.

13 Chaired by Anthony Barclay, the people on the platform were Jeremy Fox, Jean Justice, Mr and Mrs Hanratty, Paul Foot and Myke Fogarty-Waul. Source: Report of Inspector Jepson, 26 March 1970. Fogarty-Waul had made a statement to the police about a man he had seen in the Dorney Reach area a few days before the abduction and would go on to form a close working relationship with Jean Justice in his fight to prove Alphon's guilt. He would later claim that he had met the man some weeks before and had collected him from the dog track in Slough and given him a lift. Source: Statement, 1 September 1961 and Foot, 1971, p.347.

14 Dr David Lewes, a Bedford surgeon who attended every day of the Hanratty trial and who believed Hanratty to be innocent, also featured on the work of the committee but to what extent is not clear.

15 The book was republished in 1973 and 1988.

16 There are a number of theories as to where this money originated but none has any evidence to support them.

17 Michael Da Costa, Betty Davies and Trevor Dutton.
18 Disciplinary offences committed between 1955 and 1957 included damage to bedding, insolence, using obscene language and talking, laughing and whistling. He also made four escape attempts during 1958 and 1959. His last period of imprisonment included being placed on misconduct report on nineteen occasions. Source: Bedfordshire police archives.
19 The witnesses were a family from whose florist shop Hanratty had sent flowers to his mother.
20 Simpson, K., *Forty Years of Murder*, 1978, p.137.
21 Letter to Valerie, 11 May 1971.
22 Timeline – The *Storie Papers*.
23 Interview with Ken Wells, 1 February 2020.
24 New names included S.P. Terry, Kleine, Gerald Moffatt, Joseph Guinan and Gerald Murray.
25 Hawser Report, April 1975, paragraph 384.
26 Ibid, paragraph 336.
27 Transcript of C4 interview, 2001 – tape 2, p.7.
28 Adrian Hobbs was an executor to Valerie's will and it was he who provided the *Storie Papers* to allow this book to be written. He became an industrial professor in 1992 and was awarded a CBE in 2008.
29 Transcript of C4 interview, 2001 – tape 2, p.13.
30 Timeline – The *Storie Papers*, Frank Blennerhassett chaired a government committee designed to assess the effectiveness of road traffic legislation insofar as it related to drink-driving.
31 Transcript of C4 interview, 2001 – tape 3, p.11.
32 Transcript of C4 interview, 2001 – tape 2, p.42.
33 Police Review, 3 April 1987.
34 The *Storie Papers*, folder 5.
35 Timeline – The *Storie Papers*.
36 One letter in March 1989 from a well-known author, film consultant and criminologist claimed he had access to the tapes that proved an individual had been paid to separate Valerie and Michael.
37 Transcript of C4 interview, 2001 – tape 3, p.17.

Chapter Nineteen

1 Letter from Bob Woffinden to Valerie Storie, 1 December 1991.
2 Interview with Adrian Hobbs, 16 March 2020.
3 *Slough and South Bucks Observer*, 15 April 2016.
4 Letter from Jeremy Fox to Valerie Storie, 20 January 1994.
5 Transcript of C4 interview, 2001.
6 Letter from Jeremy Fox to Valerie Storie, 10 March 1995: The *Storie Papers*, folder 35.
7 *Slough and South Bucks Observer*, 15 April 2016.
8 Ibid.
9 27 January 1997.
10 Ibid.
11 Letter to Valerie Storie, 20 May 1997: The *Storie Papers*, folder 36.
12 The issue of non-disclosure of material remains a running debate in the courts today. The Criminal Procedure and Investigations Act 1996 much improved the

situation, but criticisms continue. The Commission introduced another Rhyl witness, Raymond Reed, who wrote to the Home Secretary in 1967, claiming he had seen Hanratty in the town just before his arrest in October 1961.

13 It was repeated again in October 1994 and August 1995.
14 Handwritten notes of Valerie Storie, folder 2.
15 Statement of William Ewer, 11 September 1961.
16 8 January 1998.
17 1 April 1999.
18 *Daily Express*, 29 March 2001.
19 4 April 1999.
20 Transcript of C4 interview, 2001 – tape 3, p.8.
21 8 May 1999.
22 24 May 1999.

Chapter Twenty
1 *Morning Advertiser*, 20 October 2000. Hanratty's aunt was Ann Cunningham.
2 Hanratty's body was exhumed on 22 March 2001.
3 *Mail on Sunday*, 8 April 2001.
4 Handwritten notes of Valerie Storie, folder 2.
5 Transcript of C4 interview, 2001 – tape 3, p.8. *Daily Mirror*, 4 April 2001.
6 Statements of G.M. and J.B., 24 August 1961.
7 Interview with friend of Valerie Storie, 10 February 2020.
8 *Slough and South Bucks Observer*, 15 April 2016.
9 Henry Howard.
10 Court of Appeal ruling, 10 May 2002, para 126.
11 The grounds included document analysis evidence that argued it could be shown that the police interview notes had been altered and sightings of the Morris elsewhere in the country demonstrated that its presence in Ilford on the morning of 23 August 1961 was unlikely.
12 Lord Chief Justice Woolf, Lord Justice Mantell and Mr Justice Leveson.
13 Court of Appeal judgement, paragraph 211.
14 The judges were also critical of the Criminal Cases Review Commission for incurring such expenditure on a case from forty years ago. They would expect such effort to be made in cases that were exceptional, and by implication, felt that the evidence fell far short of that benchmark. Source: *The Guardian*, 11 May 2002.

Chapter Twenty-one
1 Section 4 Sexual Offences (Amendment) Act 1976.
2 Miller, L., *Shadow of Deadman's Hill*, 2001, p.131.
3 Ibid., pp.76–77.
4 Ibid., p.82.
5 Ibid., p.145 and 146.
6 Final statement by Valerie Storie, 10 May 2002; The *Storie Papers*, folder 23.
7 *Mail on Sunday*, 28 April 2002.
8 Letters from Ken Oxford to Valerie Storie: The *Storie Papers*, folder 39.
9 30 July 2001.
10 Alphon died in January 2009.
11 *Daily Mail*, 7 April 2001.

12 25 June 2002.

13 Transcript of C4 interview, 2001 – tape 3, p.10.

14 The newspaper articles had been collected by Valerie's boss at the laboratory, Barbara Sabey.

15 Handwritten notes of Valerie Storie, folder 2.

16 Source: Pauline Hodges, 13 July 2020.

17 Source: Tracey Geddis, Stoke Mandeville Hospital.

18 Interview with Tracey Geddis, 7 July 2020.

Epilogue

1 27 April 1962.

2 Hall Williams, J.E. (1964) Review of Blom-Cooper, L. (1963) *The A6 Murder. Regina v. James Hanratty: The Semblance of Truth*. British Journal of Criminology, 4(3), pp.293–297.

3 Obsessive-Compulsive, Paranoid, Schizoid, Narcissistic, Histrionic, Avoidant, Dependent, Schizotypal, Antisocial and Borderline.

4 Statement of Terence Wilkins, 23 October 1961.

5 Statement of witness GG, 16 October 1961. It is right that the prisoner's name should not be made public since his details were never released.

6 Statements of I.O., 27 September 1961 and D.M., 29 September 1961.

7 Statement of B.T., 28 September 1961.

8 Statement of Richard Harris, undated.

9 A man called Donald Slack was interviewed about this but he maintained he never discussed a firearm with Hanratty. Source: Statement of Donald Slack, 26 October 1961.

10 It is likely that the police carried out enquiries in Maidenhead to pursue this aspect, but there is no record of the outcome.

11 This is an interesting legal argument. For a person to be guilty of murder, he/she has to have an intent to kill or an intent to inflict grievous bodily harm (a bullet through the head would almost certainly amount to that). Had Hanratty admitted to being the gunman and he had panicked and was merely reckless in pulling the trigger, his defence counsel may well have been able to argue that his actions amounted to no more than manslaughter. But he did not put himself forward for that defence and the debate never arose.

12 Bilton, M., 2003. *Wicked Beyond Belief*, p.365.

13 Oates, J., *John George Haigh: The Acid Bath Murderer* (Barnsley: Pen and Sword, 2014).

Index

The History Press

The destination for history
www.thehistorypress.co.uk